HEARTBREAK,
HEALING AND HAPPINESS

Flourishing after a heartbreak

HEARTBREAK,
HEALING AND HAPPINESS
Flourishing after a heartbreak

LARA CASANOVA

Heartbreak, Healing and Happiness

Author – Lara Casanova

© Lara Casanova 2015

www.lifeinthepink.com.au

lara@lifeinthepink.com.au

This book is sold with the understanding that the author is not offering specific personal advice to the reader. For professional advice, seek the services of a suitable, qualified practitioner. The author disclaims any responsibility for liability, loss or risk, personal or otherwise, that happens as a consequence of the use and application of any of the contents of this book.

All rights reserved. This book may not be reproduced in whole or part, stored, posted on the internet, or transmitted in any form or by any means, electronic, mechanical, photocopying, recording, or other, without permission from the author of this book.

Editing by:	Alex Mitchell www.authorsupportservices.com
Design by:	Sylvie Blair www.bookpod.com.au
Photography by:	Bruce Hobby Photography

National Library of Australia Cataloguing-in-Publication

Creator:	Casanova, Lara, author.
Title:	Heartbreak, healing and happiness : flourishing after a heartbreak / Lara Casanova.
ISBN:	9780994162939 (paperback)
Subjects:	Rejection (Psychology). Man-woman relationships. Self-acceptance. Emotions. Healing. Happiness.
Dewey Number:	158.2

To all the delicate souls out there
floundering in the raw, heart wrenching sorrow
of a breakup

Preface

"Never allow someone to be your priority while allowing yourself to be their option"

Mark Twain

Yes, I have been there. I have visited the three destinations of heartbreak, healing and happiness. I have licked my wounds, moved on and created a new life for myself. This is my story.

I spent time at the Heartbreak Manor where I checked out a little exhausted and washed out, but I graciously took my tools and lessons. I had processed the really hard parts of the pain and come to rediscover the love for myself which I had lost.

At the Healing Sanctuary I reconnected with the person I am, became truthful and authentic and slowly got my groove and my zest for life back.

The Happiness Shack is where I currently reside and it is here that I discovered my life purpose. I have created a life oozing with self love, authenticity and purpose.

My choice to complete the work required and grasp the lessons I needed to learn for me has been inspiring and empowering. I have come out the other end feeling like a whole new amazing person. I feel I have a better connection with myself and a sense of inner peace. I know who I am and what I want. I know what I deserve, and I understand why I have previously found this a little elusive.

I fell into heartbreak at forty-six. This is certainly not what I had envisaged for my life. I thought when I broke up with my previous partner many years earlier (after seven years together) I had done all the healing I needed to do. I believed I had suffered my one serious heartbreak for my lifetime, pulling myself back from more than twelve months of serious anxiety and panic attacks.

I assumed this meant that when my new prince came along I would be whole and ready to choose a partner who could provide a safe, healthy and happy relationship for the long haul. We were going to ride off into the sunset and live my version of happily ever after.

Unfortunately this was not the case. One minute we were relaxing on a boat drinking French champagne, making mad passionate love, and holidaying at beautiful resorts. The next we were yelling at each other, not caring for each other's feelings or providing a supportive environment for each other. I cried myself to sleep many nights, asking myself why he didn't love me enough.

I was presented with warning signs along the way and I choose to ignore them. I hoped and prayed things would change; I believed I could change things, or more honestly I could change the parts of him that I felt hurt by.

What I now know is that because I didn't love myself enough to believe I deserved more, I settled for less. I began to think it was normal to feel what I was feeling and instead of dealing with my feelings I instead choose to ignore them and hoped it would work out.

Suppressing feelings and emotions, being a picture of independence and strength, was a lesson I learnt in my childhood. Being the eldest of four girls, my family role evolved as the responsible elder sister, the negotiator and rescuer.

Preface

I became a master at hiding and being ignorant to my feelings in order to ensure everyone around me was happy. I was a kettle that could not express its steam, I was hot and pressure-filled on the inside with no release.

It is really no surprise I ended up in a relationship where I spent valuable time and energy trying to fix issues I believed he had rather than dealing with my own, facing up to my truth and moving on from what became a destructive environment.

Why was I continuing to stay if this was how I felt? If I loved myself, why was I here, bottling up how I felt to maintain the status quo, to stay in my comfort zone?

The longer I stayed in the relationship and allowed myself to be hurt, bigger cracks appeared not only in the relationship but also deep inside myself. The pain and suffering became too much to bear, but still I persisted, believing I could make a difference and the love we had would save us.

We both believed our love could salvage our relationship and we spent time trying to piece back the jigsaw, however sadly and after shedding many more rivers of tears, we knew this would not be the case and eventually decided on a final separation.

So I left, and learnt to love and forgive myself and access my authentic self. My spiritual journey over the previous twelve years had helped me learn and grow, so even though I loved him with all my heart, my heartbreak this time around was not as hard to navigate as the first one. I was protected by the work I had done on myself over the years, but it still hurt terribly. I felt my heart was crushed into a million pieces and I struggled to like and love myself as much as I should.

These days I do still want the fairy tale but my fairy tale is now based on reality.

I believe people have issues and differences, and we need to work together to grow as individuals and in the relationship. No one is perfect and we must accept people as they are today, not what we think their potential will create.

We need to accept and love each other's perfect imperfections, but at the same time be able to communicate through conflicting times with love and respect, supporting each other, being fully committed to each other.

Be you and only you

I am not ashamed to want to be loved; real, unconditional, genuine, be-yourself love. I want someone who will accept me for my imperfections, honour my feelings and let me be the person I am. I want someone to hold my hand walking down the street.

I want someone who will make me a high priority and relate to me as an equal. I want someone who wants to commit one hundred percent and shows this in all of their actions. I want someone who will place importance on their own personal growth, be an advocate for mine and provide a supportive environment. I want to be able to offer all the same things in return.

This was far from the relationship we had created. It was torture to live with someone you love deeply, yet everyday see the mess you have created, the failure of yourself, him and the relationship. It was like ripping off a Band-Aid slowly.

I thought if only I could change him, maybe he could do things differently. But by focusing on trying to change him, I unconsciously and conveniently took away the focus of dealing with myself.

While I remained in the relationship, I spent many months being angry every day because I thought he couldn't give me what I wanted.

Preface

Later this anger changed direction and I aimed it back at myself like a speeding bullet directed at my heart for staying where I was, accepting less than what I deserved. This is not to say we did not love each other, however instead of it being unconditional love it became destructive. It brought out the worst in both of us.

Leaving this relationship was one of the hardest decisions I have made. It created a lot of internal pain, tears and suffering and at times it became almost unbearable to sit and face the feelings.

Not only was it hard processing the break up, it also brought to the surface many other unresolved issues that needed healing. What I realised along the way is that I couldn't blame him, or myself. I had to take ownership for my life and accept and forgive.

I made a solid vow and promise to myself that this time I was going to get it right. I was going to sit back and reflect on how I ended up where I was. No distractions, no seeking another new relationship to take my baggage into. No late nights out on the alcohol hiding my feelings. I was going to do the hard work I needed to do to fall in love with myself wholeheartedly, heal the hurts from this split and any other hurts that were lingering from the past that I still hadn't cleaned up. Face the fears, shed the tears and really get to know myself, imperfections and all.

One of the most important things I learnt was that to attract the type of person that would fulfil all my needs, wants and desires, I needed to first become the type of person who would attract that in their life.

In hindsight, this whole experience helped me grow as a person and helped me mature into the loving person I believe I am today. I can now see things objectively and was able to move through the forgiveness process. I believe that when forgiveness is achieved, the love that was there flows back in.

What I have also learnt and accepted along the way is that people generally do the best they can at the time with what they know.

Heartbreak, Healing and Happiness

This became my mantra for forgiving both of us. Using this mantra saved me from many, many more conversations in my head with an internal negative voice beating me up on a daily basis.

There are many lessons I have learnt which I will share as you walk through this book, but by far the very biggest is that you must love yourself first and foremost. We must all truly understand, accept, forgive and be true to ourselves, have faith in our truth, our journey in life, trust that it is all achievable and from here we can move forward to discover our passions and live our soul's purpose.

Everything else will fall into place. When you love yourself, trust yourself and have faith in your journey, you will always make the right decisions at the right time to take you just where you need to be. You will learn, no matter how many times you stumble and fall, to pick yourself up, put on your pink high heels and keep moving forward with grace and ease, feeling stronger and wiser for the experience.

> "I believe in pink. I believe that laughing is the best calorie burner. I believe in kissing, kissing a lot. I believe in being strong when everything seems to be going wrong. I believe that happy girls are the prettiest girls. I believe that tomorrow is another day and I believe in miracles"
>
> Audrey Hepburn

Contents

Introduction 1
Your packing list 7
Pink journaling 9
The activities 'Pink time out' 13
How long will I be on this journey? 17

PART 1
HEARTBREAK MANOR

Meet and greet yourself and your emotions 21
In the Pink Process 27
Level 5 Awareness 35
Level 4 Responsibility 51
Level 3 Feeling 63
Level 2 Forgiveness 97
Level 1 Acceptance 109
Checking out 127

PART 2
The Healing Sanctuary

Welcome to the Healing Sanctuary 133
Who am I? 141
My Pink Heart Print 153
My Inner Pink Star 205

Lady Chitter Chatter 223
Meditation and me 245
Checking out 263

PART 3
THE HAPPINESS SHACK

Hello happiness 269
Self love 275
Passion and purpose 291
My new partner 303
Vision and goals 319
Checking out 331

Epilogue 339
Thank you 343
Bibliography 347

Time alone will not heal all wounds, it
is how you make use of that time that
will create space for your healing

Introduction

"I think the highest and lowest points are the important ones. Anything else is just...in between"

Jim Morrison

Do you feel like your once structured and happy life has crumbled around you? Is everything physical, mental, emotional and spiritual sprawled like rubble on the floor and you are in the middle of it, lost and scared? Do you feel you are trying to fight off a mixed bag of emotions - confusion, anger, sadness, sorrow and many others that seem too scary to face, with a nagging fear this could cause your complete demise?

Are you in the midst of heartbreak, feeling you may never experience happiness again?

You spend time romanticising and idealising the relationship by remembering the early days you spent together. If that experience was true, why are you now where you are, sifting through the rubble?

Your internal negative critical voice which I call Lady Chitter Chatter has appeared in full force. She is that little incessant voice in your head that judges you and makes you feel bad about yourself. She seems to want to undermine any positive choices. She is an expert at putting you down, berating you, creating internal doubt and, with a few sharp words, is able to deplete your self confidence and trust.

She is providing regular head mashing in all areas of your life and creating an extraordinary amount of added stress.

The self doubt creates questions. Were we ever in love? Was it my fault, his fault? Did he really love me? Should I have tried harder?

The shaming, blaming and guilt trips you place on yourself are at an all time high. Your grief is consuming every piece of energy you have, skewing your ability to look into the future. You have to hide behind your grief and still be yourself in a world that is no longer what you knew it to be.

You spend time fantasising that he will change, realise his shortcomings and come to rescue you, creating that happy together forever that you dreamed of.

Let me assure you at this point that this is all, absolutely, a normal part of grief. You are not going crazy, you are just going through a process. You are grieving.

You have two choices where you are now:

1. You can ignore the grief, push the feelings way back down and cover them up with alcohol, new partners, being busy being busy, indulging in drugs, retail therapy, late nights out or whatever your choice of distraction is at the time.

Or

2. You can choose to face up to your truth and move through the process with self love and compassion for yourself. You can do the inner work required to get yourself to your new sacred space where you love and forgive yourself. Then, and only then, will the relationship you have with yourself blossom like a beautiful flower garden in spring.

Introduction

Now this may sound like hard work, and I'm not going to lie, parts of it are hard work. It may be appealing to go with the first choice and what appears the easier way forward, but deep down you know this will not serve you well and you understand your spiritual growth will only develop and expand by taking choice number two.

Investing time now in opening up to your truth and creating an environment of self love, rather than burying it further down, will pay off in gigantic ways in your life, your future loves and your path moving forwards.

Come on the journey with me and use this book to help you move through the process and learn new tools, skills and self knowledge in order to heal your heartbreak, face your fears and fall in love with yourself. Then you can create a new bright and shiny future full of love and happiness.

This book takes you on a journey to three special places, Heartbreak Manor, the Healing Sanctuary and the Happiness Shack. Each destination holds unique gifts and lessons for you. As you move from one destination to another you will fully understand the purpose of your stay and the reason for this difficult journey.

At Heartbreak Manor you will learn to process the initial heartbreak and move out of basic survival mode. Here you will create self awareness, take ownership and responsibility for your life, meet and greet your feelings and emotions and seek forgiveness, clarity and acceptance. You will find love for yourself.

At the Healing Sanctuary we create some breathing space to help you to grow the love you have and to reconnect with yourself. You will find your truth, truly meet and know yourself, find self forgiveness and allow respite and healing from this heartbreak or any others lingering from the past.

At the Happiness Shack it is time to rediscover your talents and gifts, your passions and purpose in life. You will redesign and redecorate internally, setting goals and creating your own personal vision statement to become an amazing new version of yourself. Here you are preparing to launch yourself out into the world and shower other people with sparkles from the new spectacular you.

Redesign and redecorate internally

I invite you to take this journey, work through the processes and use the tools. Ponder at question time and complete the exercises and journaling. Take the time to invest in yourself and you will, through your journey, become a happier version of your gorgeous self.

My deepest desire for this book is to propel you forward through your heartbreak. I hope it will help you look deep into your heart and soul and allow healing internally. I hope it will help you look holistically at your life, which is ripe for redesigning and redecorating at this opportune time.

With three keys in your possession, love, truth and purpose, anything is possible. You can move past this breakup and on to many other amazing opportunities in all areas of your life.

I surround myself with many things pink. It is a part of who I am. It makes me feel at home, at ease, myself, in love with nature, being and living. It sends a warm glow to my heart in the form of love and reminds me to open it up to all experiences, pink or otherwise

Introduction

In addition, you get to do it with dignity, class and grace and in a fabulous pair of pink high heels, because, speaking from my own experience, when I am in my favourite high heels, they are often pink and they make me feel just a little bit more distinguished and classy. If your version of this is your Doc Martins, go for it. Know your truth in relation to both life and shoes and choose accordingly.

Allow me to guide you to a true sense of love, inner peace, wisdom, strength, calmness, grace, knowledge and a full understanding and acceptance of yourself, from the exciting blow-you-away good points to the imperfections that make you, you. Come with me as we move from the Heartbreak Manor, via the Healing Sanctuary, to your ultimate destination, the Happiness Shack and simultaneously transform and heal your life.

Your packing list

"It takes courage...to endure the sharp pains of self discovery rather than choose to take the dull pain of unconsciousness that would last the rest of our lives"

Marianne Williamson

There are some special things you will need to pack to be prepared for this journey:

- A pack of bright, colourful pencils
- A journal you can call your Little Pink book of Love
- Your favourite music playlist
- Phone numbers of friends you can call on when needed
- Lots of coffee and chocolate
- All your four-legged fur children
- Your best pair of pink high heels

Heartbreak, Healing and Happiness

It will get rough at times and you will need to dig deep into your inner backpack and look for one of the traits below to help you through:

- Your Inner Pink Star (inner wisdom) and the real versions of the truth
- Lady Chitter Chatter (inner negative critical voice) and the versions of her truth
- Your willingness, courage, faith and desire for change and healing
- Your trust in yourself and the process
- Your awareness and honesty to face your truths
- Your self expression, your playful and creative side
- Your heart and its readiness to be opened fully again
- Your emotions and spiritual awareness, for better or worse

Pink Journaling

*"Sometimes good things fall apart so
better things can fall together"*

Marilyn Monroe

Journaling is a personal development wonder tool. As humans, we are very able to resist what is difficult for us and hold down our feelings. We distract ourselves with a myriad of wonderful, fun people, things and activities and run away from ourselves.

We may try talking to a therapist or friends, which is an excellent outlet, but they cannot be available all the time. We need a means to sit quietly with only ourselves and be honest and truthful about what we are feeling. We need to get to know ourselves, who we are, what we are scared of, what is hurting us. The more you know about yourself the easier and more enjoyable life becomes.

Your journal, which I call your Little Pink book of Love, could be this outlet. In your journal you can let the pen sprawl across the page and express, then release, what is inside. It is amazing what is presented to you on a blank page if you let yourself open up and see what is inside.

Spend some time searching for a journal that will be right for you, one that you will be drawn to, a place you will feel comfortable to house your hurts and fears. Some people just grab a bound notebook and happily write for hours, and others like to have the perfect book with a beautifully crafted cover.

Spend some time finding your perfect Little Pink book of Love to house all your feelings and vulnerabilities

Store your journal in a part of your house where it is quiet and soothing. Create an environment that feels safe and comfortable. There will be times you feel vulnerable, so being able to go to your safe space is important to help you process your grief and heartbreak.

When you spend time in your quiet place, you can reach for your Little Pink book of Love and let the words and the feelings flow. It is an opportunity to describe how you are feeling and admit the truth to yourself. Here you can list your hopes and dreams, your biggest challenges and greatest fears.

This is the place where you can talk about what led you to take this journey, why you are here and what you hope to achieve. Scribble away and purge all the information into your Little Pink book of Love. Don't think about what you are writing - just let the words appear in front of you. Be honest, be open, be willing to unleash self discovery.

I have journals galore, as I tend to journal more when I am making big decisions in my life or am grieving for losses that have been presented to me. I am comforted that they hold all my thoughts, feelings and emotions. They have been fabulous friends because they are so non-judgemental. They allow me to purge all and everything onto the pages and help clear and release any negative energy I am carrying around. They have saved me from many emotionally destructive evenings, because once I can deliver all my feelings onto paper I can breathe and relax, knowing I have released and processed more of what has been troubling me.

Pink Journaling

They allow me just to be me. When I feel lost, scared and confused I start writing and, before long, my true self returns. I tap into my feelings and thoughts, deep below. I tap into my authentic self, buried beneath the piles of rubble. It is such an enlightening feeling when you feel you have lost yourself entirely, to see snippets reappearing. It can restore the hope and optimism in your spirit and enable you to carry on to another day believing everything will be okay in time.

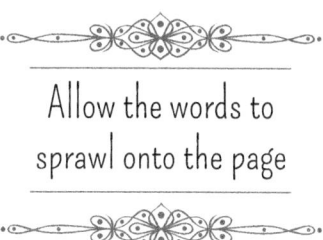

Allow the words to sprawl onto the page

The activities 'Pink time out'

"A person who never made a mistake never tried anything new"

Albert Einstein

'Pink time out' are exercises that will help propel you forward at full force in your healing. Some of these exercises take strength, will and courage; they may move you way out of your comfort zone into areas of yourself you had not visited before.

If you don't feel ready to do the particular exercises, simply reading the information is a good start. You can then revisit the activity later if you wish. However, participating in the exercises will be the cherry on top of the pie and will heal you at a much deeper emotional and spiritual level.

As your coach and guide, I will always be with you on this journey, a support and safe haven to enable you to take the risk of delving deeper into yourself to gain new insight and strength. I will give you solutions and antidotes to the worst of your fears and struggles.

When you see 'Pink time out', stop and breathe and get your Little Pink book of Love and wait for further instructions. Let's try some Pink time out right now, to get in the mood...

Pink Time Out – Promise

◦ Stop and Breathe ◦

A promise is a declaration, a commitment, a hand-on-heart sacred agreement that you WILL fulfil its action and desire. It is a pledge and vow, your word of honour, made to yourself from yourself.

For one moment, forget your yesterdays and your pain and anguish. Be in this moment only.

Take in what you have read to this point. Acknowledge how you feel about things in this moment.

Call yourself to action and make a promise to yourself. Make a promise that will move you forward, even if only a small step. A promise of how you can make a difference to create the life you desire so much, to lead from this moment onwards.

It can be as small as finishing this book or as big as transforming into the happiest person you can be. You get to decide, this is your special promise.

What is one promise you can make to yourself today to make a change to all of your tomorrows?

Write your promise in your Little Pink book of Love. 'I promise...'

Now place your hand on your heart, close your eyes and repeat out loud your promise to yourself, slowly and succinctly. Allow it to soak into your every cell, into your deep internal being. Keep repeating the promise until you

The activities 'Pink time out'

can feel it holding a place in your heart, ready to be eternally fulfilled. Honour the promise and honour yourself.

To keep your promise alive and at the forefront of your mind, post-note it on your desk, lipstick it to your mirror in the bathroom, blackboard it in the kids' playroom, magnet it on the fridge. Wherever it inspires you, ensure it is there, ready to be heard, seen, felt and integrated internally. Bring it alive and your very own miracles may start to occur.

How long will I be on this journey?

"Dance. Smile. Giggle. Marvel. Trust. Hope. Love. Wish. Believe. Most of all, enjoy every moment of the journey, and appreciate where you are at this moment instead of always focusing on how far you have to go"

Mandy Hale

What a great question, yet an extremely difficult one to answer. Every person in this universe is an individual, so the time spent at various places in the healing process will vary depending on your own circumstances, previous struggles and the level of emotional intelligence you currently have. Instead of trying to put a time on the journey, I suggest you ride with it, visit the places you need to when you need to and revisit them again later if required.

What is paramount is to regularly stop, breathe, sit back and reflect on where you have been and how far you have come. This is how you will know you are moving forward. Celebrate your successes, be they big or small, for any move forward is a positive step towards your new astonishing life.

There will be times you will feel like you have moved three steps forward and one or maybe even ten gigantic steps backwards. I won't lie to you and say this won't happen. I certainly experienced it on many occasions. Every time my journey decided to throw me backwards, I got up again and was soon catapulted even further forward. This is how I jumped major hurdles and ended up even further along in the process to realisations and recovery. I had made some serious progress and was becoming the person I wanted to be, reconnecting and falling in love with myself at an even deeper level.

> Everything you need to find self love, truth, peace, clarity, serenity and fulfilment is already inside you. Redesign and redecorate from the inside out, move forward with passion and excitement

Without the devastating lows we cannot experience the shiny bright highs. As you move through the process, keep in the back of your mind that after the lows, come the highs. After every winter comes spring, a new season with new beginnings, a fresh start, a chance to start over again, all fresh and sparkly.

The question I wish to ask now is, are you ready to begin creating new beginnings for yourself?

If so, go put the coffee machine on and brew your favourite coffee, find your most comfy chair, and let's get started. I know you don't want to reside in this place in your life any longer than you have to. I can feel your eagerness (and maybe a little nervousness) to start using the tools to bring love and truth into your life, unveiling your authentic self and finding your place In the Pink. It is time to start a fresh and move you to your happy place, all glittery and new, ready to take on your world.

PART 1
HEARTBREAK MANOR

Meet and greet yourself and your emotions

"When you break up, your whole identity is shattered. It's like death"

Dennis Quaid

Heartbreak Manor, although once majestic and full of life and fun, bubbling with social activities and love, is now run down and slightly decrepit. The big, golden door handle turns to open the large, creaky, wooden doors and reveals a greeting area that feels dark, scary, unfamiliar and uncomfortable. You peruse your surroundings with trepidation and notice that the grand chandeliers flicker on and off, highlighting the spider webs dripping from them. The carpets are clean yet old, covering the beautiful aged floorboards peeking out from the corners of the room. They ache to be exposed. The paint is dull and unattractive, yearning for a spruce up in a lively fresh colour.

The grandiose staircase to the upper levels of the Manor could have been stunning, yet the banisters are hard to hold on to, wooden chips are breaking away and splinters lie everywhere. The kitchen no longer produces the heavenly meals it was once famous for; pots and pans hang in dusty rows along the walls. The gardens are overgrown and undernourished; the rose bushes and hedges surrounding the Manor may have once suited an English stately home but are now overgrown with dead limbs and buds. The attic staircase that opens to the roof top feels eerie and cold, leaving you wanting to escape, anywhere, but at least to a lower level where everything feels marginally lighter.

You are checked into your room on level 5, closest to the eerie rooftop. It was explained at reception that all new residents begin their journey at level 5 and as they begin to heal, learn new skills and complete the exercises provided, they slowly progress down the staircase through each level, back to the ground level where reception is housed and checkout is waiting.

As you put down your bags, you ponder the reasons you were brought here. You notice a piece of paper on the fireplace that lists the activities with a perplexing reference to In the Pink highlighted at the top. Suffering from exhaustion, confusion, disorientation and fatigue, you are relieved to go with the flow and put your trust in others to guide you.

You are not sure what will happen next, but have faith the journey will bring contentment and love. You hope and pray you are where you are meant to be at this point in time and try desperately to muster strength from deep within. You hold tightly to the belief that you will leave this old scary place and move to a lighter and brighter destination at some time in the near future.

The people you meet as you first meander quietly around Heartbreak Manor seem friendly enough, yet they are all lacking in spirit and joy. They wander the halls just as you do, desperately seeking healing and happiness, unable to embrace the abundance the world had to offer. This place has a visceral sense of negative energy that flows through the people, the staff and the building.

You can see the potential of the Manor, with its underlying stunning architecture. With love, care, time and learnings, you know that redesigning and rebuilding would expose to the world a building of beauty and stature. You can see that despite its fatigue and lack

MEET AND GREET YOURSELF AND YOUR EMOTIONS

of love, it has the potential to blossom into something spectacular and sparkling.

You may not have intended to book a room or to visit, but nonetheless you are here. You have landed with a thud and have no idea how you got here, what to do here or how the hell to leave this place. Every moment is a struggle but trust that you will know in time exactly what to do, how to be and how to reconnect with your true happy joyful self.

A place here automatically opened up for you when you realised you needed help. You became willing to navigate through the terrain of heartbreak with your eyes and heart ready to be opened. I'll be honest, it gets rough, tricky and sticky moving through this part of your life, but as you strengthen yourself and your emotional muscles you will grieve, process your emotions and experiences and reflect, and soon you will get your groove back. You will redesign and redecorate your life one day at a time from the inside out.

You must be gentle and compassionate with yourself and create patience whilst you are on this journey. It is a process and unfortunately it will not magically happen overnight, it takes time and work, sometimes really hard work. If like me you have struggled with having patience, this will be another gift and learning experience you will take with you into your future. You will discover that patience really is a virtue and is in fact a necessity for a serene life.

Being impulsive all my life and wanting everything yesterday, I really struggled to have faith in my journey back from heartbreak. The two major heartbreaks in my adult life eventually taught me to trust my journey and have faith in exactly where I was in life at any time. I wanted everything fixed now, I wanted the pain to go away now. I didn't have the time or desire to delve into my emotions; they were too scary, intimidating and time consuming.

My expectation was that life was always meant to be fun. Perhaps in hindsight it wasn't a lack of time but a lack of tools to deal with grief and its crew of friends. So until I was in my early thirties I cruised around in denial, starting with my parent's separation when I was fifteen and then various small break-ups along the way. At the time, avoiding emotion seemed the right thing to do, but I tell you it waited for me and has since hit me hard, twice. Both adult heartbreaks were gut-wrenching experiences that I needed to process and move through.

Often when you experience heartbreak you keep the fear and excruciating feelings you suffered buried deep in your subconscious. You find that you have started living small and procrastinating or avoiding challenges in your life. Each time you try to rise to the next challenge you recall these subconscious feelings of fear and bring them into what's happening now. These may not even be conscious thoughts. They appear automatically as this is the story you have been telling yourself for years. You go into protection mode, operating from a fear base.

> Be gentle and compassionate with yourself

It is easy to go into denial, burying the feelings down as far as you can and pretending they don't faze you. In fact you can do this for a long period of time and get by. However my question to you is, is just getting by enough? Or do you want your heart to open up and sing, to feel the aliveness and abundance the world has to offer and the good feelings that come with living in the present moment, connected to yourself, loving, living your truth and following your passions and your purpose?

Why didn't anyone ever teach me how to live through this? Why do we have to learn the hard way and navigate through the muck of our difficult times with what little we know, too afraid to ask for help for fear of what others will think?

Meet and greet yourself and your emotions

We keep hiding behind the socially acceptable façade we have created and hope one day we will magically be happy. 'When I get the bigger house I will be happy' or 'when I get that car I will be happy'. The time to be happy is now. Now is your life, this is it. While you are hoping and wishing for the 'When I' life can quickly pass you by.

To accept yourself, you need internal validation from yourself to love yourself. You need to drop, once and for all, the false illusion that any external validation will create happiness. Shaky foundations are never a great place to build, as eventually everything just comes toppling down around us, which creates a big mess to clean up. Sometimes you need to go back to basics - redesign, redecorate and create strong, grounded foundations and from there build your tower of strength.

For tonight though, you choose to curl up in your king-size, four-poster bed and snuggle tightly in a ball under the covers to get some much-needed sleep. At least for one more night you can stay unaware and dwell in your miseries.

The musty smell of the Manor sits in your nostrils and the eerie, uncomfortable feeling remains, but gradually, as you drift off to sleep, you feel a small sense of proudness for taking the first step. You know that tomorrow when you wake up something is about to change. You know you will need to draw on all your strength and energy to move to a new state of mind and find your willingness and courage to start the process of healing.

"The privilege of a lifetime is to become who you truly are"

C.G. Jung

Heartbreak, Healing and Happiness

Let your heart open up, feel the sparkle the world has to offer and the good feelings that come with living in the present moment, connected to yourself and living your truth

In the Pink Process

"As my sufferings mounted I soon realised that there were two ways in which I could respond to my situation - either to react with bitterness or seek to transform the suffering into a creative force. I decided to follow the latter course"

Martin Luther King Jr

When you wake up, you wish you could stay under the covers, but you know breakfast is calling. You were told last night not to miss any meals as you need to maintain your energy levels at all times. Sluggishly you drag yourself out of bed, get dressed, grab the piece of paper headed 'In the Pink' from the fireplace and head out the door to breakfast, totally clueless about what is to unfold and how you will cope with it all.

Dodging the spider webs dripping down the faded walls, you feel alone, shaky and scared. Never have you had to visit a place like this before, and deep down you don't understand how this is going to help. You try to find that speck of proudness that appeared last night to help move you to the first step, but today it seems elusive. You know it would be so easy to give up and stop trying but you can't. You must move forward; it is really the only option.

No doubt you feel that grief and its friends are not very friendly. In fact they can be downright nasty and damaging, making life a total misery. The In the Pink Process will help you to process your grief and emotions and learn to work with them. After completing the process, you will find that you can be gentler on yourself when you have a grief attack. If you do not know how to become friends with your emotions and deal with them, they will keep you stuck in the mud. Blocked feelings lead to aggression, depression, guilt, low self esteem and even physical issues or disease.

What I noticed when I was grieving is that I was often stuck in the negative emotions and felt like I was going to be there forever. I didn't notice the small moments of reprieve, where every now and again I felt other emotions, like relief and empowerment. I felt like I was getting nowhere fast and this scared me to death. I used the In the Pink Process to work through my mess and chaos of emotions, until I was back In the Pink.

The phrase In the Pink was coined in the 16th century, to mean being very strong and operating well

When you are in the midst of a grief attack, you think and analyse and scare yourself silly asking yourself if it will be that way forever. You try anything to take you out of the state you are in, using distractions left right and centre until the feeling goes away.

Instead, take a moment to consider how you behave when you are happy. You don't over-analyse the situation and ask why are you happy, you just run with it, express it, let it happen and enjoy it. Now I am not saying you will suddenly start enjoying your negative emotions, but you can learn to identify them, to run with them, express them, let them happen and move past them.

Think about how children are laughing and happy one minute, then suddenly something triggers an angry or tearful outburst. Then in the next minute they are happy again. Their secret is that they felt it, they expressed it, they processed it, they moved the energy out from their body and then they moved on. The secret was obvious at a younger age and is still buried deep inside you.

In the Pink Process

As you grow older and create beliefs and become touched by society's conditioning, you have learned to repress and suppress feelings. This actually causes them to be more of a problem. The more you resist them, the more they will persist. The more you can let them go, the quicker you will return to happiness. It really is that easy, if you are willing to try it.

While you work through the In the Pink Process, be aware that it is working not only on your heartbreak but also healing other areas of your life. This process can be used in any situation you find yourself stuck, wherever you find you need to work through emotions to find your truth, peace and release. You may be grappling with a big decision to leave your job and embark on the career you have always wanted, you may be managing a house move, it could be any of the myriad of challenges life throws at us.

The tools in this process will help you evolve in your emotional development and heighten your emotional intelligence. They will stay with you forever, so you can call upon them whenever needed. They are the backbone and the foundations to rebuild yourself with love and appreciation and face challenges and new scary experiences head on, with excitement and confidence in yourself.

You will move out of acting small and protecting yourself out of fear. You will grow and move mountains, you will pursue your passions with grace and ease. Each step you conquer builds you up, which is why taking the time out after a breakup and doing the work, throws you back into life bigger and better than before. The lessons are there and if you learn from them you will GROW.

UNDERSTAND YOUR FEELINGS

"The best and most beautiful things in the world cannot be seen or even touched. They must be felt with the heart"

Helen Keller

Feelings are sensations you hold in your body. They are created by your thoughts and are individual to you, based on how you see the world. As soon as you judge your feelings, you create more difficulties in moving through them. Instead of judging them, aim to accept them for what they are.

It is important to honour your feelings and understand they are normal. Then you can look at creating healthy ways to express them, while at the same time understanding where they are coming from.

Give yourself the right to feel the way you do. You have a right to feel whatever you are feeling. Nothing is right or wrong and no one can ever tell you how to feel.

Your feelings can help you become aware of your thoughts and what you are telling yourself. You can then decide if it is healthy or not. If it is unhealthy, you have the choice to change the thought. Research shows that you have approximately 50,000 thoughts every day and 70–80 percent are negative. You may have heard of the 'monkey mind' which is a Buddhist term for an out of control mind, churning over thoughts in an undisciplined fashion.

Humans need structure and routine and when guests arrive at the Heartbreak Manor they tend to have lost this. It seems as if everything your physical, mental, emotional and spiritual self once knew has been thrown up in the air and landed all over the place. Nothing makes sense, it is a total mess, you are a total mess. There is so much emotional housekeeping to do you don't know where to start, and this creates more stress and difficulties as the clean-up task seems totally overwhelming. It can be tempting at this point to fall into a self-fulfilling prophecy that you will be here forever, and you may be if you don't get some direction and help.

Having a process, a logical, step-by-step process to work things out, makes the full task seem a little less overwhelming. A process gives you some much needed guidance on where and how to start.

To honour myself and my emotions, I found that first and foremost I needed to create awareness for where I was and what I was feeling. Awareness allowed me to reveal my feelings and my truths to myself. These revelations gave me an opportunity to take responsibility and ownership of my thoughts, feelings, choices and behaviours, and moved me on from a victim and blaming mentality. I started to feel powerful once again and I realised I was able to take control of my life.

Feeling my feelings released much internal pressure and actually initiated healing. I began to understand those feelings, why they were there and what they were telling me. This in turn provided me with a huge amount of clarity. I was able to forgive myself for feeling the way I did and behaving in ways that were not in line with my values. This allowed me to let go of my shame, guilt and negative emotions. Working through this process, I was able to forgive my ex's perceived mistakes and shortcomings and move forward with continued love in my heart for myself and for him.

This clarity and understanding led me to a higher appreciation and realisation of my heart and soul, and from there to acceptance of myself as a whole package. Knowing how and why my feelings surfaced, I was able to surrender to them and let them go rather than them holding me at gun point.

This process I used has been refined and perfected to become the In the Pink Process. I will guide you through the five levels of healing and stay beside you at every step.

In the Pink Process
Love - Truth -Purpose
5 Awareness
4 Responsibility
3 Feeling
2 Forgiveness
1 Acceptance

On level 5 you will look at your self awareness and how massively important this is to your life and your inner health. Moving down to level 4 you will look at taking responsibility and ownership for your life. Progressing down to level 3 you will feel, process and express the feelings and create some instant relief. This will lead you to level 2 where you will learn forgiveness and compassion for yourself and others. On the last level, level 1 you will gain clarity and come to acceptance.

So you have come to the end of your first day at Heartbreak Manor, and heading back to your room you feel ready to get started with the In the Pink Process. You know it may help remove some of the grief and the stress and provide relief from the constant state of hopelessness you find yourself in.

This morning you knew nothing of what was ahead in this place and now you can see that as you heal, you move down the decrepit staircase, level by level, back to reception. Once you have completed the process and arrive at the ground level you will be ready to check out and move on.

As yet though, you do not understand how your heart, soul and feelings will catch up to what your head can understand. You cannot quite believe that you will make it all the way down and actually feel better about the situation you find yourself in. At times you still feel there is no point to it all.

You do not want to remain near the eerie rooftop though, so you know you must keep putting one foot in front of the other. Your feet, your heart and the process must lead somewhere. You try to let your worries go and go with the flow but for now that seems so difficult.

You climb back into the four-poster bed for another night's sleep with a visceral sense, once again, of uncomfortableness around what is happening to you. You have so many moments of being bombarded by different emotions coming to beat you up and make you feel bad about yourself, and hope that somehow soon you will be able to get on top of them again.

Pink diamonds are some of the world's rarest diamonds. The defects that cause their pink colour make them more special, just like us

Level 5 Awareness

*"Where ignorance is our master, there
is no possibility of real peace"*

Dalai Lama

Still sluggish but awake, you take the limited knowledge you have about the In the Pink Process, gather up your courage and faith and prepare to come to terms with level 5. You figure you have to start somewhere, if you can master level 5 you know then you can move down a level. Your sensibility says to you just take one step at a time, but simultaneously your mind produces thoughts of chaos and fear.

You have become used to feeling so poorly so you access the little faith you can find and add that to the willingness lying deep within to get started so you can get healed and get happy. That is what the Manor promises and you cling to that promise for dear life.

Awareness is the first step on your journey to profound change, which is why it sits at the top level of Heartbreak Manor. Awareness in life is everything, as without awareness you stumble along in the dark, tripping over yourself, not knowing who you are, what you want, where to go, who to be or how to deal with the challenges that life presents to you.

You may not even know what you are feeling or why you are feeling it. You are held prisoner by your thoughts and feelings and leave it to chance how you feel each day. You live in a constant state of frustration, not knowing how to control your feelings or understanding how they hold you captive.

Awareness takes a few forms; there is awareness of your feelings, your thoughts, your behaviours, your choices, your personal relationships, as well as every other area of your life.

Awareness gives you the ability to take the power back and take control of your thoughts, feelings, choices, emotions and life. Taking control of your life will see you move towards being totally aware of what you are thinking and feeling at any one time, and making choices in alignment with your truth. You will be running the show, totally in charge of how you feel rather than leaving it to chance and hoping for the best.

When you make a judgement about yourself, it is said in the conscious mind. The more you repeat the same message over and over, the more it filters from the conscious mind to the subconscious mind. Once your thought has moved to the subconscious mind it becomes cemented there and can be very hard to budge.

Once it's settled in your subconscious, this judgment about yourself will pop up without you consciously thinking about it, as an automatic thought. These automatic thoughts are what can move you from happy to sad in an instant without knowing why. When your feeling state changes rapidly, it is generally because something has triggered an automatic thought that was stored in your subconscious, and has been spoken to you as an automatic thought.

Awareness is the key to profound change

Try to be mindful of what you are thinking and feeling in any given moment. When your mood changes and you start to experience negative feelings, STOP and ask yourself what you were thinking just a moment ago. Are there any obvious triggers that made your feeling state change? Learn to constantly check in with yourself to see what is going on.

These automatic thoughts are your programming which has developed over years of listening to the same negative internal network. To change the network and the programming you need to consciously flick the switch to another frequency, take in new information, and dispel the old myths, self sabotaging and limiting beliefs. Get up to date with who you now are or who you would like to be. Think and feel what serves you now, not what served you in the past, and act on that NOW.

Try becoming more aware of your thoughts and feelings. Bring them into the light, which will bring them into the conscious mind. Once they are in your conscious mind, you can challenge the beliefs you once held true and learn to replace them with new and more constructive thoughts and beliefs. These new, constructive beliefs and thoughts create new healthy messages that can filter back to your subconscious mind and help you create a magnificent new life.

A LESSON IN SELF AWARENESS

In my late 20s and early 30s, I had not yet mastered emotional intelligence and found myself wedged tightly in my first management role in the corporate world and deeply involved in my first serious, long term relationship.

Successfully moving up the corporate ladder while playing house with my first love was exhilarating. I was enchanted by the prestige and importance my business role created and the fun, connection and love the relationship provided.

Once the cracks started to appear in the relationship and the stress levels rose at work I still believed I was bulletproof. I buried my emotions, stuffing them under the surface hoping they would magically disappear.

I knew there was something missing, and sensed that my heart and soul were not being stimulated. My career provided no sense of purpose, and I was starting to feel my relationship was not healthy or providing the deep connection I sought, or the ability for me to be my authentic self. Yet I was not ready or able to create self awareness and investigate further.

I held on tight to my good salary and my perfect-looking relationship whilst my anxiety skyrocketed, until I had my first panic attack. It really scared me but it also woke me up.

Because I lacked awareness, things got much worse before they got better. Not understanding what panic attacks were, they quickly robbed me of my self esteem, which made it even harder to access a sensible decision to bring me back to some sense of normality or just inner mental health.

I had a quiet voice inside that knew I sought a life filled with passion and purpose. I wanted to wake up every day with a clear sense of what I could offer the world. I wanted a relationship that was defined by what was good about it, rather than what it was missing.

The first step was awareness to understand where I was, and this was enough for me to find my starting point. I became aware I was existing rather than thriving in this magic life I had been given. This awareness reminded me of my strength, hope and optimism for the future and helped me drag myself out of both situations and take time out to heal.

The awareness had created the consequences, as difficult as they were. Together, in time, they created the magnificent life filled with wonderful opportunities that were to follow.

Level 5 Awareness

I took a part-time role working in a book store, a job I had dreamt of for a long time. What a fabulous and soothing place to be while I navigated through my heartbreak and the landmines of my self discovery, surrounded by books galore full of information to help me heal.

Working part-time gave me an opportunity to commence my study in counselling. Every day I took baby steps to move away from the person I had become and closer to the person I wanted to be. I was on my path to find my passions and live my purpose.

I have learnt that if I continue to use my awareness and live my truth, things fall into place, every time. Not without challenges and some terrifying times, but they do. This can happen for you also, if you believe and you are willing to take risks, understand yourself and use the In the Pink Process in any area of your life that it is needed.

Sometimes the honesty that awareness brings results in hard decisions that require courage and braveness to move forward and step into alignment with your true self. Awareness is the first key to admitting the truth to yourself, to creating freedom within yourself, to start making changes, to becoming who you really are. It is like the first elusive answer to all your problems.

With my relationship breakups, I needed to become aware of how I was feeling within the relationship. For a long time I was able to bury the feelings and not really admit the truth even to myself. This kept me in a state of fear, anger, anxiety and sadness, with only snippets of gladness and joy thrown in occasionally.

By avoiding the truth, I could avoid the consequences. Through awareness, I discovered that the consequences were worth celebrating, not avoiding.

Pink sunsets appear after thunderstorms. It takes a lot of energy to make something so spectacular

Awareness is the first step in the In the Pink Process and one that will repay you in bucket-loads throughout your life. You can use it everywhere to unlock many more locks or blocks that you may want to pry open.

Even if you cannot admit the truth to anyone else, please believe me when I say, you owe it to yourself to become aware of your own truth.

 ## Pink Time Out – Question Time

∾ Stop and Breathe ∾

Throughout the In the Pink Process there are various Pink time out activities with lots of questions.

Questions enable you go inside, access your inner truth and work to find the thoughts, feelings and answers that are right for you.

Your feelings will help you access the right answer. Notice the way you feel when you answer the questions; does it make you feel good or bad about yourself? These are very helpful clues to discover the answer you are looking for that is best for you.

With all the questions, take out your Little Pink book of Love to record your thoughts and feelings. Exposing your truth on paper is a cathartic process which enables you to become more grounded, to gain more awareness and understanding of yourself.

Every now and again, a question will tap into your inner self and provide the enlightening epiphany that you are looking for, to propel you forward with clarity and acceptance.

Level 5 Awareness

Spend some time with yourself and go slowly when pondering the lists of questions provided. Notice which questions you are drawn to and which ones feel the most uncomfortable – sometimes these can be the most beneficial.

Read the list of questions below and allow time and space for self reflection. In your Little Pink book of Love, write or journal your thoughts, feelings, reactions and any epiphanies and wow moments you may have. Let the pen flow and see what appears on the page in front of you. As this may take you out of your comfort zone, remember to remain gentle and compassionate with yourself, and always come from a place of love.

1. From 0 - 10, 10 being most aware, how aware are you currently of your thoughts, decisions feelings and actions?
2. From 0 - 10, 10 being the most willing, how willing are you to create awareness in your life?
3. In one sentence, describe your ability to be aware of your thoughts and feelings.
4. Think of a time when you were totally unaware of your thoughts, emotions or a situation you were creating. How did you feel? What did it add/detract to your life?
5. Think of a time when you were totally aware of your thoughts, emotions or a situation you were creating. How did you feel? What did it add/detract to your life?
6. Write about the difference between these two experiences.
7. What distractions do you use to avoid being aware and truthful with yourself?

8. How do you feel about yourself when you are partaking in your distractions?
9. What consequences are you avoiding by remaining unaware?
10. Are you ready to accept the consequences in your life that your awareness will bring?
11. What is one small step you can take today to become more aware?

Well done on your reflection and your courage to go deeper whilst completing your first Pink time out exercise. I hope this exercise has provided you with some small snippets of clarity that you can use as you move forward through the process of healing. Every small step you take today adds to help create a new tomorrow and a happier and healthier you in the future.

Create willingness to answer questions and complete activities with your truth. From your truth you will find peace and clarity. This will lead you to a greater happiness than you could ever imagine. You are a shining bright pink star on the inside; you just need to clear the clouds to find the stars

Pink Time Out – Activity

❧ Stop and Breathe ❧

Before we can go to where we would like to be, we need to find out where we are. This activity allows you to take an emotional inventory to explore how you are feeling at the present time.

To give you a little help, I have included two lists below. One is a list of positive-feeling words and the other is a list of negative-feelings words.

As we feel and process the negative emotions, we will create more room to experience the positive ones again. When positive feelings arrive, be grateful for the reprieve. Use compassion and allow yourself to feel good, even if just for a little while.

You may want to revisit these lists on good days and bad days, depending on how you are managing. It is helpful to become familiar with the whole host of different emotions that are on your emotional radar at any one time.

Pink is the fourth primary energy centre of the heart chakra, symbolising joy, happiness and love

Negative Feelings Words

Circle with a coloured pen or highlight all the negative feelings you are experiencing during this chaotic time in the midst of your heartbreak. There will be ones that jump right off the page and reveal themselves to you and you can relate to immensely. There will be others that are important but more subtle.

With the negative feelings, take your time and note the sensations of your body as you read through each feeling. You will notice that some words make you feel uneasy or uncomfortable. These may be the ones you want to skip over as they bring difficult emotions to the surface. These however are the ones you really want to highlight. If you can identify and then address these feelings, they will create the most healing.

Experience each feeling in your body as you read its name. Let your body and its sensations tell you what is affecting you most and what is not relevant to you. Trust your body, it never lies. The feelings that are affecting you are the ones you need to work through. The ones you are most scared of could well be the ones you try to ignore and suppress through fear.

What we resist persists, it feeds and grows and works against us until we shine a bright light on it and face the fear head on. Resisting a negative emotion will bring more negativity, so shine the light as bright as you can, feel the fear, face up to all the feelings and move onwards and upwards to an enlightened spiritual journey and awakening.

Level 5 Awareness

The feelings you cannot be with, take control of you

Scared	Angry	Irritated	Wary	Sad
Afraid	Annoyed	Annoyed	Suspicious	Depressed
Dread	Furious	Impatient	Worried	Sorrowful
Panic	Irate	Frustrated	Frightened	Melancholy
Foreboding	Livid	Unhappy	Lost	Teary
Petrified	Outrage	Disgruntled	Puzzled	Hopeless
Fear	Resentful	Aggravated	Confused	Rejected
Stagnant	Reactive	Toxic	Emotional	Betrayed
Inauthentic	Under expressed	Complex	Abandoned	Scarce
Shaky	Grumpy	Bombarded	Disgraced	At wits end
Terrified	Enraged	Untrusting	Ambivalent	Dejected
Distant	Hostile	Exasperated	Flustered	Disappointed
Withdrawn	Disgusted	Upset	Guilty	Heartbroken
Miserable	Appalled	Shocked	Ashamed	Grief
Envy	Yearning	Critical	Apathetic	Crippled
Jealous	Under realised	Sarcastic	Turbulent	Indifferent
Anxious	Troubled	Surprised	Embarrassed	Hurt
Restless	Bewildered	Horrified	Lethargic	Alone
Rattled	Perplexed	Repulsed	Tired	Numb
In pain	Not interested	Nervous	Burnt out	Bored
Despair	Disturbed	Hated	Exhausted	Aloof
Worthless	Mortified	Uncomfortable	Empty	Cold
Regretful	Lethargic	Weak	Devastated	Detached
Chaotic	Heavy			

Take a deep BREATH

POSITIVE FEELINGS WORDS

Circle with a coloured pen or highlight all the positive feelings you are feeling. You may struggle to find positive feelings in the middle of your grief, but there will be some lurking around trying to be seen. They may not be there all the time but may pop up briefly even during this tough time. You may notice that you feel some guilt for having positive feelings at this time. Try to go with the flow: allow yourself to feel all the emotions, good and bad.

Now repeat the exercise circling in a different colour the positive emotions you are lacking yet craving and wish to reconnect with and take with you into your future.

The positive feelings give us a moment to appreciate and bask in the good feelings that may appear in this tumultuous time and remind us of what to look forward to as we progress through our healing.

Happy	Sassy	Interested	In awe	Concise
Pleased	Cheeky	Intrigued	Vibrant	Fulfilled
Joyful	Lively	Empowered	Calm	Optimistic
Delighted	Bold	Radiant	Placated	Full of hope
Excited	Spirited	Sexy	Peaceful	Sparkly
Glad	Blissful	Amused	Fascinated	Dazzled
Valuable	Exotic	Flourishing	Creative	Kind
Extravagant	Nourished	Transforming	Marvellous	Illuminous
Unique	Thriving	Harmonious	Magnificent	Grand
Abundant	Striving	Lovely	Limitless	Embraced

Level 5 Awareness

Grateful	Warm	Passionate	Curious	Stimulated
Thankful	Loving	Amazed	Authentic	Included
Moved	Affectionate	Safe	Blissful	Connected
Inspired	Compassionate	Serene	Tickled pink	Belonging
Appreciative	Ecstatic	Surprised	Awake	Friendly
Elated	Thrilled	Energetic	Aware	Nurtured
Pretty	Tranquil	Satisfied	Dynamic	Renewed
Synchronicity	Diligent	Significant	Desired	Delicious
Striking	Magical	Growing	Sweet	Fortunate
Serendipitous	Sincere	Understood	Savvy	Brilliant
Confident	Quiet	Enthralled	Mellow	Engaged
Relaxed	Proud	Animated	Smiley	Soft
Content	Transparent	Open	Absorbed	Enchanted
Childlike	Centred	Balanced	Eager	Relieved
Healed	Purposeful	Insightful	Responsible	Powerful
Expressive	Determined	Free	Mature	Wise
Sensitive	Introspective	Honest	Integrity	Caring
Light	Enlightened	Accomplished	Clarity	Acceptance

Well done, you have completed another exercise designed to reconnect you with yourself and move past your heartbreak. It is a great start to acknowledge and honestly accept where you are and how you are feeling. Be proud, very proud, you have done some of the work, which takes courage, willingness and time.

In your Little Pink book of Love, write the biggest thing that you learnt from this activity. "I learnt..."

Spend some time journaling a little more around what you are feeling and experiencing. It can create profound change when you become more in touch with your feelings, which in turn can create a sense of empowerment and control around your emotions.

Pink time out – Challenge

～ Stop and Breathe ～

In your Little Pink book of Love, starting today see if you can become a journal junkie. Can you commit for a period of seven days to record how you feel in general in relation to your heartbreak?

Check in with yourself numerous times throughout the day and record your findings. Notice the positive and the negative and journal around these. This will enable you to create some awareness of exactly where you are currently at. Remain patient. Draw out your truths.

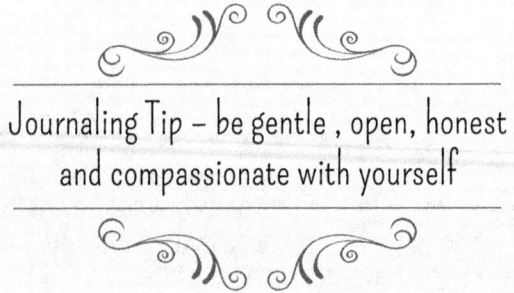

Journaling Tip – be gentle, open, honest and compassionate with yourself

I have created four codes to help you record how you are feeling each day, hour or moment. You may use something else that works for you but the idea is that you can look at the big picture and not at just the moments you feel crappy.

I did this for many weeks during the worst of my heartbreak and what I realised was as time went on that most of my ratings were one or two ticks and very few X's. Where I thought I was struggling terribly, I actually was doing better

Level 5 Awareness

than I thought. When I did have a terrible day I realised that it was a once-off, not how I felt all day, every day.

You can use this for any situation in your life to create more awareness around how you are feeling.

X = Feeling awful, terrible, the worst ever

√ = Feeling just ok, you are getting by some how

√√= Feeling reasonably good

√√√= Feeling great

Let's start now. How did you feel yesterday? Record the date and the rating in your Little Pink book of Love.

As you progress through this book, keep recording how you feel on a daily basis, using the codes above. Notice how things change as you move through the different destinations of your journey and the In the Pink Process while you are you healing.

Ouch. Trying to climb down the staircase carrying your suitcase as well as your weary body and emotions is difficult. You can feel the splinters lodge in your hands. The little bit of hope that you started with once you heard about the In the Pink Process has remained with you. After mastering awareness and completing all the activities and exercises on this level, you feel a little bit wiser and a little less chaotic inside.

Finally you are actually leaving level 5 of Heartbreak Manor. You can say goodbye to the eerie rooftop and move down to level 4. You are leaving with the gift of awareness, the ability to know yourself a little bit better. You have learnt how to become more aware of your thoughts, feelings and behaviours and it is starting to provide small amounts of much-needed relief.

Level 4 Responsibility

"In the long run, we shape our lives, and we shape ourselves. The process never ends until we die. And the choices we make are ultimately our own responsibility"

Eleanor Roosevelt

When you arrive at level 4 and find your new room, you briefly reflect on your experience at level 5 and are thankful for the time spent there. You no longer feel you need to bury your head under the covers as you did on arrival. You have started the In the Pink Process. There is no turning back - that would just be silly - you have to keep moving forward and put your trust in the process.

You still feel ordinary and your emotions are still messing and mashing with your head, causing you to tire quickly and feel foggy and weary. Still, you feel that if you do the inner work you may reap the inner benefits.

You understand from the brochure and from your discussions so far that taking responsibility is your next learning journey, so you commit to opening your heart and delving deeper inside to redesign and redecorate yourself.

You put on your shoes, put one foot in front of the other and as you close the door to your room and head into a day full of new learnings about responsibility, you hope and pray that when you return that night you will be carrying even more gifts to reflect on and to integrate into your healing and true self.

Taking responsibility and ownership for your thoughts, feelings and actions is an enormous step in the healing process. Abdicating responsibility drives you to a victim mentality, blaming others to relieve your pain and discomfort. Deflecting responsibility is usually done in the hope that you remain in the right.

It is so easy to make accusations and point the finger at everyone, everything and anything except yours truly. You construct the false illusion you did nothing wrong, enabling you to feel better about yourself and not having to look at any areas for improvements within.

It is tempting to think you are protecting yourself by believing it was all someone else's doing that created the chaos. Yet when you blame others for how you feel you are giving your power and control away.

While you are playing ignorant, you and your feelings are dependent on another person. This ultimately can send you down the road of helplessness, depression and anxiety. You are not living your truth. You are not being the boss of you. You are letting someone else be the author of your life. You are continually bound by how others act to guide you on how you feel or act. You must wait for them to change or alter their actions and behaviours in order for you to gain balance and clarity. You are a pawn in another's game and a puppet letting others pull your strings. Your life is not decided by what others say or how they act, but how you choose to respond to words or situations.

When you were a child, do you remember saying to your mum and dad "It wasn't me it was him. It's not my fault." From when we were small, we were tempted by deflecting responsibility, and some of us have taken this from the kid's sandpit to the adult playground. We want to ensure we are right. We want to avoid punishment, pain, any negative emotions, the loss of love or having to look internally.

Level 4 Responsibility

As we grow older, we become a little wiser and you may recall occasions when you had to face up to the truth and to your parents or a higher authority and say "Sorry, it was my fault. I did that". You may have to admit to your boss you messed up on an important project. Congratulations on all the times you acted from a higher source and took responsibility to solve the problem.

Deflecting responsibility keeps you in a vicious loop, as you are unable to move forward and make transformations or gain insights into yourself and your life while others are in charge. It seems easier and more comfortable than looking for solutions and taking on challenges. However this is only a short term relief from the longer term pain.

Owning up and taking responsibility for a situation and yourself ultimately means you must stop and look inwards to where you may have been a part in the situation or problem. Acknowledging you had a part to play must be done with gentleness and patience with yourself. It is important you don't just shift the blame from someone else to yourself, which can turn to self loathing and more destructive paths. As you learn to take responsibility, always explore and make discoveries with love and forgiveness.

The beauty in this situation is once you are willing to take responsibility with compassion and love for yourself, you can take a realistic picture of your contribution to the situation. This leads to transformations and new ways of being and feeling. It can produce a myriad of magical gifts in knowing and understanding yourself deeper and can launch you into new and healthier ways of being and acting.

Look at your life; wherever you are in this moment is the consequence of a decision you have made or a decision you have neglected to make. You are the boss of you, and as an adult at any time you are able to take back the reigns of your life and steer it in a different direction. Become the creator and author and design the life you truly desire to suit your wants and needs as an individual.

How would you feel if you stopped letting others dictate how your life should be? How would you feel if you made all the decisions that were in the best interests of your higher self?

You have the ability to say to yourself out loud "I own this. This situation is my creation." By owning the situation and eliminating the helplessness attitude, you are instantly moved to a place of solution finding. You can stop wallowing in the problem and start diving head first into the solution and healing.

You start to look for alternative ways of being and doing that will propel you to a new healthier place. You start putting actions, energy and movement behind your words and make changes, moving yourself from undesired situations or states of being to new improved energised happy places and spaces.

Say to yourself "I own this"

You can make a different choice. Your life is made up of the choices you make and at any time you can choose to be in a different feeling state or physical situation. Sometimes you just need to make a different choice. Are you willing to make the choice to leave being a victim and move towards being responsible for your life?

FEAR OR LOVE

Every choice you make in your life comes from either a fear base or a love base. When you come from a fear base you keep small to protect yourself. You say no to choices through fear of failing, perhaps even a fear of being successful, not being able to cope, how others may view you or many other reasons that may resonate with you. Fear shuts you down, your energy is contracted and you may have a sense of closing down. Your thoughts and feelings back this up by showing up with negative energy.

Level 4 Responsibility

Love, however, opens you up. You expand, believing you can take on anything and can cope with any disaster life throws at you. If you go into your body when you are making a choice based on love, you can feel a sense of inner lightness. You radiate an energy outwards that is loving to yourself and others.

As the law of attraction states, like energy attracts like energy. When you radiate and give love, you will receive more love graciously flowing back into your life. When you act from a fear base and pump out negative energy, that is in turn what you will receive back in your life.

When my partner and I first separated, we attended counselling a few times, and each session seemed to give us glimpses of hope to hold onto. Driving home from the last session we made a spontaneous decision to move back in together. It seemed such an easy solution to simply move back in together and start living the fairy tale once again.

The counselling had helped a little in releasing some tension, yet still left a myriad of issues and tensions unaddressed and bubbling away under the surface.

Looking back, I was not taking responsibility to access my true feelings. Rather I took a rose-coloured-glasses perspective. I was holding onto the hope that I desperately wanted to be there, but in hindsight I knew wasn't present.

I was operating from a fear base, fear of the future without him, fear of the unknown, fear of letting go and fear of losing the love we had. I was becoming small to protect myself and once we moved in together again, I felt myself contracting and withdrawing from myself and from life a little more each day.

It was no real surprise when the demise of our relationship happened six months later. We had reverted to our normal destructive dance and neither of us was happy. I continued to try to 'fix' my partner and also tried to 'fix' my attitude. I thought if I changed my perception of the problems in the relationship they would be solved.

Regardless of who had done what and who was at fault, the big learning in the situation was that I was the author of my life and choosing to stay in an unhealthy relationship was my own responsibility.

Being where I was in my life was no one's fault but my own. I had taken responsibility at last. Being at level 4 of Heartbreak Manor was teaching me about responsibility. I had moved out of blaming others to taking self responsibility.

On the night our relationship ended for the final time, I took responsibility for my life, my feelings, my behaviours and my mental health.

After the words were said that ended our relationship, I stood in our kitchen, surprised to be feeling a magical sense of peace and lightness amongst the chaos. I had never experienced such a strong feeling of peace before in my life. For two hours I did not speak but relished the experience while it lasted.

As hard as it was, I knew with all my heart and soul this was the right decision for me. I had taken the first step in responsibility and ownership for my life and was finally discovering and living my truth. That small step changed my life forever for the better.

After my two hours of enlightened peace, the emotions came. It seemed they had been stored in a box with a pretty pink bow that magically untied itself. Once the box flew open, the emotions poured out like lava, constant, fast, hot and treacherous.

Anxiety, anger and sadness flowed out, alongside guilt, shame, loss, fear, worry, despair and many others.

The time had come to feel all my feelings, positive and negative, mostly negative. They had bubbled over the surface as I knew one

Level 4 Responsibility

day would happen. Although I felt shattered, it seemed that the parts of me were slowly flowing back in. I was honouring myself. I was waking up and slowly becoming more enlightened about different areas of our relationship and being honest with myself about what part I had played.

I had taken responsibility and instead of heading into depression I journeyed into solutions. Slowly but surely I was able to move out of level 4 of the Manor and down the stairs to the next level of my healing.

Pink time out – Reflection
Stop and Breathe

Sit back, close your eyes and relax think of a decision or choice you made recently, big or small.

Reflect if you came from love or fear, and with your answer consider the questions below. Notice the feelings and sensations in your body as you reflect on the choice. Your body will never lie, even if your head is trying to convince you otherwise.

- Do you feel contracted or expanded?
- Do you feel heavy or light?
- Do you feel anxious or excited?
- Do you feel scared or at peace?
- Do you feel isolated or connected to the universe?
- Do you feel deflated or energised?
- Do you feel fear or love?

Do you feel like you are going against your deepest-held values or honouring yourself?

You can use these questions before you make a decision, to detect if you are coming from a love base or a fear base. Once you are able to determine your decision's origin you can review it intellectually and ensure it is the correct one for you.

There are two types of pink dolphins: the Chinese White Dolphin and the Pink Amazon River Dolphin. Both are full of grace and loveliness

 ## Pink time out – Promise

Stop and Breathe

Call yourself to action once again and make another promise to yourself around taking responsibility for your life, actions, feelings and self. Make a promise that will move you forward even if only by a small step. Make a promise around how you can make a difference, by taking responsibility to create the life you desire so much, to lead from this moment onwards.

Level 4 Responsibility

A promise is a declaration, a commitment, a hand on your heart sacred agreement that you WILL fulfil its action and desire. It is a pledge and vow, your word of honour, made to yourself from yourself.

What is one promise you can make to yourself today to make a change to all of your tomorrows?

This is the promise I made to myself.

"I own this; I am WILLING to take total responsibility for me. I eradicate all blame towards others or myself. I become the author and creator of my life. I actively look for solutions in alignment with my truth, with love and forgiveness from this day forward."

Write your own promise in your Little Pink book of Love. 'I promise...'

Now place your hand on your heart, close your eyes and repeat your promise out loud to yourself, slowly and succinctly. Allow it to soak into your every cell, into your deep internal being. Keep repeating the promise until you can feel it holding a place in your heart ready to be eternally fulfilled. Honour the promise and honour yourself.

To keep your promise alive and at the forefront of your mind, post note it on your desk, lipstick it to your mirror in the bathroom, blackboard it in the kids playroom, magnet it on the fridge. Wherever it inspires you, ensure it is there ready to be heard, seen, felt and integrated internally. Bring it alive and your very own miracles may start to occur.

PINK TIME OUT – QUESTION TIME

⸺ Stop and Breathe ⸺

Read the list of questions below and allow time and space for self reflection. In your Little Pink book of Love, write or journal your thoughts, feelings, reactions and any epiphanies and wow moments you may have around responsibility. Let the pen flow and see what appears on the page in front of you. As this may take you out of your comfort zone, remember to remain gentle and compassionate with yourself, and always come from a place of love.

1. Where are you deflecting responsibility and ownership in your life?
2. What are you blaming on someone else?
3. Listen to the words that fall out of your mouth, or swirl around in your head and fill in the sentences below,
    a. I didn't…
    b. I can't believe he…
    c. I can't…
    d. I won't…
    e. If only…
    f. How can I ever…
    g. It wasn't me…
    h. I'm stuck here because…
    i. I'm depressed because…
    j. I don't know how to…
    k. He always…
    l. Why can't he change…
    m. It was …'s fault. They/he/she…

Level 4 Responsibility

4. What payoff do you receive in your life by not taking responsibility for your life right now?
5. What uncomfortable situation would you have to deal with if you took responsibility?
6. Where in your life could you make a different choice in the future? Consider your emotional, spiritual, physical, mental and environmental state.
7. Where in your life do you wish you had made a different choice to what you did?
8. List the choices or decisions you made that worked for you and how you felt.
9. Say "I own this" to yourself.
10. What are you scared of?
11. Finish these sentences:
    a. I no longer wish to...
    b. I no longer wish to...
    c. I no longer wish to...
    d. Instead I wish to...
    e. Instead I wish to...
    f. Instead I wish to...
12. How well do you take responsibility and ownership of your life? Rate your ability from 0 – 10.

Well done. It takes great courage to take responsibility for your life when you are in the midst of severe heartbreak and are looking for people to blame. I hope this exercise has provided you with some small snippets of clarity that you can use to own your life a little more as your move forward through the process.

Every small step you take today adds up to help create a new tomorrow and a happier and healthier you in the future

Wow, you had no idea that responsibility would be so enlightening. From partaking in the exercises and truly immersing yourself in your learning and healing, you have learnt that this is your life, you get to make the choices, you get to decide and you get to own your life. You can honestly say that you take responsibility for your life. You feel you have received another gift.

You are by no means where you would like to be but you feel the snippets of healing bubbling up under the surface. You are allowing yourself to have mini 'proud me' moments as you learn and grow.

You are ready to leave level 4 of the Heartbreak Manor. This time you descend the staircase with a little more energy and remember not to hold the banister as the splinters remain. You feel a small skip in your step that has not been there for some time. It only appears fleetingly, but it is there.

As you descend and become more aware of your surroundings. You notice that as Level 3 appears, it does not feel so dark and scary. Everything seems a little lighter and brighter. The people you meet on level 3 don't seem to be dragging their feet around with helplessness, but are a little more engaged and a little more hopeful.

Level 3 Feeling

"I learned that courage was not the absence of fear, but the triumph over it. The brave man is not he who does not feel afraid, but he who conquers that fear"

Nelson Mandela

Level 3 may seem a little brighter and more hopeful, but you know that the lesson for this level is to feel your feelings. You know this has always been a difficult area for you and while part of you wishes you could curl up in bed take a moment to rest and tune out by getting lost in a good novel, you know you have to keep to the In the Pink Process and do the work required or you will start to move backwards again.

You wander along the corridor and become aware how old the carpet is, clean but old and ugly and in the corner it looks like it is peeling back. You stop and after checking no one is watching you tear up a little corner and expose beautiful dark jarrah floorboards.

You pull up a little more, amazed that underneath this ugly carpet is something so beautiful. Why would this be hidden? You feel a bit the same about yourself as you slowly unearth different parts of you and wonder if, once you have mastered this level, you will reveal a beautiful soul ready to take on a new life.

Feeling your feelings can be one of the most challenging and painful yet liberating steps of the process. Emotions can sometimes be scary and frightening. You may want to run and hide from them, ignore them, wish, hope and pray they magically disappear. They are inconvenient and annoying little buggers; you have other things to do, more important things, anything in fact.

You may be on your way out the door to a yoga class and don't have time to sit on the lounge and sob hysterically over a poignant memory that just planted itself at the forefront of your mind. "Go away, I'll deal with you later" you say to yourself, secretly hoping later is nowhere in sight or even in this lifetime.

You head off to your class feeling less than average, still trying to stuff the emotions down, way down. But at this moment in time pushing them down seems like a better option than feeling them. Little do you know that if you had spent the time feeling and releasing your emotions when they appeared, you may have arrived at the yoga class feeling lighter and more at peace, a little closer to being healed and true to yourself. Instead, the avoidance tactics you have mastered so magnificently have you building up more and more pressure within yourself.

When should you feel your emotions?

The question to ponder is, when is later, to deal with these emotions? Is it later once you have depression because you have left all your sadness to build up to overflowing? Is it later when you are in the midst of a panic attack because you didn't address your fears or reveal the truth to yourself? Is it later when you are yelling at people and feeling cranky all the time because you have not channelled your anger healthily? Is it later when you are so disconnected from yourself you really don't even know who you are anymore?

You may hide under a myriad of distraction techniques or just pull the warm snuggly quilt up over yourself and refuse to let the

Level 3 Feeling

feelings in. Whichever technique you use to hide from them, they are still there lurking just under the surface, waiting for you.

Think for a moment. What if you had a friend who was struggling and came to you asking for help. Would you shoo her way, ignore her, promise to deal with her later although you had no intention of doing so? Or would you sit down, give her your undivided attention and listen to what was bothering her?

I am sure you would even let her cry on your shoulder, shake with anxiety or yell and vent. Why are you willing to do this to assist your dear friend yet are not willing to do this for yourself? Are you a friend to yourself? If not, why not? You should be your biggest advocate and your own best friend forever in your lifetime.

I have been guilty of being a master avoider, forever hopeful that if I ignored my feelings they would not come to haunt me. I learnt how to distract myself and how to function on autopilot. Gradually over time I disconnected from my emotions and became lost.

The short term gain I chose actually created more long term pain. I had bottled up my emotions for so long that when the relationship breakup came they suddenly burst out as I could not contain them any more. The choice to suppress the emotions made it so much harder to deal with what was happening, so it took a lot longer to navigate through my breakup because of my own ignorance about my feelings.

I now have the ability to understand the release you feel once you process and untangle your emotional web. You start to feel lighter and cultivate an understanding and appreciation for and about yourself.

You become gentler, more compassionate and more patient with yourself and life starts to shine and sparkle again. I have learnt to express my emotions whether it be at home in private, in the car whilst a sad song is playing, in the supermarket behind my glasses or in the bathroom at work. Wherever, whenever I honour them, I honour myself and in doing this I have reconnected to the person I am.

Now I find that my negative emotions are less intense and knock on my emotional door less often. I am now able to feel the full spectrum of emotions without fear.

Try as you might, you cannot escape your emotions. They are part of who you are, they are always there waiting, waiting, waiting for you. Here is your opportunity to face those elusive and sometimes terrifying emotions once and for all.

Once you face up to them, take a stand and make a promise to yourself to take the healthy option, you will evolve, you will start feeling better. You will move past this breakup. You will create life-changing paradigm shifts and become the person you have always dreamed of being.

 ## Pink Time Out – Promise

꧁ Stop and Breathe ꧂

Call yourself to action and make a promise to yourself that rather than shooing them away till later, you will deal with your emotions when they arise, no matter how inconvenient it may be.

Create your own promise with your own wording that works for you.

Write your promise in your Little Pink book of Love. 'I promise...'

Now place your hand on your heart, close your eyes and repeat out loud your promise to yourself, slowly and succinctly. Allow it to soak into your every cell, into your deep internal being. Keep repeating the promise until you can feel it holding a place in your heart ready to be eternally fulfilled. Honour the promise and honour yourself.

A promise is a declaration, a commitment, a hand on your heart sacred agreement that you WILL fulfil its action and desire. It is a pledge and vow, your word of honour, made to yourself from yourself

To keep your promise alive and at the forefront of your mind, post note it on your desk, lipstick it to your mirror in the bathroom, blackboard it in the kids playroom, magnet it on the fridge. Wherever it inspires you, ensure it is there ready to be heard, seen, felt and integrated internally. Bring it alive and your very own miracles may start to occur.

Pink time out – Question time

Stop and Breathe

There will be some emotions you feel more comfortable with, positive and negative. Others will make you want to run, duck and hide when they show up on your emotional radar. We all have our own distraction techniques that we use so beautifully and efficiently to avoid challenging emotions.

If you can become more aware of your distraction techniques, you can start to work on being more present in the moment and feel your emotions instead of hiding from them. Be honest with yourself.

Think outside the square when you reflect on your distraction techniques. Sometimes distractions are bad for you, but in certain situations they can be good. These good techniques are only helpful at times though, and you may find yourself leaning on them a little too much, to reduce the impact of your feelings.

Some destructive techniques could be smoking, drinking too much, overeating, drugs, gambling, being promiscuous, self harm, getting involved in others' dramas and a myriad of other negative behaviours.

Other more positive distractions techniques could be going to the gym, reading self help books or helping others. These may appear to be good for you and your soul but be honest with yourself if you are overindulging in these to run away from your emotions.

LEVEL 3 FEELING

1. What form of distraction do you use to ensure you keep your emotions tied up in a pretty box?
2. What do you turn to when life becomes uncomfortable?
3. What would you like to give up that you find difficult?
4. What do you crave when you feel emotional?
5. What calms you down if you feel highly emotional?
6. What habit do you find self destructive but you continue to do?
7. What habit makes you feel bad about yourself when you partake in it?
8. What habit would you like to stop to be a better role model for your family and children?
9. When you are going through a rough patch, what do you find yourself indulging more of?
10. If you feel sad, instead of allowing yourself to cry, what do you do instead?
11. If you feel anxious, instead of feeling shaky, nauseous and powerless, what do you do instead?
12. If you feel angry, instead of allowing yourself to yell or let your anger out, what do you do instead?
13. Do others comment on what you do when you are emotional?
14. Do you have any healthy distraction techniques that you lean on?
15. Reflect on what could be a better choice when you find yourself in the midst of your distraction?

Excellent. Be proud of the work you have completed on your reflection and your courage to go deeper once again. It is valuable to understand and to be aware what you turn to when your emotions seem overwhelming and what distraction techniques you have perfected. Once you understand yourself better you can replace your habits, techniques and patterns with healthier ones to create more happiness and peace.

Sometimes a healthy distraction technique may be of benefit when the emotion is so powerful and strong you need something else to help get through the moment, while you are still learning how to feel all your emotions healthily. However it is important not to remain with the distraction and use this as an excuse not to deal with the emotion. It is important to revisit and let the emotion process and heal, otherwise it will remain trapped in your body.

This exercise can help you gain a better understanding of yourself and how you can make better choices to deal with emotions when they arise. Remember every small step you take today adds to help create a new tomorrow and a happier and healthier you in the future.

Avoidance will keep the feeling present inside you.
STOP
Be Aware, Feel, Process, Express, Heal

Level 3 Feeling

Feel and Heal

"Don't keep all your feelings sheltered — Express them. Don't ever let life shut you up"

Steve Maraboli

When your feelings arise, instead of using your much-loved distraction techniques, try the steps below. This will move the energy through you and allow your feeling to be expressed rather than bottled up with the possibly of causing more discomfort and anxiety.

1. BE AWARE - Stop, breathe and become aware of what the feeling is.
2. FEEL - Even if you are unsure what the feeling is, draw your attention to your physical self to notice the sensations you are feeling. What is your body telling you? What does the feeling mean? How are you reacting? What symptoms are you experiencing?
3. PROCESS - Sit with the emotion in the moment; don't run, don't hide, just BE with it, in the now, regardless of how uncomfortable it is. This will help you to process the emotion by letting it flow through you.
4. EXPRESS - Express it in a healthy fashion. Cry, scream, yell, laugh, jump, curse, whatever you need to do to move the energy and in turn the emotion through you and out of you.
5. HEAL - Create healing

By following these simple steps listed above you will move through the emotions more quickly and as you move through them you will start to process them and heal.

Anxiety

"Much of our anxiety and stress comes when we're focused on fear and disconnected from the voice of our inner guide"

Gabrielle Bernstein

Fear and anxiety are a normal phase of grief when you experience a breakup. Breakups can be one of the hardest and most challenging periods in our lives, where you experience a loss of structure, routine, security and predictability. You are scared and that is normal, you will take time to sort yourself out. Don't be too hard on yourself, sit and allow yourself to feel your anxiety.

Anxiety is a part of life and human emotion and can be your guiding star if you listen to it. It may emerge when you are on the wrong track as a subtle message to look at where you are headed. It may appear as growth anxiety when you are embarking on a new journey.

Anxiety becomes an issue if you ignore it and refuse to listen to its clues. If ignored it will become huge and start yelling at you in the form of panic attacks. Getting in touch with your true self and your hopes, dreams and desires and always honouring and listening to yourself will keep the anxiety monster at bay.

My grief and emotions during my two heartbreaks have been all over the place, swinging from relief, numbness, anger and anxiety to sobbing hysterically.

However anxiety for me has always been my nemesis. I can remember vividly my first experience with serious heartbreak, standing under a beautiful hot shower with water cascading down my body. This is one of life's most relaxing moments, however I found myself thinking "They are going to lock me up in the mental facility." I seriously thought I had lost my mind; I had no idea what to do or how to navigate through this part of my life. I had never

Level 3 Feeling

before experienced grief or anxiety to this level and it hit me hard. I was struggling from minute to minute, constantly in survival mode.

This became a vicious circle, as my thoughts only amplified my anxiety. I became not only scared of the physical feelings anxiety produced, but also of my thoughts, which created more anxiety and more thoughts.

The anxiety kept throwing ridiculous and ludicrous thoughts at me and at the time I did not understand the craziness of it all. I did not want to be me; I wanted to run away from myself. I hated my thoughts and myself and was frightened that my life was spinning out of control.

What I eventually realised was, that I was suffering anxiety attacks. If you have experienced these you will know just how miserable they can make you, and how you feel you are losing your mind.

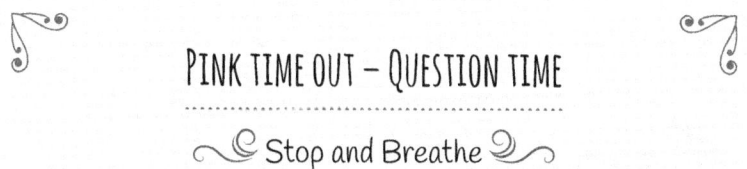

Anxiety is just your thoughts creating havoc

When you gain awareness about the physical symptoms you hold in your body for different emotions, you can utilise this as a warning that you are headed towards anxiety. Using awareness instead of ignorance can head off some of the crashes and burns in your future. When you do crash, you will find it easier to navigate back to normality with the new skills you have.

Pink time out – Question time
Stop and Breathe

Review the table below and allow time and space for self reflection. Anxiety produces numerous physical symptoms, some of which are listed below. What bodily sensations are appearing for you?

Be honest with yourself and in your Little Pink book of Love list the symptoms and bodily sensations you are currently experiencing or have experienced in the recent past. Journal your thoughts, feelings, reactions and any epiphanies and wow moments you may have around what you are feeling.

Let the pen flow and see what appears on the page in front of you. As this may take you out of your comfort zone, remember to remain gentle and compassionate with yourself as you are answering these questions, and always come from a place of love.

Symptoms

Racing heart	Headache	Pounding chest
Choking sensation	Loss of appetite	Hard to breathe
Hyperventilation	Shaking	Feeling faint
Dizziness	Exhaustion	Diarrhoea
Pins and needles	Chest pain	Sweating
Throat constriction	Loss feelings	Indigestion
Indigestion	Sweating	Heart palpitations
Depersonalisation – Feeling detached from your body	Derealisation – feelings of unreality	Neck aches
Urge to flee	Scared you will lose control	What if's – scary thoughts

Level 3 Feeling

Personally my biggest warning sign that my stress is heading towards anxiety is chest pains. Having learnt this over time, when I start to experience chest pains I know something is wrong, sometimes very wrong depending on the severity of the pain.

I need to stop and ask myself what is not working for me. It may be a situation that is not panning out how I had hoped, I may be expecting too much from myself or others, I may need to make a big decision, I may be hiding from myself.

There could be numerous other reasons or areas to consider but my anxiety equation is:

Chest pains = Warning signs = Something is wrong
= STOP = Be aware = Feel

Congratulations on completing this difficult exercise. It is really hard when you are feeling anxious to want to think about the difficult feelings that arise. You may be concerned that by thinking about them they will reappear to cause you more grief. Instead, going inside and fleshing out the feelings, facing them head on and being honest with yourself, gives you a chance to process and heal your feelings rather than running away from them. Don't run, don't hide, try to let them be.

It may be difficult to start, but the more you let your feelings be present and you sit with them rather than run and hide, the more you will become comfortable and know that an uncomfortable feeling is just that and cannot really harm you.

Why do we get anxiety?

"Learning to accept who we are is the first step to recovery, trying to rid ourselves of discomfort and distress only serves to increase it"

Paul David

Anxiety is solely your thoughts creating havoc. Your thoughts can't hurt you if you don't attach to them, align with them or believe them. As with feelings, it is not about repressing thoughts but observing and acknowledging them, viewing them with love, then challenging your thoughts and beliefs and letting them go. Anxiety is your system operating from a basis of fear, trying to protect you and keep you small to steer you clear of danger.

Become the observser of your thoughts

You will always have some fear-based thoughts so instead of running from them, aim to become more acquainted with them. Become the observer, watching when and why they rear their ugly heads.

Learn to love them for what they are and what they are trying to tell you. Through this you can acknowledge they are just thoughts, forgive them, replace them with more rational thoughts and move on.

You will be more prone to anxiety if your system is run down from trying to cope, or you have a history of being a people pleaser, trying to constantly gain others' approval, are a perfectionist, have a strong desire towards control or have low self esteem.

If this is the case, acknowledge where you need to make improvements and what you then put your energies towards to improve these areas. While you are highlighting your areas for improvement, remember to be grateful for your strengths, of which there will be many. Judging yourself to harshly will only inflame the situation.

Often when you want to please others, gain their approval or hold on tightly to a love interest, you let others crash your boundaries and lose the ability to say no. Learning who you are and what you want is the first step to being true to yourself. Being able to communicate this in the form of saying no is the next. Sometimes saying no is required in order to stay true to yourself and keep yourself safe emotionally, physically and mentally.

Don't be so hard on yourself

Another common cause of anxiety is 'shoulding'. You might say to yourself, "I should do this, I have to do this, I must do this". This creates an enormous amount of stress and guilt and in turn anxiety. Try operating from a vocabulary of "I could do this, I would like to do this, I choose to do this". Take the power back in your vocabulary. This will create more positive energy in your body. Feel how your body reacts when you use these more powerful and uplifting phrases rather than ones that come from a sense of obligation.

DO YOU NEED TO ASK FOR HELP?

"The soul always knows what to do to heal itself. The challenge is to silence the mind"

Caroline Myss

If anxiety takes a grip and you are not coping, it may be necessary to get help. Never be too afraid or proud to reach out.

I have had mixed experiences with doctors. The first one I visited told me to 'go home, relax and have a champagne'. This gave me a hangover that increased my anxiety tenfold. The next said that Cognitive Behaviour Therapy was the only therapy that could help me. I couldn't afford the therapy and became even more anxious that I would remain this way for ever.

I got a prescription for antidepressants but felt they weren't for me and didn't take them. I believe that antidepressants act like a Band-Aid and will help you to feel better on the surface, but if you don't work with your emotions to solve the underlying problems they will still be there when you come off the medication. I came to understand that healing requires an integrated focus with medications, self discovery and therapy.

It may take a while to find the best professional match for you. It is important, just like with any relationship, that a rapport and connection is built before you will trust enough to open your heart and soul to this person, which will then create the environment for change internally.

Be mindful of when your anxiety has taken on a life of its own and skyrocketed out of control. When you reach this point it may be time to ask for help.

How I Healed Myself

> "By nature, your soul is soft, gentle, loving and kind. It is forgiving, peaceful, and humble. Confident and comforting in times of despair, your soul is strong, focused, and determined in the mission called life"
>
> Debbie Ford

After trying a few different therapies I decided to take my healing into my own hands. I immersed myself learning all I could about myself and my feelings. I figured I was the expert on me and therefore the best person to help myself.

Level 3 Feeling

I became a sponge for information and took everything in as an A+ student in the course of Lara. I read books, attended seminars, journaled, did all the exercises in this book plus plenty more. I have been on my emotional and spiritual journey for twelve years now.

For me, my anxiety all boiled down to not being true to myself while I was in an extremely stressful situation.

I was a constant people pleaser, always trying to gain the approval of others and every day that I remained in this mode of operating it reinforced my anxiety. Once I let go, lifted the black veil that I had been hiding behind and became authentic, my anxiety slowly subsided and eventually disappeared. I became aware of all my emotions, learnt to understand them, accept them and forgive them. I peeled back many layers of wallpaper to reveal the person I truly was.

So, yes I did recover; I became anxiety free many years ago after my first heartbreak. During this heartbreak there were a few minor anxiety moments at the end that I put down to normal anxiety considering the situation. I still had the opportunity to address residual fears which gave me new and delicious diamonds of truth and wisdom. I can now drink champagne freely and relax.

Pink champagne is delicious

Anxiety has in some ways been a huge gift for me as it has been my teacher and guide back to my true inner peaceful self. Even though I fall off the wagon at times, when my anxiety starts to speak to me, I know I need to reassess where I am at and where I am not honouring myself.

I have an extensive collection of personal development books from different stages in my journey and I refer back to them as needed. Some people laugh but I find it much smarter to house this wisdom in my home rather than house hundreds of receipts from empty bottles and retail therapy blowouts.

This healing led me to gain qualifications and experience in Counselling, Life Coaching and other modalities including Remedial Massage Therapy, Pilates instruction and various business courses. I started following my passions and my dreams and my life eventually became an awesomely amazing journey and adventure full of fun, laughter, love and enjoyment.

Pink time out – Question time

Stop and Breathe

Read the list of questions below and allow time and space for self reflection. In your Little Pink book of Love record your thoughts, feelings, reactions and any epiphanies and wow moments you may have around anxiety. Let the pen flow and see what appears on the page in front of you. As this may take you out of your comfort zone, remember to remain gentle and compassionate with yourself, and always come from a place of love.

1. To acknowledge your anxiety, complete the sentences
   a. I am scared that...
   b. I am scared of...
   c. I am scared if...
   d. I am scared...
2. List three areas in your life where you are not living your truth.
3. List three areas in your life where you are living your truth.
4. Where in your life are you letting people crash your boundaries?
5. Are you able to say no when you need and want to?

Level 3 Feeling

6. Where would you like to say no more?
7. Where in your life are you a people pleaser?
8. What is the cost to you to please others all the time?
9. How would your life feel if you said yes to your intuition every time?
10. Reflect on where in life you are looking for external validation and approval from others over internal validation.
11. Acknowledge where you have already mastered internal validation.
12. Are you a perfectionist? If so, where can you be gentler on yourself?
13. What are you trying to control that you could let go of?
14. What unresolved issues are surfacing as you go through this heartbreak?
15. What areas in your life are you using the word should, must, have to instead of could, want to, choose to?
    a. Change 'I should' to 'I could...
    b. Change 'I must' to 'I want to...
    c. Change 'I have' to 'I choose to...
16. What is your anxiety trying to tell you?
17. Rate your anxiety levels from 0 - 10.

Find the true person inside and let her free, be yourself, be authentic. Freeing yourself from the shackles of your negative emotions and anxieties will allow you to blossom and become the person you were destined to be.

Pink time out – Challenge

⁐ Stop and Breathe ⁏

Over the next week, be more mindful and aware of the times you feel anxious. When the anxiety arises, observe what the thoughts are that come right before the anxiety. Reflect on these thoughts and challenge them for their truth. Are they rational or irrational? Can they be replaced with more useful true thoughts?

Are you attaching or aligning to unhelpful thoughts and creating a vicious circle with your anxiety?

Allow yourself to record this in your Little Pink book of Love and see what it highlights for you.

Any time your anxiety levels start to rise, try one of the activities below to help you move through it. These are good to keep in the back of your mind so you can pull them out any time you need to:

- Take ten long deep breaths
- Sit with your anxiety and let it pass through you
- Go for a walk around the block
- Go for a run
- Sit still in a silent meditation
- Move your body
- Do some stretches
- Go into a downward dog yoga pose
- Call a good friend who is good at listening

LEVEL 3 FEELING

- Listen to some relaxing music
- Do some dance moves in your lounge room
- Put on your best feel-good movie
- Do some gardening
- Clean the house
- Go for a drive
- Hug your dog
- Read your favourite personal development book
- Sit in your garden, listen to the birds and try to get back to the present moment

I am sending you big outstanding congratulations on your reflection and your courage to go deeper around anxiety, one of the more difficult emotions to clear. I hope these exercises have provided you with some small relief from a difficult emotion and that you see the benefit as you move forward through the process of healing. Every small step you take today adds to help create a new tomorrow and a happier and healthier you in the future.

Anger

> "Holding on to anger is like grasping a hot coal with the intent of throwing it at someone else; you are the one who gets burned"
>
> Buddha

As women in society, it is no secret that a lot of us have been taught to hide our anger and act nicely. "Good girls don't behave like that" I hear mothers say to their children. Do you recall being told not to yell, calm down, be quiet, go to your room and an array of other messages that imply it is not acceptable to express your anger? Not even Father Christmas will visit unless you are good.

It is no wonder you became conditioned to appease your family and society. You don't want to suffer the pain of rejection or isolate yourself from the ones you love the most, so you learnt to push your anger away and pretend it does not exist.

This repression and the suppression of emotions build over time. You start to doubt yourself and your feelings, telling yourself you are bad for feeling the way you do and in doing so, destroying the trust you have for yourself.

You bury your anger as far down as possible, packed in an emotional box that is bursting at the seams, tied up with a pretty bow. You hope the day never comes that the box will be opened, causing these unsightly emotions to be let loose to run rancid throughout your life. This is not healthy, in fact it is downright dangerous.

Others may have grown up on the flip side of this experience. They have been given different messages and overtly display their anger. They will become defensive, scream, yell and hurt others emotionally, mentally or even physically.

Level 3 Feeling

These women will share that they can often not even remember what they said when they were in the height of their anger. It can be frightening for both the recipient and also the person exploding. Just like the first group, they are unable to process and vent their anger in a healthy fashion.

Anger can be healthy, warning you of something that is not working in your life that needs to be addressed, or highlighting areas where people have crossed your boundaries. However anger can also be a powerfully destructive emotion and can cause lifelong bitterness and resentment if not handled appropriately.

Learning to let it go

> "For every minute you are angry, you lose 60 seconds of happiness"
>
> Ralph Waldo Emmerson

There is a nature versus nurture debate here, as you may have passive and aggressive children in the same family, however there is no doubt your upbringing can play a major role in how you display your anger.

When you are a child you are a little mirror of your parents, so the type of role model you had while you were growing up will play a large role in how you view and deal with your anger. As an adult, though, you can make a choice; you can learn new skills and improve your relationship with anger and how you express it, accept your imperfections, love yourself and take the healthy option each time.

Delving into the past is interesting and highlights patterns, but be mindful not to be stuck there and use this as another distraction from moving on and finding new solutions and ways of behaving.

When you are sitting in the midst of your breakup there could be hundreds of reasons to feel angry and it's important to find a healthy medium to express it and let it out so the feelings don't start eating you up.

Do not be one of those people we all know who are still stuck in the breakup ten years later, cursing their exes, stuck in limbo, losing friends, family and any sense of peace and happiness.

Holding on to anger interferes with the way you live, your ability to connect to others, and your ability to show love and appreciation to yourself and others. Every day can be a struggle as you are forever bound in your mind and your heart to your ex. You have the option to let it go.

Anger that you hold inside only hurts you, no one else. Read that again and take it in. If you never see your ex again but remain in an angry state, he would not even know. It has nothing to do with him and everything to do with you.

Let it go

Sometimes this may create a convenient holding pattern. While you still hold anger for your ex you have something to focus on. This is a good excuse to not move on when you have no idea what to move on to. You may be scared of what might be next, so instead of excitedly going out and finding out you stay angry, which means you don't have to try.

Your friends want the fun you back and are happy to help move you to that place. Friends are there in the heart of the breakup and are willing to discuss everything that happened to help you move through the grief haze to a happier place. Be mindful you do not overstay your invitation though; people will get tired of hearing the same stories if they feel you are not making an effort to process and move forward.

LEVEL 3 FEELING

Anger also deflects responsibility. Blaming others conveniently takes the focus off you, places it on others and enables you to play the victim role. This is a self destructive place to reside and takes away your power, peace and happiness.

As my relationship broke down I continued to be the peacekeeper, always biting my tongue. I didn't feel heard whenever I tried to speak up, so I stopped trying and kept it inside. Even though I was coming from a passive standpoint and didn't generally partake in screaming matches there was a huge welling of anger growing inside me.

I can recall getting up every morning at 6am and taking my gorgeous puppy for a walk. From the moment I opened my eyes till the moment I came home I was in my head, cursing my ex and having imaginary conversations of what I would say if only I got the chance, replaying them over and over in my head like a song on repeat.

When I arrived home I would act like nothing was wrong as I did not want to lose his love by saying what I really felt. However I had lost the love for myself by not expressing myself willingly and assertively or openly asking for what I wanted and needed.

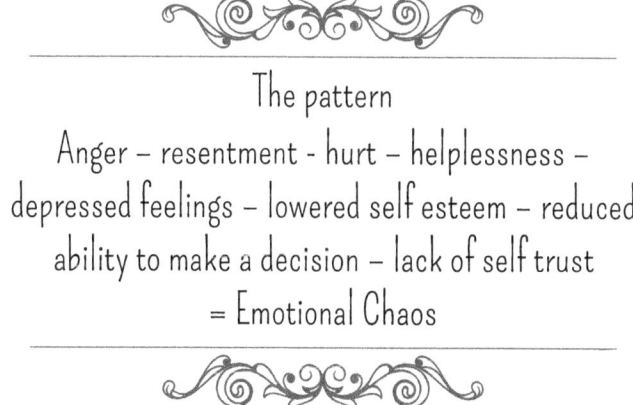

The pattern

Anger – resentment - hurt – helplessness – depressed feelings – lowered self esteem – reduced ability to make a decision – lack of self trust

= Emotional Chaos

This went on for months and became really self destructive, as I didn't have any healthy ways to process my frustrations and anger.

Although I had mastered assertiveness in many areas of my life I have always found it more difficult in romantic relationships. After much reflection I discovered my pattern and it all started with anger. I would feel angry at a situation and then become resentful as I was giving my power away.

I discovered that under the anger I felt incredibly hurt and raw because I didn't feel heard. Being unable to make a sound decision, I started to doubt myself and lose my self love and trust. This then led to depressed feelings which lowered my self esteem more and prevented me from taking responsibility and making the decisions I needed to make. Suppressing the anger sent me on a downward spiral that was dangerous and self destructive. My pattern held me in an unhealthy relationship beyond its expiry date.

Luckily, somewhere deep down I did love myself, I believed I deserved a healthier relationship, a healthier me. I discovered this was my pattern and had experienced it before in relationships. This awareness allowed me to take responsibility and feel the feelings, which catapulted me into my healing journey and on to new insightful miracle moments.

Anger was my protection mechanism to prevent revealing all the hurt I felt inside. Anger is often a cover up for other emotions waiting to be sought out.

Pink symbolises being rare, romantic, heart and soul centred, joyous, happy, exquisite, well and unique

LEVEL 3 FEELING

PINK TIME OUT – QUESTION TIME

❧ Stop and Breathe ☙

Read the list of questions below and allow time and space for self reflection. In your Little Pink book of Love, record your thoughts, feelings, reactions and any epiphanies and wow moments you may have around your anger. Let the pen flow and see what appears on the page in front of you. As this may take you out of your comfort zone, remember to remain gentle and compassionate with yourself, and always come from a place of love.

1. Acknowledge your anger
   a. I am angry that...
   b. I am angry with...
   c. I am angry because...
2. What are you avoiding when you do not express your anger?
3. What is the payoff for holding onto your anger?
4. How do you attack other people?
5. What are you angry at yourself about? Reflect with compassion.
6. How do you attack yourself?
7. What damage do you inflict on others when you release your anger inappropriately?
8. What damage do you create internally when you do not express your anger?
9. How is anger interfering with your life?
10. What is your pattern?

11. What does your anger reveal to you?
12. What other emotions is anger covering up?
13. If you were in a room with your ex and could say anything without reproach, what would you express about your anger?
14. What ways do you currently express your anger? Discuss healthy ways and unhealthy ways.
15. Rate your anger from 0 - 10.

Good job on your reflection and your courage to address your anger and its effect on you. I hope this exercise has provided you with some small snippets of clarity that you can use as you move forward through the process of healing and moving your anger through you. Every small step you take today adds to help create a new tomorrow and a happier and healthier you in the future.

Anger eats away at your happiness and destroys your spirit. It leaves you feeling empty, longing for peace and quietness within. Anger is the veil that prevents and protects you from feeling hurt and fear.

Set yourself free and reach out to your true self. Know yourself, learn to love yourself, express yourself, feel the anger and dispel the negative energy from within to release the light that follows the dark.

LEVEL 3 FEELING

SADNESS

> "Do not apologize for crying. Without
> this emotion, we are only robots"
>
> Elizabeth Gilbert

Sadness was the gift I relished beyond the anger and the fear. It allowed me to reveal and feel my hurt and vulnerabilities. I sat with sadness comfortably, immersing myself in the warm safe haven it provided. I treasured and cherished its message, listening intently.

I felt the physical sensations, including the cascading waterfalls that poured from my eyes. It was for me the final step in connecting with myself. In giving sadness permission to be felt I finally allowed myself to go deep inside and reconnect to my true authentic self with love and compassion.

Sadness creates tenderness within, as the anger and anxiety that held it at bay have been released and you are left with the raw emotion that enables you to reach out to others. Society finds it acceptable, especially as a female, to call a friend and let the tears flow. Sadness promotes a cathartic release that creates a healing inside you. Crying releases toxins and endorphins, reduces tensions and stress hormones, which is why you feel better after you have had a good tear-fest.

Not only does this reconnect you to yourself, it also reconnects you to others. Where the anger and anxiety may have created a disconnection, sadness brings you back to needing others and allowing them to help you.

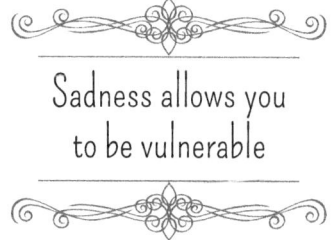

Sadness allows you to be vulnerable

Holding back the tears and the sadness takes an enormous amount of energy and is exhausting, leaving a false illusion of yourself internally and to the world. It prevents the release of deep-seated emotions that are welling inside.

Can you remember a time when you needed to release your tears and instead kept them inside? Do you remember the energy taken to repress the tears? Can you remember a time when you just let the tears flow unabashedly, and how much better you felt afterwards?

There can be a fear that if you allow yourself to fall into the sadness you will be consumed by sorrow and loss, by grieving for the relationship. In fact it needs to be released so you are not held in a dark place, struggling to control the emotions.

Preventing the expression of emotions risks a move towards more serious mental health issues, whilst expressing them is a way to set yourself free.

It is important, though, to distinguish sadness from depression. While you are grieving and feel sad, you will still have moments of peace and joy and appreciate other areas of your life. You will be able to continue to function with some normality.

Once depression sets it may feel like you are in a black tunnel. There is no hope, and you do not see any point in carrying on. Nothing brings any joy to your life and it is hard to leave your bed in the morning. If you fear you have moved from grief into depression, it is time to seek professional support to help you escape the hold it has on you and to return to a happy and healthy life.

The ability to hide my feelings from myself and from others had become habitual and it was not until I experienced this heartbreak that I let the flood gates truly open. I cried for the loss of my best friend and lover and the hopes and dreams we had created. I cried for the loss of a previous long term relationship. I cried for

LEVEL 3 FEELING

my parents' divorce thirty years ago. I cried for myself who I had abandoned over the years. I cried because I was finally feeling my sadness and allowing myself to heal.

I came to enjoy and welcome sadness, as it provided a warm, safe nurturing environment to fall into. I was creating a surrounding of love and ultimately I started to feel like my own best friend. The tears of sadness eventually turned into tears of joy and happiness for rediscovering and honouring my true self.

Emotions wait for you, they waited so patiently and this was their time to shine. I had given permission for them to be felt. I knew I could now handle the enormity of them and feel and process them just as they needed me to.

Sadness and other negative emotions are a normal part of the grieving process. As you move through the levels of the Manor you have the opportunity to feel your emotions in a positive and healing way so you can move to the acceptance and healing stage, when life starts to sparkle once again.

In the Pink

By honouring your anger you can learn to love
By facing your anxieties you can flourish and thrive
By feeling your sadness you can feel your happiness
By acting responsibly for your grief
you will start to move past it
By expressing your emotions you will become unstuck
By walking through the darkness you will
find the shiny, sparkly places once again

Pink Time Out – Question Time

ᓚ Stop and Breathe ᓗ

Read the list of questions below and allow time and space for self reflection. In your Little Pink book of Love, record your thoughts, feelings, reactions and any epiphanies and wow moments you may have around your sadness. Let the pen flow and see what appears on the page in front of you. As this may take you out of your comfort zone, remember to remain gentle and compassionate with yourself, and always come from a place of love.

1. Acknowledge your sadness
   a. I am sad that...
   b. I am sad with...
   c. I am sad because...

2. What are you avoiding when you do not express your sadness?

3. What is the payoff for holding onto your sadness?

4. What vulnerabilities are exposed when you release your tears?

5. Think about how you feel after you have released your tears. List the benefits.

6. What does your sadness reveal to you?

7. How do you express your sadness?

8. Whose shoulder are you able to cry on?

9. If you are struggling to release your tears, listen to some sad love songs. This is a sure-fire way to help express your sadness.

10. Rate your sadness from 0 - 10.

Level 3 Feeling

11. Has your sadness turned into depression? If you are concerned, please be honest with yourself and seek medical advice as soon as possible. There is help out there and the sooner you acknowledge this and get started, the sooner the darkness will start to lift.

What an exceptional reflection to go deeper and a good use of your willingness and courage to look at your sadness. I hope this exercise has provided you with some small snippets of clarity that you can use as you move forward through the process of healing. Every small step you take today helps create a new tomorrow and a happier and healthier you in the future.

Anxiety prevented me from living in my truth and accessing self love. My energy was small and contracted, I feared making a decision and taking responsibility for myself and the consequences that, deep down, I knew were unavoidable. I was scared.

Anger buried the sadness and protected me from fully experiencing the hurt and vulnerabilities that lay beneath. It kept me in a destructive situation feeling helpless, lowering my self esteem and self trust, fighting and blaming rather than thriving in a peaceful knowing state that I knew existed just beyond where I was surviving. I was angry.

Sadness reconnected me to myself, it helped me create acceptance, enabled me to accept reality, grieve the enormity of the loss and move onwards and upwards. I was sad.

One day I woke up. I felt glad, happy, empowered, enlightened, inspired and grateful for my entire feeling experience for better or worse. It had taken me through the dark tunnel of heartbreak

I feared enormously and placed me gently out at the other end a brand new version of myself. I had become an awakened, healed, happy individual, carrying and embracing the essentials: self love, my inner truths and my new best friend - ME.

> *"A tear is one percent water and
> ninety nine percent feelings"*
>
> Anonymous

Back in your room at the Heartbreak Manor you fall into bed exhausted after all the feeling you have done today. As you drift off to sleep you know you have got in touch with your feelings and, for the first time in a very long time, you feel a little more vulnerable but a little more yourself. You feel somehow lighter and your heart feels a little more open.

You have begun to understand that if you feel your feelings rather than letting them bubble way under the surface, you will process them and move through them and begin to heal. The Heartbreak Manor has, despite its rundown state, provided a safe haven for you to do just that.

The next morning as the sunlight drifts through the small windows and the chandeliers help light up level 3, you say a quiet thank you for the gifts you have received here and know you are ready to descend the staircase to level 2.

Level 2 Forgiveness

"The weak can never forgive. Forgiveness is the attribute of the strong"

Mahatma Gandhi

You have more of a skip to your step as you arrive on level 2 hoping to discover forgiveness. You are starting to process your feelings, take responsibility and create awareness.

You now trust the process because you can feel the lessons, see the gifts and your inner self is starting to feel lighter and brighter. It's still hard but you have moved out of survival mode into creating understanding and awareness for yourself.

Your energy levels have risen to the point that you feel like going into the Manor kitchen, dusting off the pots and pans and cooking a nice dinner for the other women who share this place with you. You know, however, that your energy is better spent completing the In the Pink Process before you commit to other projects.

Forgiveness was one of the hardest levels for me to move through, as it had always been a challenge through my life. I had always been mindful of this, however it wasn't till I put it into practice in a life-changing situation that I realised just how tremendously difficult it could be.

I was very hurt and for a period of time was holding onto the pain and retelling my story rather than choosing to let go. Once forgiveness finally descended on me I felt my heart open up with warmth and love.

It was the biggest gift I could have given myself. I found I was able to not only let go of the negative emotions that had been haunting me, but could also release destructive pressure from myself and relinquish all the blaming. This enabled me to transcend to a more peaceful and truthful state creating space for soul growth. I had untied myself from my bonds and was left with an enlightened feeling only possible once I had accepted the beauty of being able to truly forgive.

Forgiveness is the kindest and most compassionate thing you can give yourself. Forgiving is not necessarily a gift to the other person or an acceptance or approval of wrongful behaviour bestowed upon you, it is a lifelong gift to yourself and allows you to set yourself free.

It enables you to untie the attachments that tie you to the other person. It erases the bitterness and resentment from your life. It eliminates the damaging energy and venom you carry around internally and facilitates good health and longevity of life.

As humans we make mistakes continually, and everyone is at different stages in their spiritual and emotional journey. Despite how it seems at times, most people do not intentionally try to hurt you. People are usually doing the best they can at the time with what they know, how they have been raised and how evolved their emotional intelligence is. When they make mistakes, people will normally feel some level of remorse and will be processing their own feelings even if you remain unaware.

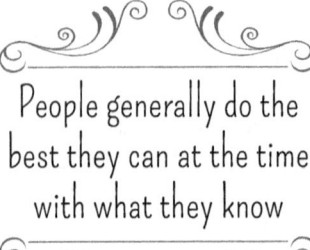

People generally do the best they can at the time with what they know

Level 2 Forgiveness

Learning to forgive

"Forgiveness is a virtue of the brave"

Indira Gandhi

Think about all the good qualities your ex possesses and remove the focus from his limiting factors.

Focussing on the good helps you realise that he was not all bad, even if he did something bad to you.

Using your new-found responsibility, you can accept ownership of the situation and choose to acknowledge he did the best he could with what he knew. He is the person he is. He is another human who made mistakes, and most likely regrets the hurt it caused you even if he has not vocalised this to you.

It is a choice we make to forgive.

If it was he who ended the relationship, he was doing the best he could at that point in time. Maybe he no longer felt he could be in the relationship, and saw leaving as better than staying and not investing a full commitment.

If it was you who ended the relationship, accept that you took control of your life and accept your perception of his limiting factors. Responsibility, understanding and compassion help to create forgiveness.

Think back to a time where you craved forgiveness for a hurt you caused someone. Maybe you did not intentionally hurt them, maybe you had a lapse in judgement, made a mistake or were not thinking clearly or rationally at the time. We have all made mistakes and required forgiveness.

When we put ourselves back into a situation where we needed forgiveness, this creates empathy and compassion. It can help us to understand why forgiving another might be worthwhile. Try putting yourself in your ex's shoes for a minute.

Think about where he is at in his life, why he was not able to live up to your expectations. Think about where his emotional intelligence lies, and who he truly is as a person. Think about what his abilities are to act the way you want him to. This can create an environment of compassion for your ex.

You may realise his limitations in being the person you wanted him to be. You may realise the demands you were placing on him were too high. You may realise you were trying to change him and this was not your role. These are all lessons waiting in the wings for you to discover when you are ready to move towards forgiveness.

You may realise that you are not so angry at him but angry at yourself. You always have a choice to be somewhere or not. How and who we let into our lives and how long we let them stay is always our choice.

Forgiveness does take time and it requires awareness, responsibility and understanding your feelings. This is why it sits on the level 2 of Heartbreak Manor – you need to move through the other parts of the process before you are ready to forgive.

Being ready to forgive can sneak up on you. One day you realise that you no longer carry as much negative energy towards your ex, and a small part of the forgiveness process has been achieved. In this way, you may forgive in small stages before overall forgiveness is possible.

If you are finding forgiveness elusive, try focusing on the lessons you are learning along the way. This may create shifts in perception and initiate appreciation and thankfulness for the lessons. Life lessons build your emotional muscles and empower you to become stronger and wiser.

Level 2 Forgiveness

It is often in the most gruelling situations that we learn the most and have the most extensive emotional growth spurts. The process you are going through involves big lessons, so be thankful for them even though they hurt so much. Think about what the silver lining is in all of this.

Think back to when you have forgiven previously. Think about the wrongful behaviour that was directed towards you in that instance. Think back to an old ex that may have hurt you and how you feel about it today. More than likely you have stopped carrying that old hurt with you in your day to day life. You fostered forgiveness. What helped you to forgive on that occasion? Can you take any learning from that situation to help you forgive in this instance?

Forgiveness is a gift

Forgiveness can change your life. It does not assume that you forget what happened or erase the past. It does not infer you agree with what happened. What it means is you have let go. You make the choice and give yourself permission to be free.

You may need to work hard at forgiving and struggle with it for a period of time. Make a commitment to yourself that you want to be free. Once you have made a commitment you will begin the forgiveness journey even if it has a rough start.

Forgiveness for me had a rough start. I knew I had to forgive and I wanted to forgive but I continued to tell my story in my head over and over, blaming him for our relationship's shortcomings. I felt he had left me with no option but to leave, so I remained in blaming mode. I loved him and I had been hurt. I found it very hard to let go of him, the love I had for him, and the love I wanted from him.

I created a mantra in my head when Lady Chitter Chatter started the blame game. "He did the best he could with what he knew." I repeated it over and over many times a day and after a while I found small forgiveness moments. But I still lacked the ability to truly let go, forgive and release myself.

One day I was driving and heard a song my ex and I had listened to a hundred times together. It was poignant as it symbolised a very difficult period in his life, and we bonded whenever we heard the song together.

Hearing the song again, I had to pull the car over I was crying so hard. It brought back so many memories but also it reminded me of the beautiful and gentle soul he had underneath all the expectations and limitations I had placed on him.

It was as if my insides were rising up and spilling out through my eyes. All the negative energy and emotions were being purged out into the ether. My heart went out to him and how he felt when the song played. It was like our hearts and souls were joined at that moment in time, even though I was sitting in the car alone. That fleeting moment took me from blaming to forgiveness in an instant.

Everyone needs forgiveness

"If we really want to love we must learn how to forgive"

Mother Theresa

Unfortunately once I had forgiven him, I still had the hurt, and still believed someone was to blame for what had happened. So the next person in line was me. Although I had gained compassion and forgiveness for my ex I had neglected to create it for myself.

I started to point the finger towards myself and look at all the ways I had helped co-create the demise of our relationship. If he was not to blame, I must be. I was looking for a reason why the relationship had failed and was still hiding behind blame rather than creating acceptance for what was.

LEVEL 2 FORGIVENESS

For a period of time this mindset created self loathing. Not only was it now my fault, I was angry at myself for having been so angry at him. I was angry for hurting him. I was angry for betraying and losing myself in the relationship. I felt I had let us both down. I felt I was disloyal for leaving him; we had made a commitment to each other and I had broken it.

To pull myself back from this vicious, destructive circle my new mantra became "I did the best I could with what I knew." Eventually this worked on me just as it had on him, even though I did not have a monumental moment where I forgave myself. I moved slowly towards forgiving myself and began to appreciate all the wonderful things about myself. In the end I realised the relationship breakdown was no one's fault, it was just the way it was.

I came to understand that being loyal to myself was more important than beating myself up over not being loyal to him. This was a hard realisation for me, as loyalty is one of my strongest values, but it was healthy and self loving.

We were just two people in the world, in love, trying to co-exist. Our individual imperfections created a relationship that did not enable us to be the best version of ourselves. Ultimately we were better off apart and having a chance of being the best version of ourselves on our own.

From that moment of forgiveness onwards, my new life started to blossom. I still experienced negative emotions on occasions but they were far and few between; I knew I was moving towards my shiny new life. When I had forgiven, I had released the negativity and love began to flow in. Love for all the dogs I saw on the street, the roses in the gardens, the trees in the park. Even love for the people who were grumpy, because I knew they were doing the best they could.

For a long time I had been shut down to being with others, socialising, or feeling happy, never mind giving or receiving love.

Once I had forgiven, I was set free. Freedom was peaceful and tranquil. What a blessing I had created in my life.

Pink is delivered with a sense of grace and beauty

You can only love another as much as you can love yourself. You can only give away what you have inside. I had found love again internally and so had been reunited with the side of myself that was able to give love away and also receive love again.

Pink time out – Question time

~ Stop and Breathe ~

Read the list of questions below and allow time and space for self reflection. In your Little Pink book of Love, record your thoughts, feelings, reactions and any epiphanies and wow moments you may have around forgiveness. Let the pen flow and see what appears on the page in front of you. As this may take you out of your comfort zone, remember to remain gentle and compassionate with yourself, and always come from a place of love.

1. What would you be able to let go of if you were able to forgive?
2. How would your life benefit if you could forgive?
3. What is not forgiving stopping you from achieving?
4. What feelings does not forgiving create for you?
5. Who have you forgiven in the past for wrongful behaviour towards you? How did you move towards forgiveness in that situation?

LEVEL 2 FORGIVENESS

6. What have you needed forgiveness from, from others?
7. Complete the sentences
    a. I would like to forgive...
    b. I can't forgive...
    c. I need to forgive...
    d. I'm sorry that...
    e. I'm sorry for...
    f. I'm sorry if I...
8. Try saying "I'm sorry, I forgive you" over and over towards your ex and see if your feelings towards him alter.
9. Create a mantra of "He did the best he could with what he knew." Repeat it over and over, letting it sink into your essential being.
10. If you had an opportunity to speak to him, what would you like to say to him to vent, clear your emotions and move to forgiveness?
11. Create a mantra of "I did the best I could with what I knew." Repeat it over and over, letting it sink into your essential being.
12. Reflect on self forgiveness and how you can be more gentle and compassionate with yourself.
13. From 0 - 10, rate your ability to forgive.
14. From 0 - 10, rate your willingness to try.

Well done on your reflection and ability to contemplate forgiveness. I hope this exercise has provided you with some tools to help you begin to forgive yourself and find forgiveness for others. Every small step you take today helps create a new tomorrow and a happier and healthier you in the future.

Pink time out – Letter writing

～ Stop and Breathe ～

Take out your Little Pink book of Love. Light some candles play some soothing music to prepare yourself to write two beautiful letters of forgiveness.

One letter is to your ex, where you can write down all the things you forgive him for.

The other letter is to you, where you can write down all the things you forgive yourself for.

When you are ready, release your feelings onto the paper. Go deep inside and access your feelings. Let the words flow onto the page, itemising all the situations that require your forgiveness.

Be free to use your creative energy and decorate the letters with colour and warmth. Let the words and tears flow, bask in the experience letting the feelings wash over you. This is a cathartic experience, so don't rush, take your time, be honest and open and you will reap the rewards.

Level 2 Forgiveness

Pink time out – Art expression

Stop and Breathe

Draw a big pink love heart on a blank piece of paper. In the middle of the heart write the word love.

Now that you have found forgiveness, connect to your true self and feel what your heart is saying to you. What do you love about life? What does love represent for you? What warms your heart? Who do you love the most? What makes you feel loving?

Write all these thoughts and feelings in the spaces around your pink love heart. Include everything that feels like love to YOU. The things that make you, YOU. Bask in the sunshine of love, appreciating it for the wondrous miracle it is. Use your coloured pencils, or use a canvas with paints, or finger paint. Do whatever feels right for you. Be yourself. Have fun. Let this art be a loving expression of who you are.

When you are finished you will have a beautiful piece of art that you can keep with all the words, thoughts and feelings that symbolise what love means to you as you find forgiveness.

Heartbreak, Healing and Happiness

You are getting ready to leave level 2 and realise that you have found forgiveness and have allowed yourself to receive its gifts. You have removed the blame and the shame, you have freed up an enormous amount of mental and emotional energy by forgiving your ex and, more importantly, forgiving yourself.

Tonight the chandeliers appear to be even brighter as the natural light fades and the sun disappears for the night. You can't work out if it is the chandeliers that are shining more or you are just more awake, aware and alive. Whichever it is, you know you are ready for level 1, the last level of your stay here at the Heartbreak Manor.

Level 1 Acceptance

"Understanding is the first step to acceptance, and only with acceptance can there be recovery"

J.K. Rowling, Harry Potter and the Goblet of Fire

You are nearly back on solid ground! As you skip down the stairs to level 1, your bags seem lighter and you are eager to learn the last part of the In the Pink Process. You notice a small part of you would actually like to swing on one of the chandeliers but that is probably a little unladylike.

You realise this light-hearted feeling is symbolic of you having more energy, more understanding, more awareness, more responsibility. You have found forgiveness and are more in tune with your feelings. You notice you experience your feelings very strongly; one moment you are happy, the next sad, the next angry and the next a little anxious.

You understand this is normal while moving through grief. It does make you feel a little crazy and you wonder what others may think but your inner being is thrilled to be able to express the emotional energy that has been stored and stuck within. You feel more like your authentic self each time you process a little more.

Now you have an understanding and awareness of your feelings and have begun to take responsibility for them and forgive yourself and others, you are in a position to truly accept yourself and where you are in life.

This acceptance will bring clarity and the process will be able to come to its grand finale. Through moving through these levels of Heartbreak Manor, you have surrendered. You have stopped fighting and resisting your feelings. You have also stopped fighting and resisting the end of your relationship.

Throughout the In the Pink Process you no doubt have had many miracle moments and diamonds of discovery. You will take these with you when you leave Heartbreak Manor and delve deeper into them at the next point in your journey, the Healing Sanctuary, where you will raise your emotional intelligence ever further.

Being at the level of acceptance gives you the opportunity for total transformation, to review yourself, redesign and redecorate from the inside out. You have fought and struggled through the hardest levels of the process and are still standing and breathing. With acceptance you will feel a whole lot more confident and calm than the day you first walked through the door of Heartbreak Manor.

Choosing a New Pattern

"Remember that sometimes not getting what you want is a wonderful stroke of luck"

Dalai Lama

Acceptance, clarity and understanding can transform your life. Clarity is defined as 'clearness or lucidity as to perception or understanding; freedom from indistinctness or ambiguity'. You begin to understand why you have done the things you have done, why you act the way you do. You begin to see your patterns,

Level 1 Acceptance

where they originated from and why they have played out in your life the way they have.

The beauty is that once you understand where the patterns came from, you can start to look at making some changes. This is the key to profound and lasting transformation in your life.

When I walked down the winding stairs of Heartbreak Manor after completing level 1, I realised I had finally stopped wondering if he would arrive at my front door on his big white horse and profess his love and ability to commit, admitting it had all been a big mistake. I had stopped wondering if maybe we could work it out one day. I had found acceptance.

I had let go peacefully. I was feeling grateful for the lessons, and had learnt so much. I had lots of energy and a clear head for the first time in a long time. I had dived into my new life and was feeling fabulous. My life was starting to sparkle again. I was starting to get really excited.

What I hope you are saying at this point is "I understand now why I did that". Reflect on what you have learnt and document your miracle moments in your Little Pink book of Love. You are strong enough now to admit the truth to yourself, where you contributed to the demise of the relationship and how you felt in regards to it, what you could have done differently and how you can address certain areas of your life to lessen the feelings of catastrophe.

Regardless of what happened in your relationship, you realise you are the source of the love you receive in your life. Without this you will attract another partner with a different face and name but the same qualities you fought so hard to recover from.

Choose to learn the lessons your ex was sent to give you, move forwards with the lessons learnt, choose a different style of partner, one that is healthier for you and will bring out the best in you.

PINK TIME OUT – DEEP, DARING MARATHON QUESTION TIME

~ Stop and Breathe ~

Read the list of questions below and allow time and space for self reflection. In your Little Pink book of Love, record your thoughts, feelings, reactions and any epiphanies and wow moments you may have around creating acceptance into your life. Let the pen flow and see what appears on the page in front of you. As this may take you out of your comfort zone, remember to remain gentle and compassionate with yourself, and always come from a place of love.

Allow this to be an enormous brainstorming session drawing out ALL the learnings, and there could be many.

It is the marathon of questions. When you get to the end I hope you will feel really proud to have reflected so deep, although you may be exhausted, but it will be worth it.

This exercise will highlight areas that were lacking in your relationship, as well as what you would like to see in your next one, to help you arrive at a healthier space for the future. Let's spend some time looking at your miracle moments and any diamonds of discovery.

Think deeply about these questions and don't skim past any that are uncomfortable. Ponder each one; ask yourself the question and then sit with it or go for a walk and let it process. Answers will come if you keep asking the question and give it permission to sink in, then allow space for the answer.

This is a tough exercise, so complete it with compassion and love for yourself. This is not an opportunity to let Lady

LEVEL 1 ACCEPTANCE

Chitter Chatter go berserk with insults and accusations. It is an opportunity to observe yourself and learn about yourself with love. Life is a continual learning experience, so appreciate it for what it is and go forward to this exercise with excitement. Be willing to learn more and more about yourself each time you delve deeper into yourself.

Don't be scared, be consistently honest and endlessly loving with yourself.

1. How did you contribute to the relationship downfall? Even if you were only 5 percent to blame, what was the 5 percent?
2. If you could go back to when the relationship was still good, what would you do differently?
3. Would you go back to the relationship tomorrow, if you knew nothing had changed? If yes, why? If not, why not?
4. What caused you to feel resentful in the relationship? Consider how you gave your power away in these moments.
5. Did you give too much in the relationship? If so, how?
6. Did you feel you were not respected? If so, what could have you done differently to receive the respect you deserved?
7. Do you feel you sabotaged your relationship in any way? If so, how?
8. Where could you have taken a stand in your relationship and chose not to?
9. Where do you feel you betrayed yourself within the relationship?
10. Were you able to express yourself openly and honestly within the relationship and feel safe doing so?

11. Were your feelings dismissed, stonewalled or laughed at? How would you prevent this happening again?
12. Where did you go against what you knew were your truths in your relationship?
13. What are the top three areas in the relationship where you did not trust yourself?
14. Were you constantly trying to change or fix him? If so why did you think this was your responsibility?
15. List the areas you wanted change in the relationship. This will highlight where you were not getting your wants and needs met.
16. Did you have a connection with your ex, physically, mentally, emotionally and spiritually? If not, which areas were lacking? Rate each area from 0 - 10.
17. Did you bring any past fears into your relationship?
18. Were you scared he would leave you?
19. Were you scared you would leave him?
20. Did you trust him wholeheartedly, 100 percent?
21. List the 5 most hurtful times within the relationship.
22. List the 5 things that you regret that you created in the relationship.
23. What warning signs are obvious now that you ignored at the time? When did the warning signs start? Why did you ignore them?
24. Do you feel like you settled for less than you deserved in the relationship?
25. Did you fall into the victim mentality? If so, at what point did this take place? How could you have prevented this from happening? What would you have needed to do differently?

LEVEL 1 ACCEPTANCE

26. Did you become needy? If so, think about what inside you prompted this, rather than what was done to you.
27. Did you lose your self respect? If so, what could you have done to maintain it in the relationship?
28. Did you remain loyal to yourself or did you put loyalty to others above loyalty to yourself? Why?
29. Where did you blame and shame?
30. Have you resolved all resentment, anger, sadness and anxiety around this relationship ending? If not, what are you still struggling with? How will you actively overcome this?
31. Have you forgiven your ex?
32. Have you forgiven yourself?
33. What is your pattern with the type of men you attract? Are they unavailable, abusive, controlling, narcissistic, boring, lazy, immature, childlike etc?
34. Do you feel like you have any of those character traits yourself? Were they a contributing factor?
35. If you woke up tomorrow and your past was erased, what one thing would you be glad you left that you seem to struggle with regularly?
36. Are you still living in the past in any areas of your life?
37. Are you able to healthily express your emotions?
38. Are you able to in an assertive way ask for what you need and want?
39. What are you unhappy with yourself about?
40. What do you not like about yourself?
41. What is the biggest thing you despise in others, that may be a projection of what you dislike about yourself?

42. What do you feel ashamed about?
43. What did you feel guilty about?
44. Did you feel unlovable, not enough, not important, invisible, pushed away, a burden?
45. Where do you sacrifice yourself?
46. What will you NEVER do again in a relationship? List a few here if you wish.
47. What do you wish you could change for your next relationship?
48. When you look at other's relationships or traits, what do you admire about the way they act, feel and behave that you would like to emulate?
49. Visualise yourself in the perfect relationship. How would you be acting that is different to how you acted previously?
50. What is the one biggest thing you can change, reinvent about yourself that may prevent you from falling into the same relationship pattern again?

WOW and phew. I send you a colossal well done on your intense reflection and your courage to go deeper and answer the long list of questions I provided. I hope these questions have provided you with some miracle moments and added clarity that you can use as you move forward through the process of healing.

Just in case you are feeling a little challenged and overwhelmed, below I have some fun exercises to help you dream up your new ideal life.

Level 1 Acceptance

Pink is a very common colour of flowers;
it is believed to attract the insects and
birds that are needed for pollination

Close your eyes and visualise

*"To accomplish great things we must first dream,
then visualise, then plan... believe... Act!"*

Alfred Montapert

Thoughts are created in the conscious mind and with enough repetition they sink into the subconscious mind. Your brain is like a computer and will only work with what you feed into it. If you feed it negative thoughts it will believe this to be your desired reality and create more negativity. If you feed it positive thoughts, it will produce more positivity.

This is really exciting because it means you can train your brain to create anything you desire. If you think about the things you want, and visualise them as if they are real, your subconscious will soon believe you already have them and will create more of the same.

You can use your imagination to create a bright, vivid and colourful picture of how you want your life to be. Your conscious mind will filter this to the subconscious mind and try to match the reality. Visualisation works better than thoughts, because the primary language of the subconscious mind is images.

When you feed your subconscious with positive energy, thoughts and experiences, the universe will provide, it will filter back the same and more to your daily life and situation. You may feel like this is a bit of a leap of faith, but give it a try and enjoy some time visualising all the nice things you want, how you want to behave and act. Continue this over time and start to see if you can notice the differences.

To visualise, you need to be really clear and concise on exactly what you want. Think about incorporating all of your senses into the visualisation; see it, hear it, smell, it, touch it and taste it. Picture yourself in the visualisation, behaving how you would like to be in your dream life.

When you start visualising, it is important to note that you visualise on the bigger final goal, don't worry about all the details, just visualise the final result.

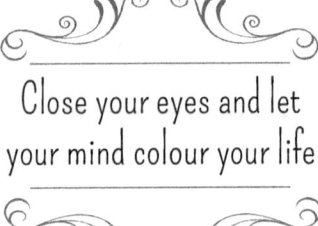
Close your eyes and let your mind colour your life

To help create more power when you are visualising your dream life coming true, hold yourself in that moment and feel the feelings you will feel once this has come true. Pretend it has already come true and access what you feel and include them into your visualisation.

Feel the proudness, the excitement, the calmness, whatever feeling you hope to achieve. Stop, breathe, close your eyes and think about feeling exactly how you want to feel once it has come to reality.

A quick recap:

1. Focus on the end goal, not the details
2. Be very clear and concise about your goal

LEVEL 1 ACCEPTANCE

3. Feel the desired feelings you hope to achieve when it is a reality
4. Use your five senses
5. Make it bright and colourful
6. Repeat the visualisation on a regular basis

Changing your reoccurring thoughts and images can and will have the power to change your reality. Let's give it a go.

PINK TIME OUT – MAGIC WAND

Stop and Breathe

Pretend I am a fairy godmother and have a beautiful pink magic wand. Whatever your heart desires I can make come true; all you need to do is ask me and I will make it appear. I'm a really lovely fairy godmother and want the best for you.

Imagine I have waved the pink magic wand and now you can be whoever you want to be. You are free of any self sabotaging patterns and negative beliefs and have all the attributes you admire in other people.

Make a list of all the qualities you want for yourself. You may already have some traits and there may be others you desire to incorporate into your being.

Who are you? Who is that person? What does it feel like? What attributes do you have? What are your thoughts? How do you hold yourself? What do you think about yourself? How do you portray yourself to others? What do others say about you?

Use these sentence starters for some help. Dream away, think outside the box, visualise yourself being this person. Who are you?

I am...
I look...
I feel...
I am so good at...
I am proud of myself for...
I stand for...
I believe in...
I know that...
My best attributes are...
Others comment that I am...
Others feel jealous that I...

Reflect and think about the person you have created on paper. Does the image you have dreamed up feel right for you? Do you get a warm feeling when you think about this person and have an internal excitement to grow into her over time?

Knowing and creating awareness about what you want is the first step to creating your new life and in becoming the person you wish to be. Listening to your heart and intuition aids you in knowing when we are headed in the right direction or when we are veering off path.

At our next destination, the Healing Sanctuary, we will delve more into this and how we can become this person we hope and desire to be.

Excellent work on your reflection and your courage to start to create the person you wish to be. I hope this exercise has provided you with a starting point and an idea of who you may wish to become as you are creating the new version of yourself as you heal and move forwards.

Level 1 Acceptance

Every small step you take today adds to help create a new tomorrow and a happier and healthier you in the future

Pink time out – Self love time

 Stop and Breathe

When I was trying to rescue our relationship, I made my partner a list of the 100 things I loved about him. I thought it was a special gift at the time, but now realise I was more focused on what I loved about him than what I loved about myself.

Don't let the chance go by to appreciate what you love about YOU. Even though there are areas you know you need to improve, there are simultaneously plenty of good qualities, even amazing qualities, you have.

Get your Little Pink book of Love out and write a list of 100 things you love about yourself:

1. I love...
2. I love...
3. Continue through to 100

It may take a few days to think about all areas of your life. As you go, colour up your list with pencils, dress it up with decorations, make it fun and pretty, frame it if you wish.

The amount I learnt through this exercise was astounding and started to create internal excitement. Without this process there is no way I would have had the wondrous discoveries I have about myself. Like you, I also had a big list of things I wanted to improve, but that's great because it provides clarity, which brings acceptance.

Acceptance gives you somewhere to start. Now you can look at improving areas of your life to prevent the same old patterns repeating. Be proud of yourself for completing these exercises. You are coming into your spiritual awakening and becoming aware of who you want to be moving into your future. The years ahead can be as fabulous as you choose them to be. Continue to move through your healing process and things will all fall into place.

Pink Time Out – Reflection
Stop and Breathe

The lessons we learn as we go through our breakup are the silver lining for all the pain and suffering we have felt. With no appreciation for the lessons, it is easy to remain in bitterness and resentment and remain stuck. Ensure you give yourself

Level 1 Acceptance

enough time to understand and honour the lessons you have learnt and the gifts these lessons have taught you.

In your Little Pink book of Love, list the biggest learning lessons you have received going through this breakup so far. Record your thoughts, feelings, reactions and any epiphanies and wow moments you may have. Let the pen flow and see what appears on the page in front of you. As this may take you out of your comfort zone, remember to remain gentle and compassionate with yourself, and always come from a place of love.

1. I learnt...
2. I learnt...
3. I learnt...
4. I learnt...
5. I learnt...
6. And so on until you exhaust yourself of all your learnings

You should be really proud of yourself for completing this. Sit with your feelings for a moment after completing this list of self discovery and be grateful and compassionate for how you feel. This is an empowering exercise and acceptance of what has occurred and what has been learnt can bring some control and power back into your life.

Once you know your lessons, you can put strategies into place to prevent having to learn the same lesson again. If you learn the lessons and move on with awareness and acceptance, you can make different and wiser choices for your authentic self in the future.

The colour pink takes its name from the flowers called pinks

Acceptance for me came in an instant, just as forgiveness had. I had visited him to wish him a happy birthday and our conversation was reminiscent of many others we had had. It wasn't so much what was said, but the joking way he talked about our breakup that made me feel that he just didn't get me.

Acceptance washed over me, as I realised he did not have the capacity to give me one of my deepest wants, needs and desires - a committed partner who was an advocate for their own personal growth alongside advocating for mine. He was not in the wrong but he was wrong for me.

Like forgiveness, acceptance is a choice, a liberating choice. You have the chance to start your life fresh. You are the author of your life, you make the rules. Make a stand for yourself move through the last level of the Heartbreak Manor and see what exciting opportunities lie waiting just on the other side.

You can't quite believe that you have finished the last level in the In the Pink Process. You sit and reflect for a moment on your brave adventure into yourself.

Tomorrow you will descend the last flight of stairs and arrange your checkout. You say thank you for your gift of acceptance you received on this level as you drift off to sleep at the last night at Heartbreak Manor.

Level 1 Acceptance

Make the choice now to ACCEPT.
I have awareness of my feelings, my thoughts,
my behaviours, my grief and my experience
I have taken responsibility for myself and
my life. I am the author of my life
I have felt, processed and expressed all my feelings
I have forgiven, stopped blaming and removed
negative emotions with compassion
I have acceptance and clarity
I have emotional freedom, I have self love, I have
my truths, I have myself and my life back

Checking out

"The best way out is always through"

Robert Frost

You have made it to check out day. You manoeuvre the staircase from level 1 to the ground floor a little wearily, but also a little excitedly. You walk slowly, appreciating and taking in all that has happened in Heartbreak Manor. It has been a challenging yet rewarding journey and although you are excited to leave, you stop to bask in the memories of your stay here one last time. You are grateful for everything the Manor has given you. You are proud of yourself for making the choice to stay here and work on yourself, to spend time in a place that many people refuse to visit.

When you arrived you had no idea you would be given such special, intangible gifts to take home. Your gifts are awareness, responsibility, feelings, forgiveness and acceptance. Now, alongside your weariness, you are also leaving with snippets of joy, happiness and excitement about what is to come.

You look around the Manor and even though it looks the same, it feels different. It no longer feels unfamiliar, uncomfortable, dark and scary. It seems brighter and happier and even though it is still run down you realise that when you feel good about yourself it doesn't matter where you are because you feel solid and balanced internally. Heartbreak Manor to you is beautiful and magical as it has provided a safe and nurturing environment through this tremendously difficult time.

You meet the new residents coming through the doors and recognise the looks on their faces, the same look you had on arrival. You try to share your enthusiasm with them but can see that they are not able to understand the positive adventures ahead. They appear numb and lifeless, trapped in their pain.

You smile to yourself as you know in time they will be standing where you are, holding the gifts the Manor has given them and with a new exciting life in front of them. You know that they are at exactly the right place even though they are yet to realise it.

You have rebuilt your foundations and started to actively redesign and redecorate from the inside out. The experience has changed how you feel and who you are as a person. You no longer struggle to get through each day. You occasionally reflect back and revisit memories yet you accept you are where you are and it's okay. You will be okay. You are actually more than okay.

Your hope and optimism have returned and you are living life once again. You look forward to discovering your passions and purpose and in time create a new loving relationship based on your new self.

As you check out of Heartbreak Manor you are asked some final questions by the staff:

1. What is the one thing you can share with others about your stay here?
2. What did you like most about your stay here?
3. What is the biggest lesson you learnt during your stay here?
4. Would you revisit in the future if you needed to?
5. Do you take responsibility for everything you learnt and who you have become?

CHECKING OUT

6. How will you acknowledge how far you have come in your journey?
7. Please rate your stay from 0 – 10, 10 being the best.

PINK TIME OUT – SONG CHOICE

Stop and Breathe

Music and songs are very powerful, helping us access our emotions as we submerge ourselves in the tune and the words. Different songs touch people differently. I found it beneficial to have a song that represented my journey and my pain and my healing.

Pick one song that relates to your stay here. Choose a song that is symbolic of how you felt when you arrived, what you achieved and how you feel now. Play it over and over and let it sink in.

In your Little Pink book of Love, record the name of your song.

Let it be your reminder for ever and always of the time you spent here. Remind yourself often of the tremendous work you achieved and the amazing journey you have been on.

At Heartbreak Manor you have learnt how to process the initial heartbreak and move out of basic survival mode. Here you have created self awareness, taken ownership and responsibility for your life, felt your feelings and emotions, sought forgiveness and found clarity and acceptance. You have allowed yourself to love yourself a little bit more.

You are handed the brochure to the Healing Sanctuary and are overcome with a warm fuzzy feeling. This will be your home for the next little while and you can't wait for some relief and time out from all the challenges so far. You look forward to learning more about yourself and emerging further into the person you would like to be and the life you would like to create. You can only imagine how divine it must be there.

You pick up all your gifts and open the large creaky wooden doors one last time. You stop for a minute and look back at the chandeliers. For you they symbolise lighting you up internally. You exit to the shuttle bus waiting just outside the door to transfer you to the Healing Sanctuary.

Thank you for staying at the Heartbreak Manor.

Love – Truth – Purpose

> My lover is gone and my heart feels lost
> With work to do I embrace the fear
> Slowly I awaken and my soul starts to shine
> I realise my true potential that I nearly left behind
> I choose to find myself and live my life free and clear
> My soul is now dancing and singing its tune
> My lover may be lost but I have found
> true love as I have found me

PART 2

The Healing Sanctuary

Welcome to the Healing Sanctuary

*"Find yourself first, appreciate your own worth
and next time you are in a relationship never get lost again"*

Dodinsky

You arrive at the Healing Sanctuary feeling small snippets of joy and peace bubbling up gently from a place deep inside, following the intense personal development work at the Heartbreak Manor. Once again you are feeling slightly nervous at what to expect at this new destination, but generally carry a more positive outlook. You have a knowing and a feeling that you are on the right path for yourself and are starting to find faith that life will work out and you will grow out of this dark period.

There is a persistent feeling that the worst is behind you; you have moved out of the depths of despair and there is finally some space in your mind. For now, this space can be best used to process how you ended up where you did. You can process what you contributed to your relationship's ending and how you may be able to return to your authentic self with self love and ensure you follow your truth in the future.

It is common after a relationship ends to say, "I lost myself" or "I don't know who I am anymore". Without a solid foundation of self you can easily lose yourself in a relationship. You may feel you have betrayed yourself or abandoned yourself for others and battle confusion as you try to find your way back.

At this stage of your journey you may be feeling empty and bereft, lacking self love, however this is fairly normal after a heartbreak. It's what you choose to do next that helps and heals or hurts you.

Many people believe the way to refill themselves is to find love straight away and use the new love to heal their pain. By doing this you are at the mercy of once again losing yourself and your feelings.

If you feel empty when you start a new relationship you are counting on your new partner to make you feel good about yourself. In the initial pink haze of the relationship you may feel better than you have in a long time as the compliments are flying and everything your new partner says helps you feel good about yourself. However what is really happening is that you are relying on external validation to feel good as you lack internal validation.

In this type of relationship your emotions and self esteem will ebb and flow depending on how the other person treats you. If they are attentive and loving you will feel good and when inevitably the focus is taken off you, real life gets in the way or a struggle arises, you may feel even lower than before. You did not develop a solid sense of self to take into the relationship, and without loving yourself fully you cannot love someone else in a healthy fashion. The secret here is to nurture strong and solid internal validation before you enter a new relationship.

Welcome to the Healing Sanctuary

Time to love yourself

*"Life's not about waiting for the storms to pass...
It's about learning to dance in the rain"*

Vivian Greene

By taking respite rather than living in avoidance, you can love yourself again. Then when you meet someone, they are not filling up an empty vessel but instead will be adding to a full life. Your feelings will not ebb and flow based on another person's actions, as you will have built a solid foundation of who you are and what you want and need. You will be able to look at your new partner and evaluate in a mature and loving fashion if they meet your needs and wants in a relationship. You can then build your relationship with love and growth instead of neediness and insecurities.

A good indication of how long you will need to stay at the Healing Sanctuary is to check in whether you are happy in your own company. When you leave the Healing Sanctuary you should feel truly comfortable and relaxed, not looking for the next exciting venture to fill you up or replace the love you are lacking. You are happy being instead of doing, you are busy getting on with your life and creating your solid structure and internal love and appreciation for you and the world.

The place you are in life now is an opportunity to feel good about yourself on your own. We all come into the world alone and we all die alone. People come and go in our lives but we can really only ever rely on ourselves. So if you learn to love, honour and be proud of who you are, you will create independence for yourself and be ready for interdependence when the right person appears.

You will only attract the love you desire when you are able to be that love yourself. We attract into our lives people that are a reflection of ourselves. There is no accident when choosing to be in a relationship. If your partner is unavailable, maybe you are unavailable. If they are aloof, maybe you are needy. If they are abusive and you feel you cannot leave, perhaps you so desperately need their love that you will sacrifice your own wellbeing. Whatever the pattern, you will continue attracting the same type of person till you learn the lessons and do things differently.

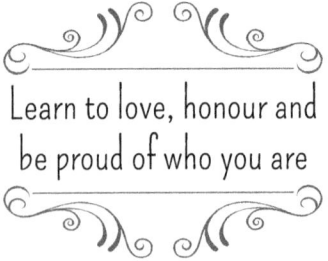

Learn to love, honour and be proud of who you are

The way to the life and love you really want is through healing, self love, awareness and authenticity. When you are honest with yourself, stop blaming others and take responsibility you will be in a position to learn more about yourself and you will flourish.

Your surroundings at the Healing Sanctuary

"Be the change that you wish to see in the world"

Mahatma Ghandi

Arriving at the Healing Sanctuary, for a moment you feel serenity and calmness wash over you. You are not yet sure why but this space oozes a radiant loving feeling. You pause to embrace the warm and fuzzy feelings that well up inside you and wash over you. Feelings that have been absent in your life for some time, feelings that you believed you would never feel again. Feelings you deeply wish will frequent your emotional repertoire more regularly.

At this stage you may be afraid because you know these glorious feelings will pass and in their place the tough ones will return again. It is an emotional rollercoaster you are on and you feel out of control. Someone is pushing the buttons and you are just along for the ride. You have not yet mastered the ability to sit comfortably with your feelings and accept them for being a part of you, learnt to observe rather than attach, to process and feel rather than avoid. Once you master this, the hard emotions will pop their head up less regularly and when they do you will know how to deal with them. Through this gentle transition life becomes more flowing, manageable and serene.

You take in your new surroundings like a child on an amazing adventure. As you pull into the driveway you cannot really see what you are yet to experience, but anticipation is building inside you. You move towards big, black, iron gates that have a beautiful love-heart woven through the ironwork.

The gates sweep open slowly and quietly to unveil luscious grounds; an awe-inspiring sweep of colour, with a hint of pink and the smell of jasmine that intensifies your senses. The grounds are immaculate with soft, green grass cascading between the flower beds. The ambience creates a calm inner feeling and you can imagine sitting quietly amidst the garden reflecting on your life.

You see villas amongst majestic oak trees, with views of stunning hills all around. The villas are secluded and separate from each other, but joined by winding pebble paths dotted with benches, inviting quiet contemplation of the tranquil surroundings. It is such a serene and inspirational sight.

Up a steep flight of stairs and positioned precariously on the hill, you spy what looks like a glass room with a 360 degree view. You are feeling very curious about this inviting-looking space. You notice a pool on the outskirts of the garden, surrounded by daybeds and umbrellas. Guests are slowly ambling around with teas pots and books while others are relaxing quietly.

There appears to be another area behind a white picket fence and you wonder what lies waiting for you on the other side.

As you walk to reception you pass a day spa with a pretty pink front door and tall candelabras on either side. You sneak a glance at the spa menu and are delighted to see that massages of all kinds are available, a service made all the more inviting by the aromatic essential oils that caress your sense of smell.

The reception area is open and light, with cool, marble flooring and walls of greenery and plants instead of bricks and mortar. There are white leather lounges and coloured ottomans scattered with Balinese-style throw rugs. Candles glow enthusiastically from magnificent chandeliers and pink and white lilies burst from vases. Buddha statues keep watch as you savour the moment, slowly heading towards the main desk.

At the marble reception desk you are greeted by a beautiful, friendly, caring individual. You share your details and are given a new In the Pink Process brochure that you hold close to your heart, hoping it will bring the secret of peace and freedom you so desperately seek.

You are escorted to your own private villa where the double doors open to expose a table ready with some healthy snacks and a pot of herbal tea in a colourful Moroccan tea pot. You sit quietly and allow yourself to be in this special moment, just you, your feelings and your liquorice tea.

You read the brochure and reflect how differently you feel about the process than when you arrived at the Heartbreak Manor. Now you know and feel this experience will be gentle and divine. You know you must go with the flow, and give yourself the opportunity and permission to relax. You feel safe and secure here and have faith this environment will bring health and healing.

The brochure reveals five main spaces of the Healing Sanctuary and the promises they hold.

Welcome to the Healing Sanctuary

In the Pink Process
Love – Truth – Purpose
Who am I?
My Pink Heart Print
My Inner Pink Star
Lady Chitter Chatter
Meditation and me

1. The Pink Spa guarantees a soothing touch, fragrant oils and an opportunity to delve into the 'Who am I' question that you find at the forefront of your mind.
2. The pool area vows tasty treats and calming tea and also an intriguing opportunity to develop your own Pink Heart Print.
3. The Pink Studio you saw perched on the hill encourages truth and enlightenment through Pilates and yoga. There is also the assurance you will become familiar with your inner wisdom, or as I call her, your Inner Pink Star.
4. The main grounds and its special seating spots pledge to help you understand Lady Chitter Chatter, your inner negative voice. Here you will learn ways to help integrate her into your life and reduce the chaos she produces.
5. Finally the mysterious area behind the white picket gate you learn is called The Flower Garden of Love. This intimate garden holds a secret and promises more lessons to carry forward into your new life.

Your sense of peace and calm is intensified after reading through the brochure and the map. You can see that at each space there will be activities to shift you further into your healing helping to create added internal transformation.

You sense calm and excitement are battling for space in your heart, so you decide that tonight you will nurture yourself with a spa bath and order a scrumptious meal from the room service menu.

When you are washed and nourished you will hop into the king size bed surrounded by flowing white curtains to embrace and relax your body, heart and soul. You are preparing yourself for a bright and early start to what you are sure is to be a big adventure of learning and growth.

WHO AM I?

"Be who you are and say what you feel because those who mind don't matter and those who matter don't mind"

Dr Seuss

The next morning you feel rested and ready to plunge deeper into your healing. The gentle walk from your villa to the Pink Spa takes you through the grounds to the pretty pink door; the entrance to what you hope will be a relaxing and serene experience. You gaze for a minute at the tall candelabras either size of the door and feel inspired by their size and stature; they appear so quietly calm and powerful.

Opening the pretty pink door, the mood and aromas overcome you as you realise you have a whole morning here to bask in the tranquillity, the massages, the spa baths and the essential oils. While your heart prepares for deeper healing, you will be able to let your physical body savour the attention it so desperately deserves, attention that has been long lost while dealing with such difficult heartbreak.

Sitting in the foyer admiring the décor and basking in the calming ambience, your name is called. You are shown to a subtly lit, warm room where soft and relaxing music is playing. The massage table is swathed in pink towels folded back waiting for you. You slowly sit and allow your body to sink into the massage table and lie silently while waiting for a set of magic hands to do their work.

Only a few moments later you can smell the aromatic oils while simultaneously you feel a set of warm hands on your back which slowly start massaging your tired and needy body. What seems like a few minutes but is actually over an hour, the magic hands are removed from your body and replaced with a set of warm towels.

After your massage, you spend the rest of the morning in pampering bliss and are indulged by the steam room, the sauna, the spa baths and take in the magical atmosphere that you find yourself immersed in. At the end of your pampering gift, you shower and dress and are escorted to the veranda where a scrumptious lunch, water, herbal teas and the first exercise at the Healing Sanctuary, 'Who am I?', awaits you.

Even though it's your first day at the Healing Sanctuary you are required to work hard and challenge yourself. Who am I? You might think it is a pretty straight forward question. When asked this, many people would reply 'I'm a doctor', 'I'm an Office Manager', 'I'm a mother' but that is what we do, it is our label, not who we are. 'Who am I' could in fact be a deeper question, requiring insight and reflection to answer. Do you really know and understand yourself at the core of who you are?

Delving deeper into yourself will expose what really makes you tick and awaken who you truly are. Who you are at your deepest level is about your strengths and your areas for improvement, your values and beliefs, your passions and fears, your likes and dislikes, your limitations and intolerances, your insecurities, your moods, your habits, your deepest desires and hurts, your body and your relationships.

You will also need to consider that now you are in the place of making changes in your life. Through your experiences of this heartbreak, you know you do not want to remain as you were. At this point you are able to make a choice about the person who you would like to become in your future. It is helpful to look at the past and look at your habits and traits, then choose to bring with you only what you wish to keep so you can feel, act and behave in the way you have envisaged for your future.

'People can't change, leopards don't change their spots' you may be thinking. This can be true but only if you choose to remain ignorant and unconscious to life and yourself. This may sound harsh but it's true. If you live without creating awareness around what it is you want, you could coast along, hiding behind a false façade, being busy being busy but getting nowhere, hoping that life will magically change without having to actually take responsibility and make those changes.

In this state you are unaware of your deep core essence and live in fear of change, fear of everything. You are happy to think the way you have always thought and look outwards for blame and persecution rather than inwards for growth and change. Unfortunately for others, you will not be inspiring or uplifting to be around. Those who have created awareness will feel their energy drain just being in your presence.

You could, however, choose to live life with awareness and enthusiasm for growing and emerging into the person you dream yourself to be. You could actively spend time discovering your values, making hard choices and changing your life, challenging your negative chitter-chatter and replacing it with positive self talk.

You would feel deeply and process what is needed to come through to a more peaceful and serene state of mind. You would look at where you have created struggles in your life in order to avoid falling into the same patterns and routines. You change all the time; you are constantly growing and evolving. You take risks and move towards your dreams and passions. You ooze optimism, friendliness and love; others want to be around you and are attracted to your uplifting presence.

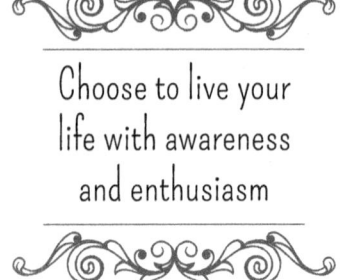
Choose to live your life with awareness and enthusiasm

Now be honest but gentle and ask yourself which best describes you? Which would you rather be? Do you want option A or option B? Or is there a little bit of you in both? Do not beat yourself up internally if you think you are doomed to being in option A. The place you are now is perfect, because here is where you are able to choose. You do not have to do what you have always done, you can choose something else. Like many things in life you just need time, practice and a few tweaks of your mindset. This is what life is all about, learning and growing. It is actually quite exciting, because when small changes are made you can start to feel very proud of yourself; things change, you change and life begins to sparkle.

CHOOSE WHO YOU WANT TO BE

"Everybody is a genius. But if you judge a fish by its ability to climb a tree, it will live its whole life believing that it is stupid"

Albert Einstein

The good news is that you do not have a predestined future. It is a CHOICE, YOUR CHOICE. You get to choose which group you would like to be in. Your future is not your destiny, it is not who you are, it is what you choose. It is not always easy to take responsibility but everything in your life is your choice. You can choose to play victim and stay negative or choose to be bursting with optimism and enthusiasm and find the good things in life. You can choose to take risks to improve the areas of your life that don't currently live up to your dreams.

Discovering your true self does not happen overnight and may be the start of a soul-searching lifetime journey for yourself. You need

Who am I?

to be ready and willing to come face to face with yourself - the darkness and the light and all the areas for improvement alongside the fabulous amazing traits, skills and talents, some that may not have even emerged yet. Once we are no longer frightened of the darkness within, the light begins to shine ever so brightly.

One baby step today can change all of your tomorrows

After I had come out of my dark period of grieving over my relationship, the light began to shine and I became enthused to learn more about myself and grow into the person I wanted to become. I knew I was over the worst of it and was ready to discover me again, to go back to my core basics. I was ready to make a choice about who I wanted to be. What did I need to work on or be more aware of? What areas did I want to improve? Which values and beliefs would I leave behind, and what would I replace them with?

I made the choice I was going to be one of the enlightened individuals that grows, shapes and changes, becomes more enlightened, regains enthusiasm for life, builds a solid foundation, redecorates from the inside out. I was going to find my authentic self and add improvements to create the person I want to be in this world. Phew! It was a big task to do this without becoming overindulgent and overly internalised or introverted, to do it while also living life and having fun along the way. It's a balance, but I did it and so can you if you wish and prioritise. A bit of time out at this stage will create miracles in your future.

Here at the Healing Sanctuary you will firstly look at who you are, unlocking your core to reveal the good and not so good. You will explore where you are now and where you want to go with your family, your career, your history and your future. By surrendering to all the parts of you and your true self and giving up resistance, you will move to your authenticity that is so desperately waiting to emerge so you can begin a peaceful flow with life and love.

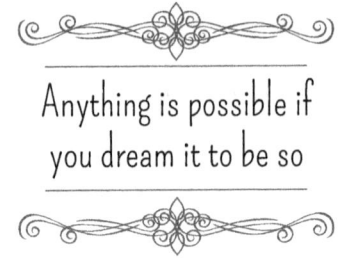

Anything is possible if you dream it to be so

You know now how important awareness is in your life. While finding the answers to the 'Who am I' question, you have the chance to put that awareness in to action. Use it with the questions and sentence starters below to start to highlight parts of yourself that may be hidden.

Pink time out – Question time and sentence starters

Stop and Breathe

This list of questions or sentence starters will help you start to discover where you stand now and where you want to go. Don't dwell on the answers for too long, write what comes into your mind first - it is often the deeper truth. Take it seriously but not too seriously. Getting to know ourselves can be a very rewarding and also fun pastime. Enjoy the process and have a bit of a laugh if it reveals the old habits that will never die.

In your Little Pink book of Love, record your thoughts, feelings, reactions and any epiphanies and wow moments you may have. Let the pen flow and see what appears on the page in front of you. As this may take you out of your comfort zone, remember to remain gentle and compassionate with yourself, and always come from a place of love.

1. My family is...
2. What I would change about my family is...
3. My current career is...

Who am I?

4. What I would change about my career if I had the chance is...
5. My friends are...
6. What I would change about my friends is...
7. I live in...
8. What I would change about where I live is...
9. How I act/behave in social situations is...
10. What I would like to change about how I act in social situations is...
11. My favourite social activities are...
12. The person I love spending the most time with is...
13. I feel... when I am around this person
14. My style and dress sense is...
15. What I would change about my style if it didn't matter what others thought is...
16. What I do for exercise is...
17. What I would like to add to my exercise routine is...
18. What I do to relax is...
19. What I would like to add to my relaxation routine is...
20. My daily spiritual practice is...
21. Traits I do not like in others are...
22. My financial situation is...
23. If I could change my financial situation I would...
24. My body is...
25. If I could change my body I would...
26. I am sick and tired of...

27. For fun I...
28. My health is...
29. I would like to improve my health by...
30. The last time I cried was...
31. I cry when...
32. The one thing that makes me really sad is...
33. I hate it when...
34. I get angry when...
35. The last time I got really angry was...
36. The one thing that makes me really angry is...
37. I manage my anger by...
38. My worst habit is...
39. I suffer from exhaustion when...
40. My energy is drained when...
41. My energy is uplifted when...
42. I still feel guilty about...
43. I have forgiven myself for...
44. I feel most confident when...
45. I feel most insecure when... because...
46. I always worry that...
47. I am scared that...
48. The last time I felt really anxious was...
49. I manage my anxiety by...
50. I feel overwhelmed when...
51. I always get jealous when...

52. I am envious of others when...
53. ... bores me to tears
54. I really hope that...
55. When I feel rejected I...
56. I feel a sense of belonging when...
57. I get really excited when...
58. I get really depressed when...
59. My best assets are...
60. My favourite movie is...
61. The three most fabulous experiences I have had are...
62. The three saddest experiences in my life were...
63. I was most hurt when...
64. My deepest wish is to...
65. I am happiest when...

WOW, if you made it to the end of this extensive list you are doing well. You may have clarified which parts of yourself you know well, and perhaps found some traits that previously had been hidden or locked away. Take some time out to digest what you have just tackled and learnt; relax and breathe in all that you have unearthed. Be proud of yourself for investing energy into yourself and creating enthusiasm and passion for your life. You are creating change every moment you delve deep and meet yourself head on with softness and compassion. You are moving forward to be the person you desire to be.

Nobody is perfect and we are all unique exactly as we are, with all our scars and imperfections

PINK TIME OUT – PROMISE

Stop and Breathe

Call yourself to action and make a promise to yourself. Make a promise that will move you forward by a small step. A promise that will move you closer to becoming the person you desire to be.

It is important to make a commitment to yourself in regards to change. You may not yet know exactly what all the changes may be, what they may look like or how they will play out. The vital part is to make a commitment to that first baby step. Use your intuition to help decide what your steps may be and make a promise to yourself to take them one by one.

A promise is a declaration, a commitment, a hand on your heart sacred agreement that you WILL fulfil its action and desire. It is a pledge and vow, your word of honour, made to yourself from yourself.

Write your promise in your Little Pink book of Love. 'To work towards becoming the person I want to become,

Who Am I?

I promise the one thing I am going to do today to start creating this is...'

Now place your hand on your heart, close your eyes and repeat out loud your promise to yourself, slowly and succinctly. Allow it to soak into your every cell, into your deep internal being. Keep repeating the promise until you can feel it holding a place in your heart ready to be eternally fulfilled. Honour the promise and honour yourself.

To keep your promise alive and at the forefront of your mind, post note it on your desk, lipstick it to your mirror in the bathroom, blackboard it in the kids playroom, magnet it on the fridge. Wherever it inspires you, ensure it is there ready to be heard, seen, felt and integrated internally. Bring it alive and your very own miracles will start to occur.

Leaving the Pink Spa via the pretty pink door, you return to your villa and your comfy chair. As you sip on your herbal tea you reflect on the day and your journey so far at the Healing Sanctuary. Your body feels soothed, peaceful and pampered while your soul feels a little more connected to your heart and mind.

You pull your knees to your chest and hug them tight, feeling a sense of warmth and fuzziness. Something has shifted - you are meeting yourself again and honouring and respecting the person you are, imperfections and all. For a while you sit and just be, something you have for a long time been unable to do. It's just you and your thoughts and feelings and you are starting to enjoy the solitude, now that the barrage of negative thoughts is subsiding.

Another restful night awaits, after you wash off the oils from today's massage in a warm shower. You dress in glorious crisp yet snug pyjamas and slowly lay yourself down on the warm and comfy bed, preserving the love you have provided for yourself today.

My Pink Heart Print

"The unexamined life is not worth living"

Socrates

Looking out the window of your villa before you leave for the day, you feel blessed to see the sun is shining. It's still early but you sense it will evolve into a beautiful summer's day, you can smell the warmth in the air. How perfect, as today you will be heading to the pool for the day.

You follow the path through the beautiful grounds, and as you move and nurture your body you ponder what you learnt from yesterday's 'Who am I' question. It has left you wanting more; you want to learn more, understand more and meet more of you. It feels like a long-lost friend has reappeared and you are discovering so many new things about her.

As you enter the pool area, you look for the right day bed and umbrella to spend your day with. You find the perfect spot where you will ponder, drink tea, eat yummy food and hop into the pool when it gets too hot. You relax and wait for all that this space has to offer to descend upon you.

Today's activity is to develop your own Pink Heart Print. This is like the blueprint of a building but is all about you. It is about your heart, your soul, the real you. The you that is like a race horse at the starting gate desperately waiting to be let loose on the world, no holds barred, no masking parts of yourself to pacify anyone else.

The Pink Heart Print is comprised of 14 sections. You will be prompted to find the relevant information to complete each section with detailed facts and data about you..

This will build on the awareness and understanding you now have of yourself to be able to walk forwards and remain true to your essence. This exercise will cement your foundations so you are ready for anything. In essence the Pink Heart Print is like a user manual of you.

You will look at your strengths and areas for improvement, your values and core beliefs, your passions and fears, your likes and dislikes. Then we will move onto your deepest hurts and desires, your intolerances, habits and moods, where you get most upset with yourself and your grandest dreams. Finally we will look at your triumphs and achievements, your blocks, what you are grateful for, your purpose and three adjectives to describe yourself.

It is a big list and, yes, you will need to be gentle with yourself and allow time to dive deep inside. It will highlight places within that may have been buried for a long time and help you to understand and know yourself inside out. The Pink Heart Print is preventative medicine for the heart and soul to ensure you find yourself, remain true to yourself and never abandon yourself or treat yourself with disrespect.

Often we spiral around our head spinning in chaotic circles and we go nowhere fast as we can't distinguish which way to turn, which way to focus our attention. Questions are raised in our ever busy minds 'If I knew who I was maybe I would know what direction to take'. We impulsively look for quick fixes out of testing and messy situations, often finding we have just landed in another cow pat without realising it. Trying to escape one situation, we find ourselves back in the same one, only slightly different.

This is why it is so crucial to build the solid foundations, go back to basics, do the deep inner work and discover who you are before making massive changes in your life. Then when you make the changes they will be in the best interests of your true self, not just the self that wants to escape their current situation. Why spend energy moving in circles when you could make one or two well planned changes so you can work towards being your true unique self and find your true unique purpose in life?

Once you can be the person that is uniquely you, that has your Pink Heart Print, you can have trust in your journey and yourself, life stops being a struggle and you can master living in the flow. This synergy with life creates abundance and glory, jubilation and synchronicity with everything that materialises in your life. You will achieve quantum leaps, attract your higher callings, respond to your true yearnings for life and see where the magic starts to sparkle.

You will cultivate the awareness you gained at Heartbreak Manor at a deeper level to draw more from the 'Who am I' mystery. You are capable of limitless and infinite potential in this lifetime and nothing is stopping you except you.

Meeting a new man and learning all you can about them is so much fun. It's exciting, thrilling and exhilarating. This process will allow you to meet yourself with just as much excitement.

When I was amidst my heartbreak I was fed up with feeling crappy about my relationship demise, so I decided in that moment that I was going to list the areas I believed I needed to work on. Then I could slowly work towards improving them and coming back to my true self. As the list grew, it flowed into the creation of my Pink Heart Print to get to know all the nooks, crannies and crevices of myself.

Miraculously, once I had written my list and created my Pink Heart Print, people and situations I needed started to emerge in my life. I asked for them and 'poof' they appeared. But in reality it was not magic, I asked for change and believed so hard that I started to attract and manifest what I needed into my life.

Once I attracted what I need to change, I began to transform from a caterpillar into a beautiful butterfly, spreading my new-found wings and flying gracefully away to a better place.

When developing your Pink Heart Print, record your answers in your Little Pink book of Love. Go all out, write everything and anything that comes to your mind, make it creative and arty or structured and orderly, whatever works best for you. You are creating a resource that will travel along with you.

I often look back on my Pink Heart Print when I feel a little lost or suffer a minor setback. My notes help me remember who I am, and how proud I am to be me. I use my Little Pink book of Love to keep me on track, consciously valuing and celebrating my strengths while working on areas that I would like to improve.

Begin your transformation

You dive into the pool, the sun warming your skin through the blue serene water as you contemplate what you have just learnt. After a few laps you surface dripping with water feeling enthused to get started to see what gems arise from your own Pink Heart Print.

"The most terrifying thing is to accept oneself completely"

C.G. Jung

Step 1 - My strengths and areas for improvement

Knowing the positive as well as the areas for improvement is invaluable in life, love and your career. It enables you to have a deeper understanding of the authentic you, why you do the things you do and what you can achieve in the future. Values help bring all your personae into the open to be acknowledged for the part they play in your life. Awareness empowers you to create change, potentially profound, amazing change.

This exercise will give you the opportunity to be proud of yourself for who you are, what you have achieved and what is still to be achieved. You can rejoice in the successes and strengths that are individual only to you.

It can be hard to clearly see your strengths if you have been on autopilot for a while, or if you were bought up not to celebrate your own successes. In fact it is natural and healthy to voice your strengths so you can more clearly see what you have to offer yourself and those around you.

Identifying your areas for improvement and examining the submerged fragments of yourself may seem scary or even terrifying. But it is only once your limitations are accepted as part of you, that they can no longer harm you. It is only once your limitations are unveiled that you can design strategies to improve these areas.

While working on your areas for improvement you can leverage your strengths and so work towards the person you want to become.

Pink time out – Question time

Stop and Breathe

Read the list of questions below and allow time and space for self reflection. In your Little Pink book of Love, record your thoughts, feelings, reactions and any epiphanies and wow moments you may have. To define your strengths, you may need to think further outside the square. Let the pen flow and see what appears on the page in front of you. As this may take you out of your comfort zone, remember to remain gentle and compassionate with yourself, and always come from a place of love.

Through this exercise can you create a list of at least 20 strengths, maybe more. Each question may have many answers; the more the merrier! If you cannot answer all the questions in one sitting, don't panic; sleep or meditate on it and come back and add to your list later. You might need to ask others for help to answer some questions, which could open up ideas you hadn't considered. Some of your answers might be physical things you are skilled at doing, or they might be personality traits, or emotional strengths. It's up to you!

1. What comes easier to you than to others?
2. What do others compliment you on?
3. What have you received awards for?
4. What does your employer praise you for?
5. What do your friends say you are good at?
6. What do family say you are good at?
7. What do your children say you are good at?
8. What do you feel competent at training others in?
9. What do you love doing where you lose time and feel in the flow?
10. What do you believe you do well?
11. What do you really love?
12. What are you really passionate about?
13. What makes you proud of yourself?
14. What makes you feel excited when you talk about it?

Reviewing your answers to the questions above, are you able to compile a list of strengths you hold? Try to list 20, or as many as feels right for you.

Next, in your Little Pink book of Love, use the questions below to help you list 10-15 areas for improvement. Some of these questions may also prompt you to add to your strengths list.

Once you highlight and bring into the open these areas it becomes a lot easier to deal with them. They are no longer buried, they are no longer so frightening, and this is the first step to improvement and change. Keep in mind that everyone has their own list of areas they would like to improve. Be kind and gentle with yourself and answer with compassion not harshness.

1. What do you really struggle at?
2. What do you dislike doing?
3. What do you avoid doing?
4. Do you process all your emotions?
5. What emotions do you avoid?
6. What makes you angry and frustrated?
7. Do you suffer anxiety or nervousness in certain situations?
8. Are you able to process your grief when required?
9. Where and how are you hard on yourself?
10. What negative chitter-chatter goes on in your mind?
11. Do you look after yourself?
12. Do you love yourself?
13. Do you have a passion and follow your purpose in your life?
14. Do you have life balance?
15. Are you able to create awareness in your life?
16. Are you able to take responsibility for your life?
17. Are you comfortable in your own company?
18. Are you able to sit still with only yourself and evaluate and look internally?
19. Are you able to voice your concerns, needs and wants in an assertive way?
20. How do others push your buttons?

21. What constructive criticism do you receive from others?
22. Are you able to deal well with conflict?
23. Are you able to set boundaries and deliver consequences if they are broken?
24. Do you use and trust your intuition?
25. What patterns emerge repeatedly in your life?
26. Do you self abandon?
27. Do you trust yourself?
28. Do you become defensive easily?
29. Do you use humour and sarcasm as a front for dealing with life?
30. Do you feel self pity rather than take responsibility?
31. What are you intolerant of?
32. Do you take pride in your appearance?
33. Do you learn lessons from situations in your life?
34. Are you able to comfortably make big decisions in your life?
35. Are you able to move on from destructive situations?
36. Do you accept yourself?
37. Do you show gratitude for your life?
38. Are you able to show forgiveness to others?
39. Do you spend too much time trying to please others?
40. Do you need others' approval?
41. Are you able to say no to others nicely?
42. Do you surround yourself with people that sap your energy?

43. Are you judgemental of others?//
44. Do you indulge in gossip?
45. Are you able to be kind and tolerant to others?
46. Are you a perfectionist?
47. Do you doubt yourself?
48. What are your fears?
49. What makes you cringe?
50. Do you procrastinate?
51. Do you fall into helplessness?
52. Do you play the victim in certain areas of your life?
53. Is your thinking negative more often than positive?
54. Are you too focused on your achievements rather than your efforts?
55. What avoidance strategies do you use in your life?
56. What one thing would you change about yourself if you could wave a magic wand?

Reviewing your answers to the questions above, are you able to compile a list of your areas for improvement? Try to list 10-15, or as many as feels right for you.

Some answers may give you an obvious area for improvement and others you may need to think about a little longer to highlight what it is that is holding you back in life. It may highlight patterns or areas that you would like to change.

Read your lists and take it inside to your internal being. Sit with it and see if it feels right. Stand up to the fears you have awoken internally and know that knowledge is power. Knowledge gives you the opportunity to create change, which creates the power within. You have uncovered buried parts of yourself that can no longer harm you. Now you can take on challenges and be totally honest with yourself.

Well done; after spending quality time examining yourself at a deeper level you should now have a more solid idea of the strengths and areas for improvement that make you, you. Honour yourself with a reward, something really nice you can do for yourself that honours and respects who you are becoming and what you are learning. Consider something that you may not do very often but is special. Maybe you could have a massage, enjoy coffee and cake at your favourite café, then movies with a friend, go on a trip away or spend a day at the beach. It does not need to be extravagant, just something that is a treat for you to relish and enjoy whilst appreciating and reflecting on the hard work you have done.

Creating this list of strengths and areas for improvement is how I got started when I didn't know where to start. Sometimes you have to just start the journey somewhere. I felt I had a fairly good idea of my strengths; I could list them and was told often by others what they were, yet I still didn't feel great about myself. I was trying every day to leverage my strengths but it was only through this process I was finally able to be honest with myself about what was holding me back.

My areas for improvement were lurking below, waiting to surface and I was holding them down with all my might. By using this process to let them surface, facing them and being honest with myself, I realised that they couldn't hurt me, they were just buried parts of myself wanting acknowledgement.

Surrender and let go

I discovered a list of fifteen areas I needed and wanted to improve. Yes, it was scary and yes it was a big list. But once I had created the awareness, the solutions were able to flow. I kept the list handy and revisited it regularly as I probed deeper into each area every day. Life was finally starting to take shape for me, my days became brighter, my thinking became more positive and I became gentler on myself. I had gained a lot more knowledge and awareness into who I was as a person and what made me, me.

Pink time out – Art expression

◦‿ Stop and Breathe ‿◦

Now that you have two lists, one for strengths and one for your areas for improvement, let's create an art piece. Use your coloured pencils and self expression to document your strengths and areas for improvement. Celebrate each and every one with colour and positivity.

You could have one page for strengths and another page for areas for improvement, or join them together. Use your internal creativity, make it your own and acknowledge what you have learnt from this exercise.

Be proud of your strengths and be proud of your ability to unearth your areas for improvements. Be proud of your desire to make positive changes in your life.

As you read through your two lists, you may find that some of your strengths and areas for improvement are things you were already aware of and working on as part of your self improvement. There may be other areas that were a bit of a surprise, and you are yet to discover how to implement changes internally.

Get out your Little Pink book of Love and keep your art piece near. Let your art piece help you as you journal around these areas; journal around your strengths, areas for improvement and the feelings around each as they come up.

If you find you are being hard on yourself, remember the focus is to be self loving. Create an internal sense of gentleness and forgiveness to self. Remember to say, 'I am sorry and I love you' to yourself.

Take a break to celebrate the hard work you have done with this first step of your Pink Heart Print. Don't try to be superwoman and get through this whole chapter at once. Rest, recuperate and reward yourself with a wondrous surprise. You deserve every little smidgen of it and the happiness it brings you.

Step 2 - My values

Values are who you are. They are not things you have but a record of what is most important to you. By clarifying your values you will be able to create an internal map that will guide you through the major decisions in your life seamlessly. You will have the ability to make a stand for yourself. If you honour your values in your life decisions, you will feel a sense of fulfilment like never before.

If you aren't aware what your values are, your life can head in random directions, turning down wrong roads looking for something that feels wrong inside when you find it. You may be living the life that you think you should lead, or that others tell you to lead, but you are not living the life you want, as you don't know what is important to you.

Continuing to ignore your values and staying on the discomfort path can lead to more serious emotional issues like anxiety and depression, and once you reach that point it is a lot harder to turn it around. Your intuition can help you with your values if you sit still long enough to listen to it.

Once you have a list of your top values you can look at your life and see where you are not living congruently with them. Sometimes you may learn that the decisions you need to make are bigger than you thought, so you need to take one step at a time. Once you can do this you will automatically feel a sense of inner relief, like you have come home to yourself again. Life starts to become a whole lot easier and shinier.

You can then lead the life that is sincerely true to yourself; you can start living in the flow doing what you love and feeling enthused and rewarded each and every moment. It is a glorious feeling when you get it right.

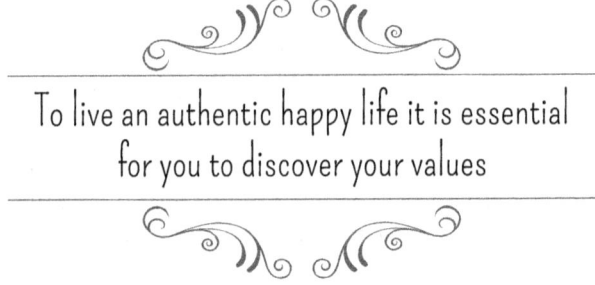

To live an authentic happy life it is essential for you to discover your values

PINK TIME OUT – QUESTION TIME

⸙ Stop and Breathe ⸙

Read the list of questions below and allow time and space for self reflection. In your Little Pink book of Love, record your thoughts, feelings, reactions and any epiphanies and wow moments you have around your values. Let the pen flow and see what appears on the page in front of you. As this may take you out of your comfort zone, remember to remain gentle and compassionate with yourself, and always come from a place of love.

1. What are your favourite activities – ones that you currently do often or ones you wish you could spend more time immersed in?
2. When do you currently feel happiest? Who are you with, what are you doing?
3. When do you feel most in the flow, so you lose track of time?
4. When are you most fulfilled?
5. What do you feel gives your life most meaning?
6. What is most important to you?
7. In your ideal world, what personal qualities would you like to see/experience/have?
8. Think about people you admire most; what is it that you admire?
9. Think about people you are envious of, what is it that you are envious of?
10. What do you always find room in your life for even when you are pressed for time?

11. What do you dream about that has not yet materialised in your life?
12. What do you think about a lot?
13. What do you like to talk to others about?
14. What do you talk about that lifts your spirits and creates excitement?

At this point you are discovering what is most important to you in your life. You have started to create your values in alignment with your truth.

Pink time out – Values list

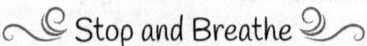

ᙚ Stop and Breathe ᙚ

The second step is for you to use the list below to circle the words you relate to deep inside. Just go with what feels right to you.

Abundance	Closeness	Flexibility	Passion	Service
Achievement	Compassion	Freedom	Purpose	Simplicity
Accomplishment	Contribution	Fun	Patience	Significance
Adventure	Coolness	Focus	Peace	Sincerity
Altruism	Correctness	Growth	Perfection	Stillness
Authenticity	Courage	Gratitude	Perceptiveness	Silliness
Acceptance	Credibility	Generosity	Power	Skill
Adaptability	Curiosity	Grace	Popularity	Sophistication

My Pink Heart Print

Adoration	Decisiveness	Giving	Polish	Spirituality
Advancement	Discovery	Happiness	Pleasure	Stability
Affection	Diversity	Healing	Playfulness	Strength
Affluence	Discipline	Heart	Persistence	Success
Ambition	Dependability	Helpfulness	Persuasiveness	Support
Alertness	Desire	Honesty	Poise	Sympathy
Amusement	Depth	Honour	Practicality	Space
Approval	Dignity	Hope	Privacy	Status
Appreciation	Devotion	Humour	Precision	Teamwork
Art	Diligence	Harmony	Pride	Tolerance
Awareness	Determination	Integrity	Presence	Thankfulness
Availability	Direction	Independence	Punctuality	Thoughtfulness
Accountability	Dream	Individuality	Purity	Thoroughness
Beauty	Directness	Influence	Preparedness	Trust
Balance	Duty	Inspiration	Proactivity	Tranquillity
Belonging	Equality	Insight	Reliability	Truth
Boldness	Excellence	Introversion	Respect	Tidiness
Bravery	Ease	Intuition	Rationality	Tradition
Brilliance	Education	Intellect	Realness	Unity
Bliss	Excitement	Interest	Reasonableness	Usefulness
Calmness	Efficiency	Inquisitiveness	Reflection	Vitality
Cleanliness	Effectiveness	Introspection	Recognition	Variety
Challenge	Empathy	Involvement	Richness	Vivaciousness
Communication	Encouragement	Impact	Rest	Vision
Commitment	Energy	Improvement	Resilience	Vigour
Change	Elegance	Innovation	Religion	Virtue
Collaboration	Elation	Joy	Relaxation	Wisdom
Community	Enjoyment	Justice	Refinement	Warmth
Competition	Enthusiasm	Knowledge	Safety	Wealth
Certainty	Exploration	Knowing	Stability	Will
Charity	Experience	Kindness	Solitude	Winning
Charm	Extroversion	Keenness	Security	Wit
Competence	Fairness	Loyalty	Sharing	Worth

Control	Feelings	Love	Sensitivity	Wonderment
Connection	Family	Learning	Sensuality	Youth
Cooperation	Faith	Leadership	Satisfaction	Zest
Creativity	Fame	Lightness	Serenity	Zeal
Clarity	Fear	Liveliness	Sexiness	
Cleverness	Fidelity	Logic	Shrewdness	
Comfort	Firmness	Organisation	Safety	

How many words have you ended up with on your list? These are all the values that are important to you, however some will touch you more deeply than others. In the next part of the exercise you can narrow down this list of values to see which really shine out.

Use the answers to the questions and the circled words above to help you narrow down your value words to your top ten. The answers to the questions will give insight into what's important to you, and ideas about which value words feel right. By narrowing your list of words down to ten this does not mean that the others are not important and are not values in your life. It is that we are just looking for the top ten at this point.

Spend some time thinking about each word, say it out loud. See which ones resonate with you deep inside. Your top values will just feel right.

Write the top ten words you have chosen in your little Pink book of Love. Remember this is your own personal values list and you can alter it at any time.

Take a breath and a moment's rest. When you are ready, come back to your top ten list and put your values into an order 0–10. Think about each of the top ten words and choose which are more important to you than others. Put them into an order of importance that feels right for you.

Now that we have the top ten in order of importance, I am going to ask you to cut the list in half and put the second five words aside. Once you have done this are you still happy with the top five on your list? Do the top five you now have in front of you speak to everything you do in life, or do you need to reshuffle your order to get a new top five?

You should now have a list that feels right and has highlighted the top five values in your life. The top two should be the things you just could not live without. These top two values are what underpin every major decision you make. Previously it happened subconsciously, but imagine how much more powerful your decisions will be now you know what drives them.

Some time ago I was offered the potential to invest in a successful small business. This amazing opportunity looked excellent and the financial reward was good. Yet trying to make a decision around this opportunity sent me into a big tail spin; a part of me was so tempted as I thought about the prestige and the financial element for my future.

Yet another more authentic part of me was yelling at myself saying 'No, don't do it!' Family and friends were asking why I would not take such a great opportunity, which put even more pressure on me.

To solve the dilemma I revisited my values and trusted my intuition. Bringing my values to the forefront of my awareness helped me make a decision in alignment with myself.

My top ten values are:
1. Authenticity
2. Family
3. Inner harmony
4. Love
5. Life purpose
6. Integrity
7. Personal growth
8. Balance
9. Vitality
10. Security

Nowhere in my top values is competition, prestige, prosperity, wealth etc. Now this does not mean that I don't want these things, but they are not in my top ten. The promotion was in a field that was not my deepest passion and the long work hours would leave no time for family and balance. The added stress of the role would not lead to peace or inner harmony.

So I turned down the opportunity, but the process led me to a further exploration of my life purpose. If I had decided I didn't want that opportunity, then what did I want for my life?

Through checking in with my values I realised that creating a business around my passion, meaning and purpose in life would fulfil me and tap into my authenticity and life purpose values. It may also bring an added bonus of prosperity and wealth, but this was not the most important thing. I would be happy doing what I truly loved for no or little financial reward.

It is not easy to find what you were put on this earth to do but knowing your values adds an intense knowledge and understanding to help discover your passion and purpose.

I live and breathe my values every day. This does not mean I don't stuff up and wonder why I am dissatisfied, it just means that I can understand why it has happened and then bring my direction back to one that is in alignment with my values.

Live and breathe your values

Pink time out – Top ten values

Stop and Breathe

As you have probably noticed from the previous exercises, knowing what your values are doesn't mean they are magically reflected in how your life looks right now. Finding out what is and isn't working is the key to establishing what changes to make.

This next step in the process will help you evaluate how satisfied you are with how each of your values is currently incorporated into your life.

1. Take out your coloured pencils and draw a circle in your Little Pink book of Love.
2. Draw lines through your circle to make ten segments, like pieces of a pie.
3. Write each of your values on a different pie piece.
4. Ask yourself the same question for each of your values "How satisfied am I with this value in my life right now?"

5. Rate your satisfaction from 0 - 10, with the centre representing 0 - not satisfied, and the outer edge of the circle representing 10 - very satisfied. Colour in from the centre out to the point that represents how you rated how satisfied you are with this value.

6. Go around your circle, assessing how well each value is showing up in your life at this point in time. Colour in up to the number in each pie as you rate each value.

7. Once you have assessed and coloured in each value you can visually see where each one sits in your satisfaction levels.

8. Your reality may well be different to your ideal; for example your value of family may be very important to you, yet you are currently not very satisfied with how it is focused on in your life, and have given it a rating of four. Sit for a minute and take in what this exercise has revealed to you so far.

9. Now ask yourself, what rating would you prefer each value to be?

10. Place a dotted line on the pie piece representing what level of focus you would like to have on that value in your life. Now you can visually see the gap between the actual and the ideal.

11. Lastly, ask yourself what you could do differently to raise this value from your original number to the number you wish it to be. Document your findings in your Little Pink book of Love.

12. Keep your pie handy and as you feel you are moving closer to your values, return to the exercise. See if you can colour in more of the pie between the coloured plotted point to your dotted line, and celebrate moving closer to living in tune with your value.

You are brilliant for coming this far. Spend some time reflecting what this exercise revealed for you. Check in where you have highlighted the values you are living well, and where you would like to make some changes. You can use this exercise at different stages of your life to reflect and review how you are advancing with living authentically, in alignment with your values.

The exercise may have highlighted values that you hold and the gaps in your life where they are not being fulfilled. It may highlight where you have unconsciously tiptoed off course and now awakened the opportunity to revisit your life, your choices and your future direction.

It may present you with decisions that need to be made and goals that need to be set. At the Happiness Shack you will have the chance to set those goals and develop your vision to move forward to a life you can feel tickled pink about.

Step 3 My core beliefs

Values bring about core beliefs. A core belief generally develops in childhood, being a belief you hold deep internally, that feels so fundamentally true based on your life experiences. It is generally rigid and inflexible and has a major impact on how you live your life day to day. Each individual will hold their own set of core beliefs depending on their upbringing, significant life experiences and circumstances they have found themselves in.

Core beliefs then translate to automatic thoughts that appear in your mind at an unconscious level. These in turn affect your emotional state on a daily basis. To improve your thoughts you must first identify and challenge your core beliefs. When you have identified your core beliefs you can assess how healthy and rational each of them are. You can open up and probe into a deeper understanding of yourself.

If you continue to have negative beliefs and thoughts about yourself it is definitely time to challenge and expose them for what they are. You can then set about replacing them with new, healthier ones, which will in turn change your negative thought patterns to more positive ones. This will translate into a healthier and happier life and promote self love.

The first step to unearth your core beliefs is your emotions. Once you have identified a particular emotion you can work backwards to find the thought that preceded the emotion. This thought will then help you work backwards again and will ultimately lead you to the core belief. Once you are familiar with the core belief you can go about assessing it and deciding whether to challenge it.

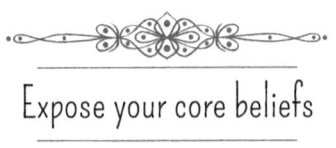

Expose your core beliefs

By looking at your thought patterns and paying attention you will become mindful of what you are telling yourself. Creating awareness of your thoughts will enable you to delve deeper to the core belief that lay deep underneath. The core belief can be many layers underneath the actual automatic thought, so be prepared to look deeply to gain the most benefit. This is not work for the faint-hearted but will produce such rewarding benefits and bring about profound change to your life.

Pink Time Out - Emotions, Thoughts and Core Beliefs

⟶ Stop and Breathe ⟵

This exercise will allow you to unearth your core beliefs through the following steps:

1. Document a situation, list the emotions find the automatic thoughts
2. Challenge the automatic thoughts
3. Replace the automatic thoughts
4. Identify the core beliefs and challenge the core beliefs.

1. **Document the situation, list the emotions and find the automatic thoughts**

    Think about a situation this week when you felt you were not operating at your best, felt low or encountered an uncomfortable emotion. Think about how you felt; think about what was going through your mind straight after the event. A thought diary is good way to capture these scenarios. In your Little Pink book of Love, create a table like the one below to document your discoveries. List the emotions that surfaced and then list the thoughts that popped into your head.

    Example:

Situation	Emotion	Thoughts - automatic
I was walking down the street and saw a friend on the other side of the road. I waved to her in an enthusiastic manner, excited to see her and yet I received no response.	Felt sad, concerned, worried, low, rejected.	What have I done wrong? Maybe I have upset her. Maybe she doesn't like me anymore.

2. **Challenge the automatic thoughts**

   The next step is to challenge your automatic thoughts by asking yourself some questions. This will help to see if you just trust your emotions and thoughts without giving any consideration to their truth.

   1. Is there any evidence to support my thoughts being true?
   2. Could there be another explanation for her not responding to me?
   3. If my thoughts are true, what is the worst thing that could happen?
   4. If my thoughts are true, what is the best thing that could happen?
   5. How does believing my thoughts affect me?
   6. Is there anything I can do about this?
   7. If a friend came to me with this issue, what advice would I give her?

3. **Replace the automatic thoughts**

   Look at replacing your automatic thoughts with new, more rational ones. In this scenario, you could try:

   1. Maybe she did not see me.
   2. Maybe she did not have her glasses on.
   3. Maybe she was on the phone.

   By considering alternative thoughts, you will feel your emotion change to a more positive one to replace the negative thoughts.

   There could be a number of reasons why she did not acknowledge you. The automatic thoughts that came into your mind are most likely based on a core belief that you hold, rather than an actual truth of the situation.

4. **Identifying and challenging the core belief**

   By sourcing the core belief you can bring about real change rather than just attempting to change the automatic thought.

   To find the core belief, go through this process with your question:

   1. Question - What does it mean to you if your friend does not acknowledge you?
      a. Answer - It means that I may have offended her
   2. Translate the answer to a question - What does it mean if I have offended her?
      a. Answer - It means that she may not like me
   3. Translate the answer to a question - What does it mean if she does not like me?
      a. It means that I am not loveable

   I am not loveable = CORE BELIEF

In this process you continue to ask yourself what it means to you, until you get down to the deepest layer underneath it all: the core belief.

Think about someone with a different core belief, perhaps someone who feels loveable. Her situation would probably be very different. If her friend did not see her, her automatic thoughts may be 'She didn't see me; oh well I'll speak to her later'. In this situation there are no negative emotions, no concern, worry or sadness. She has a core believe that she is loveable, so the situation did not have a distressing meaning for her. The way we interpret a situation with our emotions and thoughts is all about our deepest beliefs about ourselves. This is why it is so important to uncover our core beliefs and challenge the ones that do not serve us, to live a sparkly happy life.

At this point if you have discovered the core belief to be that you are not loveable you can then challenge this belief. You can learn to replace a negative core belief with a more positive one that will benefit your future.

1. Think about who loves you in your life.
2. Think about whether it is necessary to be loved by everyone you meet.
3. Think about feedback you get from friends and family regarding how loveable you are.
4. Think about how much you love yourself.
5. Think about how you can love yourself more.
6. Document what it means to be loveable.

This exercise is exceptionally tough as it draws out our deepest, negative core beliefs if done correctly. This is, however, what we need to do to create the awareness and get to the actual negative belief and to the root cause of our suffering. Until we know what our true negative core beliefs are, we are still operating at a superficial level and it is not until we go really deep and find the root cause do we start opening doors to immerse ourselves in deep healing.

When I was having monthly appointments with my Life Coach and trying to gain perspective around my relationship demise and my healing, we went through this exercise a number of times. It took me a long time even with my professional experience to access and acknowledge that there was a part of me deep inside that felt unloveable and had done so since childhood. This was the part that allowed me to stay in destructive circumstances and not expect better for myself.

It was daunting and scary when I finally accepted this is how I felt, but on the other hand a part of me was excited because now I understood how I responded in certain situations. The answer to many questions was being presented to me. I had finally dived deep enough and was getting to the root causes. I could sense that this was going to make a difference to my future.

From here I had some work to do, but I had a plan, I could see a change in my future. I knew now that I knew what was holding me back I could work at improving it. I needed to introduce self love, I needed to love myself, I needed to believe I was loveable. Once I started to work towards this, things started to change for the better.

Remember it is not until you have been immersed in the darkness that you can start to see the light. A life of highs and lows is so much more satisfying that one in a straight line.

Pink Time Out – False Beliefs

Stop and Breathe

The American psychologist Albert Ellis developed this list of twelve commonly-held false beliefs. Peruse the list and notice the ones that apply to you. This is another opportunity to unearth your irrational or false core beliefs.

1. I must be loved and approved of by all significant others.
2. Everyone should think and believe the way I do, especially those close to me.
3. I should never make mistakes or fail.
4. I should never let anyone down, especially those I love.
5. My life must be conflict free, especially with those close to me.
6. I need to be accepted by others at all costs.
7. My life should always be happy.
8. Everyone needs to understand me, especially those close to me.
9. Everyone needs to agree with me, especially those close to me.
10. I need to perform to be loved.
11. No one can dislike me.
12. I can't change the way I am.

Reading this list, I resonated with some and not others. There were some statements I had issues around, which helped me unearth core beliefs that I wanted to improve.

If you find some of your own feelings and beliefs on this list, be reassured that they are twelve of the most common beliefs out there. You are not alone.

Pink Time Out – Question Time

 Stop and Breathe

Read the list of questions below and allow time and space for self reflection. There are just a few questions that may help to pinpoint those core beliefs that are holding you back from happiness and fulfilment. In your Little Pink book of Love, record your thoughts, feelings, reactions and any epiphanies and wow moments you may have. Let the pen flow and see what appears on the page in front of you. As this may take you out of your comfort zone, remember to remain gentle and compassionate with yourself, and always come from a place of love.

1. Where in life do you feel least loveable?
2. With whom in your life do you feel least loveable, least important or insignificant?
3. Where do you feel not good enough?
4. Do you ever get angry when others have a different viewpoint to yours?
5. Can you accept others' opinions without judging them?

6. Are you able to make mistakes and use them as learning opportunities rather than being hard on yourself?
7. Do you seek others' approval at all costs?
8. Are you able to let others down in order to say yes to yourself?
9. Do you accept life has its ups and downs?
10. Do you believe you can grow into the person you want to be?
11. Do you accept that conflict is part of life?
12. Do you need to control yourself or others?
13. Do you trust yourself?
14. Do you need to be perfect?
15. Do you love yourself?

Outstanding reflection. I hope this exercise has given you once again a deeper insight into yourself and helped you gain a better understanding of you. Keep moving forward with the exercise as you are now ready to create your own list of beliefs.

Pink Time Out – Beliefs Table

~ Stop and Breathe ~

It's now time to create your own list of positive beliefs; beliefs you hold dear and will share as you move forward in the world. This exercise will again provide a great and deeper understanding of the magnificent person you are.

I will share some of mine as a starting point. Currently my list is sitting at sixty and it is an evolving document as beliefs come and go from my life. How long will your list be?

1. I believe we are capable of things we have not even yet dreamed or believe we are capable of.
2. I believe there is the authentic you in each person that lays dormant until you make the choice to be awakened and enlightened.
3. I believe the ego is your friend, and can be loved for who it is, if you get to know and understand its purpose.
4. I believe your Inner Pink Star (intuition) is bigger and brighter than you can ever imagine.
5. I believe the most important relationship is the one with yourself.
6. I believe sitting quietly with yourself in mediation on a regular basis will unleash and tap into your authentic and powerful self, where you can embrace the silence and the answers to all your questions will be given to you.
7. I believe each and every one of us is put on this earth with a special purpose that brings us passion and delight and in turn helps change the world.

8. I believe animals are one of the many amazing gifts and treasures on this planet and can teach us more about unconditional love than most humans. They deserve a life free of suffering and full of love.
9. I believe by feeling all your grief, your heart opens up and lets more love inside.
10. I believe in going barefoot in the park and connecting with the earth.
11. I believe in being able to say no when I want to.
12. I believe in love, romance and the one.
13. I believe there is someone, somewhere looking after the ones I have loved and lost through death.
14. I believe in me.

Now that I have shared my beliefs with you, I ask that you get out your Little Pink book of Love and start creating your own list of beliefs that are individual to you. Start with ten to twenty and over the next week as you are thinking about your beliefs, try to increase the number to a final fifty.

I believe...

Phew. If you have got this far and are still breathing and focused you have done some significant work on yourself. At the Healing Sanctuary the healing comes through hard work and we get our hands dirty straight up. You have achieved a breath-taking task to arrive at this point.

Don't forget to rest and recoup when you need to. You have completed some powerful and intense soul discovery, so remember to reward yourself and take respite to allow this information time to digest. Sometimes it is when you are focused on another area of your life that you suddenly feel a miracle arise out of nowhere. This is the wow moment you have been seeking and will evoke the most epiphanies.

So go rest, walk in the gardens barefoot, swim in the pool, meditate amidst the serene gardens. Do whatever creates a warm and fuzzy feeling inside and allows the love you are holding to spill out into the world. It is there just waiting for you to unleash it, and every moment you spend healing yourself allows a little more love to be exposed to the world. This enables you to feel loving inside and the world accepts and welcomes this gift with pleasure and thanks.

Step 4 - My passions and my fears

Passions propel you forward and fears pull you backwards in life. Getting to know yourself again, you need to become familiar with both. Moving towards your passions and including them into your life will make your days more fulfilling and fun. You want to be able to walk forward towards these passions despite your fears. You need to know what your fears are and come to understand them, so you can be aware when they pop up to throw you off track, or when they pop up to highlight a genuine concern.

Read the list of questions below and allow time and space for self reflection. In your Little Pink book of Love, record your thoughts, feelings, reactions and any epiphanies and wow moments you may have. Let the pen flow and see what appears on the page in front of you. As this may take you out of your comfort zone, remember to remain gentle and compassionate with yourself as you are answering these questions, and always come from a place of love.

Pink time out – Question time

⸺ Stop and Breathe ⸺

Answer the questions below to discover your passions:

1. What are you totally enthused about?
2. What do you love doing?
3. When do you feel in the flow with life and time passes without you noticing?
4. What do you love talking about to others?
5. What have you always talked about doing?
6. What did you love doing when you were a child?
7. What books topics do you love to read about?
8. Which section of the book store do you gravitate to?
9. What interests do you have just for yourself?
10. What lights you up internally?
11. What makes you jump for joy?
12. What do you walk away from and feel your energy has lifted substantially?
13. What do you see others doing that you are envious of?
14. What do you do whenever you get the chance?
15. If you knew you would succeed, what would you do?
16. When you are most happy what are you doing?

17. When you are totally enthralled what are you doing?
18. What makes you feel most alive?
19. If you won the lottery tomorrow what would be the first few things you would do?
20. If tomorrow was your last day on earth how would you fill your day?
21. If you had one year to live what would you ensure was on your pink bucket list?

Answer the questions below to discover your fears:

1. What do you procrastinate about?
2. What are you scared of?
3. What would you love to do but don't, and why?
4. What makes you feel insecure?
5. What do you avoid thinking about?
6. What emotions do you run away from?
7. What are you struggling to keep buried?
8. What do you resist?
9. Where are you defensive in your life?
10. If you had 10 minutes with the Dalai Lama, what secrets of his would you want to know or would you ask him to help you with?
11. What makes you consider attending counselling?
12. What makes you tremble and shake?
13. What brews anxiety internally?
14. What holds you back?

Add your fears and your passions to your Little Pink book of Love with the rest of your Pink Heart Print. Continue to compile your information and structure it in a way that is in accordance with you and your creativity so you are able to refer to it when needed.

Step 5 – My likes and dislikes

We all like and dislike different things. Often we try to like things because others like them. Sometimes we feel uncomfortable openly stating what we dislike in fear of what others may think. Sometimes we just don't know at all.

This is an opportunity to be honest with yourself what you like and what you dislike. We all need to be ourselves, be individual and feel comfortable with our likes and dislikes and then have the capacity to share them, with others honestly to remain authentic.

You could list little things, like my own dislike of paperclips and italic font, or big things like my dislike of arrogant people, inappropriate sarcasm, defensiveness, pretension, shallowness and saying goodbye. My personal list of likes includes dogs, reading, skiing on water and snow, yoga, bookstores, personal development, coffee and being around positive people.

Create a list in your Little Pink book of Love of all the things you like, that bring you happiness and create that warm fuzzy feeling inside. Feel free to be creative and use your coloured pencils. To gather ideas, think about what you do in a typical week, what Facebook pages you like, or flick through magazines to draw out ideas.

Create a list of everything you really dislike and would rather not do or be. Think about what you complain about to friends. What triggers you and sets you off? What makes you angry? What type of people do you avoid being around? What activities do you hope you never have to do ever again?

These lists make up another section of your wonderful Pink Heart Print.

Step 6 - My deepest desires and my deepest hurts

We all house, deep inside, a list of people, places or situations we desire. You may keep these secret from others and yourself or perhaps you openly discuss and are aware of them. As part of your Pink Heart Print you want to draw them out and celebrate them.

You also house deep hurts that have been with you since childhood or are more recent like this heartbreak. Some of your deepest hurts may lie dormant until you seek honesty and closure. This exercise creates another opportunity to be honest with yourself and bring any hurts to the surface to be healed.

Create a list of your deepest desires for your life, the things that you seek most desperately. Think about what you have always wanted. What do you dream about, wish and hope for when you have a silent moment in your busy life? What do you see in others and envy?

When you think about your deepest desires, try to go below the surface. Many people desire a house with a pool but I am looking for something closer to the heart. For example, one of my deepest desires is to have a deep sense of belonging and a sense of inner contentment and self love. Having an understanding of this helped me realise the suffering I had in my life and where it originated from and why and when it continued to raise its head.

To balance this, create a list of the deepest hurts you have suffered in your life; the things, people or situations that really hurt you. Think back to when you were little and what created raw pain for you throughout your life. By ensuring you know and understand your biggest hurts you can investigate if you have healed them. Drawing these out also gives insight into what makes you who you are and what creates pain for you. It helps you move in a direction free from pain and instead seeking things, people and situations that make you content.

Be gentle with yourself with this one because it can be hard to acknowledge your deepest hurts and, no doubt, they still may cause you pain. Be kind and self loving while you explore this area. After you have unearthed a couple of points, take a break to do something on your 'likes' list to feel better and bring you out of the pain that may be surfacing.

These lists are particularly special and may create vulnerability, so keep them close to your heart. Add them to your Pink Heart Print, be proud of yourself and move onto the next section.

Step 7 - My intolerances, habits and moods

We all have various idiosyncrasies that make us who we are. We have traits, intolerances, habits and moods that we hide from ourselves and others. It is okay to be who you are. If you are honest about them, then you can decide what to do with them.

Be gentle with yourself and remember everyone has intolerances, habits and moods they are not proud of, but each person's list is different.

First create a list of everything you are intolerant of. Think about what sets you off, making you angry or frustrated. What makes your blood boil? I have no tolerance for incompetence or time-wasting. This usually shows up when I am speaking with big companies like a telecommunication company, or waiting in line at a bank while the teller is chatting and not moving the line along. I cannot hide my frustration and turn into a person that I do not like. It is something I am aware of and try to be better with every day.

Next create a list of all your habits, good bad and indifferent. We all have habits, some we are proud of and want to create more of in our life and others we would like to stop. Awareness of what your habits are means you can actively move towards reducing the ones that cause pain and frustration in your life.

I had a terrible habit of smoking and through this process gained the awareness that I did not like the person I was whilst I was continuing to smoke. I was scared of giving up, but once I had this awareness it was the biggest and best motivation and quitting wasn't nearly as difficult as I'd anticipated. I was creating self love in my life and wanted to love myself, so the smoking had to go. Because of this exercise, changing the habit was easy. When we like ourselves more we treat ourselves better.

Finally, create a list of your moods; when, why and how they appear. Sometimes it may be hormones that make you moody and at others times there is another influence that creates the mood. Again by using awareness you can start to pinpoint what creates your moods and then put some strategies into place to reduce the negative moods.

Add these lists to your Pink Heart Print and move forward to the next section.

Step 8 - My attributes I get most upset about

As humans we can be very hard on ourselves. If you stop and think about it, you probably treat yourself much worse than you would treat a friend. Now is the time to start to be your own friend, treat yourself better and create a more harmonious internal experience.

By becoming aware of the attributes that make you most upset, that you beat yourself up for, you can introduce some gentleness into your thought pattern to lessen the chaos that is created inside. It is when you get upset and are really hard on yourself that your thinking becomes negative and your emotions follow, producing sadness, anger, anxiety and depression.

So let's find out what triggers you to not like yourself. List what comes up for you and see if you can be gentler on yourself.

Once you have your list you can refer back to your beliefs and see if they are motivating you to use behaviours that don't serve you. You may still be relying on internal beliefs that are irrational, for example believing you need to be happy all the time. If this is the case, the solution is to create a more healthy belief system.

One of the attributes that I got upset with was not listening to my intuition and abandoning myself for others. To work on this attribute I needed to create more self love and be more compassionate and trusting with myself.

Another one for me was getting impatient and cranky on the phone with the telecommunication people. Now each time I am on the phone with them I focus on staying present and reminding myself to be patient and tolerant. This makes the whole experience a lot nicer for them and I like myself much more once I get off the phone.

Gather your list together in the Pink Heart Print in your Little Pink book of Love. When you have everything written down move to the next section.

Step 9 – My dreams

Oh, this is such a lovely section. We all have dreams, those nice thoughts that pop into our heads before the fear appears. Your dreams show you how you would like your life to be, who and what you would like in it and how you would like to live. They are the thoughts that pop into your head when you have a few days off or are on a holiday and allow your mind to rest from the mindless, unnecessary chitter-chatter.

Dreams are the first step to planning your reality. If your dream is rational, there is no reason not to turn your dream into your reality. It is possible. It may entail a lot of hard work, it may involve sacrifices. It may demand you to move past your fears, it may require you to take a chance on yourself and take some risks.

So the question then becomes, how much do you want it?

You may have forgotten how to dream, as you have become so beaten down by the situations in your life and are living a life within your comfort zones, afraid to make any changes. Your happiness levels may be diminishing daily. Perhaps you are living as a victim and not taking responsibility for improving your life. I hope as you move past your heartbreak and start integrating the tools you learnt at Heartbreak Manor, you are starting to bring your dreams to fruition.

Find a comfy chair and pretend you are sitting on a beach with the sun warming your body. Let your mind be creative and dream away. Start to document the things that bring you most joy. How would you want your life to look if you had all the time and money in the world? What would you do?

Think about everything you have dreamed about and wished you could do, if only…

We will use this again when we move to the next destination on our journey, but for now start your list. Document all your dreams, let them take up some space in your mind and move forward to the next section.

Step 10 - My triumphs, achievements and moments I am most proud of

A true act of self love is to think about what you have achieved and what you have done well. You have done many good things in your life that you should be proud of, no matter how big or small. The feeling of proudness is amazing and touches your heart.

It is important to look back and reflect on what you have done well, to appreciate yourself, to bask in the triumphs, celebrate the achievements and plan for more for come.

Allow yourself to enjoy these moments. Stop and live in the present with your achievements. Appreciate them and be mindful of what is happening in your life rather than being so busy that you are onto something new without being thankful for what you have just finished.

The more love you create for yourself as you move forward, the more you will find to appreciate. Loving yourself more will see you stopping to appreciate, be thankful and value who you are and what you have accomplished.

Add to your Pink Heart Print some of the triumphs, achievements and moments you are most proud of in your life. Bask in the memories and the proud feeling as you add them to your list. Enjoy, be thankful now, and appreciate these moments even if you did not at the time.

Take time for a special treat or memorial before you move forward to the next section.

Step 11 – My blocks

We all have blocks that create difficulties for us to move forward. The blocks may be different for everyone but we all have them. Become mindful of your individual blocks and use this mindfulness to walk into your future.

Pink time out – Reflection

Stop and Breathe

What are the blocks that stop you from being your best self, that remain hidden till you catch them out? See below a list of common blocks to help you uncover what is relevant to you. Which ones touch your buttons? Are there others not listed here you know are holding you back?

- Worrying about others' opinions
- Fear of disappointment
- Limiting beliefs
- Unhealthy values
- Uncertainty
- Lack of time
- Injury or illness
- Fear of hurting others
- Not following a true goal

- ❋ Not connecting to your feelings
- ❋ Not trusting yourself
- ❋ Not being true to yourself
- ❋ Self doubt
- ❋ Finances
- ❋ Guilt or shame
- ❋ Lacking support
- ❋ Religion
- ❋ Overwhelm or stress
- ❋ Procrastination
- ❋ People pleasing
- ❋ Others' drama
- ❋ Distractions
- ❋ Addictions

Record your blocks as part of your Pink Heart Print and review what you have discovered in this step.

Did you highlight any new information or did you already know what blocks you had? New information can create an opportunity to create new changes internally. Old information can create an opportunity for you to look at it with new fresh eyes.

You are doing really well as you come to the final few steps in your Pink Heart Print.

Step 12 - My gratitudes

What are you grateful for? Being grateful has the ability to change your mood from negative to positive in an instant. If you stop and allow yourself to think about what you are grateful for in your life and pay tribute to it, your energy can change instantly and allow good feelings to surface.

It is proven that being grateful in your life not only lifts your happiness levels. It will also give you a host of health benefits. It boosts your immune system, creates a feeling of connectedness with others and helps you feel better about yourself and your life.

Being grateful can bring you back to the present. When you have your morning cup of coffee, allow yourself to appreciate the warmth of the cup, the way it warms your insides, the lovely taste and the down time to enjoy this moment. It becomes a mini coffee meditation, keeping you in the moment and allowing other thoughts to rest or just pass through while not attaching to them.

It is an amazing miracle that you are here in your human body to experience all that the world has to offer. Yes, there are horrendous things that happen and grief you will endure in life but there are still amazing things happening every day. There are wonderful individuals in your life that make it fun and special.

Try to focus on the good, not what you are missing, to keep your thoughts producing good feelings more often. Research shows that gratefulness can improve your immune system, keep you healthier for longer, help you sleep better, create better relationships and ward off negative emotions.

Focus on the good, not what is missing

Put aside your negative thoughts and think gratitude. Create a list of everything you are grateful for. Think about people, places, situations, things and also think about yours and others' characteristics or traits. Add these to your Pink Heart Print.

Step 13 – My one thing

There is one little question that can make a big difference. I want you to read the question and answer instinctively without thinking too much about it. For a moment, pretend you have all the money in the world and all the time in the world. Go with your intuition and trust yourself.

What one thing do you believe you have been placed on this earth to do, carry out, achieve, be?

Did you come up with an answer?

If you come up with a blank, remember to be gentle with yourself. There are very few people who know instantly what their life purpose is. A large majority of people are seeking this, the reason for their existence. You are in a healing and learning phase right now and at your next destination you will do more work around your life purpose to help draw out the answer to this question or point you in the right direction on your journey to finding it.

We are all on earth for a purpose. Once you discover what yours is and start to implement it into your life, everything begins to change and sparkle begins to happen. The days flow easier, you become more content and a lot of the internal negativity you have carried around slowly fades away.

Sit with your answer and let it settle, and then put it into your Pink Heart Print. You can always come back and amend it if necessary. Everything you find out about yourself is another little piece of the jigsaw. Some pieces fit perfectly and some you need to come back to later to get them just right. Be patient and have fun through this process.

Step 14 - My three adjectives that best describe me

You are now on the last step, one that could be challenging or fun, depending how you approach it. It is often hard to list adjectives to describe yourself, so it can be easier to list three that your friends would use to describe you.

Isn't it strange that it is easier to be honest when you come from your friend's perspective than your own? When you describe yourself, you don't want to appear big-noting yourself, so you may dull it down, but deep down you know what your friends would say about you.

Pink time out – Reflection

Stop and Breathe

Try these three steps to look at the question from different angles:

1. List the three adjectives that would be best used to describe you.
2. List the three adjectives you think your best friend would use to describe you.
3. If you want to have some fun, actually ask your friends, so you can see how on target you were!

I send gigantic congratulations your way. You have come to the end of the Pink Heart Print so you can now take a big breath and allow it to permeate softly into every cell. Inhale from the depths of your ribs, allowing your lungs to fill with air and then slowly exhale the air along with any remaining negativity within you.

I hope from the self discovery you have so bravely undertaken, you have revealed and explored many parts of yourself that were hidden under the surface. I also hope you have re-awoken and acknowledged all your strengths, talents and the miraculous parts of you that make you, you.

It's okay to have flaws and imperfections because that is what makes you human. The important part is that you are aware of them, accept them and integrate them into who you are rather than have them loitering under the surface causing grievous emotional harm at every turn in your journey.

Sitting in your comfy chair back in your villa, overlooking the beautiful scenery, you feel mentally exhausted. What a huge day; who thought it would be so tiring sitting by the pool? However your body feels nourished from the healthy food you consumed and your soul feels soothed from the calming teas. You feel mentally prepared and aware for what is to come in the following days, but look forward to your bed tonight.

You hold your Little Pink book of Love close to your heart and think of the Pink Heart Print that now sits safely inside it. You are looking forward to adding to it with more discoveries and epiphanies in your new flourishing life. You reflect on how far you have come from day one when you were in a big pile of rubble on the floor. You are starting to rejoice in your progress thus far and revel in the footsteps you are taking, steps to become you.

My Pink Heart Print

You are starting to acknowledge what an amazing individual you are with an enormous amount to offer yourself, others and the world. You look forward to the day your insides are bathed in serenity, peace, calm and contentment.

You are starting to tingle with this feeling more regularly and you will know when you are there, perhaps through a feeling, a knowing, a sense or a visceral knowledge that you have arrived.

When you are there you have been reunited with her, your Inner Pink Star.

My Inner Pink Star

*"This above all – to thine own self be true.
And it must follow, as the night the day,
Thoust can not then be false to any man"*

William Shakespeare, Hamlet, Act 1 Scene iii

Nestled into the leather lounge at reception, surrounded by a multitude of colourful Balinese rugs, you think about the day ahead. As your herbal tea is placed in front of you, your eyes wander to the people going in all different directions through reception. People-watching is so much fun; you observe how much more energy is in their step than those at the Heartbreak Manor. Their souls seem to have more of a purpose.

Going inside to your own soul for a moment, you notice how much more enthused and energised you feel by each lesson you internalise and each epiphany you encounter. The ambience of these surroundings certainly helps yield calmness and peace, fuelling your desire for change and creating space in your life to look within and heal. Through allowing time, space and resources you are able to honour yourself with this gift of healing.

Bringing your focus back to the reception area, you notice the chandeliers that you love so much. At Heartbreak Manor, despite their tatty look the chandeliers still symbolised the lightness and brightness that you were rediscovering inside yourself and the same feeling appears here. However here they are even more impressive and grand, well cared for, sparkling brightly for all to see even in the daylight hours. They seem to take on a life of their own, demanding respect and delivering a sense of grace, proudness and class.

You look up the hill to the steep staircase to the Pink Studio perched on the hill. You know you have the energy to make it to the top and trust that once there, the studio will offer stunning views and gift you in added vitality that will be derived from the Pilates and yoga classes that are on offer.

Leaving reception and navigating up the hill, you arrive to the steep staircase and realise that right next to it is an interesting outdoor elevator. Things are not always as they seem to be; you had been expecting a difficult trek but realise there are always options. You stop for a second and wait for the elevator but with a burst of determination decide the stairs are for you and up you go one foot in front of the other.

Entering the Pink Studio, you are completely overcome. The stunning, colourful view all around you takes you out of all your anxieties and worries and brings every part of you back into the present moment. You feel overawed by the beauty of this space. Candles emit an aromatic smell, the soft relaxing sounds of harps and other exotic instruments echo from the ceiling and walls, water trickles into fountains while Buddha statues on the dark jarrah floorboards face the centre of the room, silent in their gaze.

Stop and be present

The vision makes you really stop and be present, something you are still struggling to maintain regularly. You remind yourself that this space encourages inner scrutiny and steps towards truth and enlightenment, with an assurance of becoming more familiar with your inner wisdom, your Inner Pink Star. You honour the sacred space and let go, in order to allow what will happen to be.

Hello Inner Pink Star

"The most creative act you will ever undertake is the act of creating yourself"

Deepak Chopra

You may know your Inner Pink Star as your inner guidance, intuition, inner wisdom or gut instinct. It's part of you, a part you have ignored and forgotten. And yet this part of you is still there quietly in the background, patiently waiting for acknowledgement once again or maybe for the very first time. You may have neglected to listen, you may have overlooked the fact that you always know the answer. You just need to listen. You are here now and ready to listen, so let's go.

This is where life starts to get all seriously shiny and sparkly. The three steps forward and one step back starts to become ten gigantic steps forward. You hear a voice and you know it's your Inner Pink Star. You follow her voice and voila, magically situations change, life starts to flow effortlessly and choices become easier.

She is born from love and houses all your internal creativity and power. She knows every step of the way how loveable and pure you really are. She knows immediately, without hesitation, what is best for you. She is the gateway to happiness and serenity; once you walk through you will never turn back. What was once a swirling chaotic confusion, not knowing which way to turn, becomes a calm, evaluated mindset that works perfectly for you.

She doesn't judge, she doesn't put you in harm's way, she always knows what's best for you. She is quiet and often gets overshadowed by Lady Chitter Chatter, your ego and inner critic.

Lady Chitter Chatter is born from fear; she is the loud, arrogant, overinflated part of you that is scared, holding onto past events and allowing them to affect the present moment. She is the part that has irrational beliefs and values, irrational thoughts about your identity. The part that gossips, labels and judges yourself and others. The part that can't say no and looks for others' approval, constantly telling you that you are not loving enough, pretty enough, skinny enough or smart enough. Lady Chitter Chatter, although part of you, is not the real you. She can harm and cause serious emotional distress to your inner world if left to run wild.

Your Inner Pink Star is your gateway to happiness

So twinkle twinkle, let's learn a little more about Your Inner Pink Star and Lady Chitter Chatter in the upcoming chapters. You will learn how to tune in so you can get all the answers you are so desperately seeking. You will learn how to observe and separate from Lady Chitter Chatter to lighten the pressure she exerts over you.

Let your Inner Pink Star guide you through the darkness into the light.

HOME SWEET HOME

"If you think something is missing in your life, it is probably YOU…"

Robert Holden

I learnt the hard way. The For Sale sign went up on my gorgeous cottage after spending ten glorious years there. 'Cool and Classy' was its description on the signboard. This was more than just a house, it was my safe haven, and the first house I owned by myself. I had redesigned and redecorated every inch with my own hands. It was my sanctuary that oozed love and happiness; like a child I would wander around it deliriously and tell the rooms how much I loved them, not just the first year I was there, but the whole ten years. I couldn't have been happier in my real estate heaven.

We were together for three years before he decided to move in to Cool and Classy. I was ecstatic. Logistically we worked fabulously together; we were a match made in heaven, and it was what I had been waiting for. However cracks started to appear and things started to not feel quite right. I sensed a lack of a deeper commitment.

My house was small and impulsively two months later we decided to purchase a bigger home together. My Inner Pink Star tried to speak up during the house negotiations but I silenced her, hoping everything would work out for us.

The day of the auction of Cool and Classy, I held my head up high and held on tight to my partner as the hammer went down yielding a great price but stealing my soul in the process. I could feel deep down I had done the wrong thing; we were not ready.

Moving day came and the tears flowed for the Lara I was leaving behind at Cool and Classy and the Lara yet to be born at the new house. I had one month before settlement and visited my empty nest daily, watering my garden and trying to come to terms with the move, trying to convince myself and my Inner Pink Star I was doing the right thing. On settlement day I visited for the last time, I said goodbye and thank you. Again the tears flowed as I closed the doors on the house, my intuition and my inner feelings. I made a conscious decision to put one foot in front of the other and keep moving forward into my new life.

I grieved for the sale of Cool and Classy for two years. I had let go of more than just a house but a part of me. I would attend Pilates and fantasise during the class about being in my old house. I wondered why I loved it so much, why I didn't feel the same at our new dream home with my dream man. I experienced feelings that would cover my heart with sadness and tears would flow.

Sadly my worst fears came true. I had ignored so many signs and after it was all over, I finally realised I needed to come back to me and my Inner Pink Star for guidance. I was raw, wounded, sad and grieving the loss of the relationship. I was tremendously hurt and there were scars to heal. Scars from the relationship demise and more scars because I had allowed myself to be in this position. I hadn't protected myself.

Wow what a lesson to learn; it exhausted me mentally, physically, emotionally and financially, all because I chose not to listen to her, my Inner Pink Star. She knew every step of the way and yet I shut her down and ignored her. Thank goodness that when I finally chose to listen she was right there standing beside me, ready to hold my hand and help me put my life back together piece by piece. No judgements, no labels, no putting me down, just offering a tender heart allowing me to access my true self with compassion and love.

No judgements, no labels – just truth, love and compassion

It was not till after the relationship break up and I purchased my new home that I realised what I was really grieving for the most was not the house I had owned but the person I was whilst I was in the house. I had allowed a part of myself to shut down. I had stopped following my Inner Pink Star.

When I returned to me and looked inside and trusted myself I slowly found myself again and allowed myself time to grieve for the loss of the first house and the loss of the relationship, and abandoning myself. I spent time to reflect on the lessons I had learnt. During this time I also allowed my Inner Pink Star to speak more than she ever had before.

I learnt to listen to myself and ask myself what was right for me, and I realised that each time I knew the answers. For the first time in a long time I was starting to feel happy; the constant ache of sadness, anger, frustration and anxiety was no longer part of my every waking moment.

If I had listened to my Inner Pink Star it would have saved me a tremendous amount of pain. I had ignored her and shut her down so I could stay in the relationship. It seemed easier than feeling the grief I knew I would feel if I fessed up to the truth. So instead of leaving him I left me, which created a whole lot more dark feelings.

My Inner Pink Star had been overshadowed by fear, and now I was moving forward with my life, I felt her jumping with joy and excitement, like a little child that has been let out to play after a long dark dreary winter.

You will know when you have accessed your Inner Pink Star because you will feel different. You may experience snippets of it when you are even unaware you have accessed her to help you make a decision, or you may feel her presence growing gradually as you heal. You will feel calm, relaxed, and peaceful, you will trust yourself fully and this will produce an internal sense of knowing and fulfilment. You will feel an inner proudness.

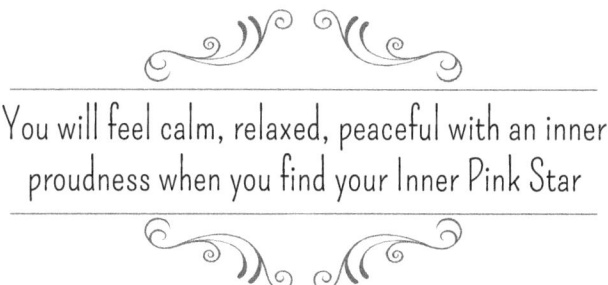

You will feel calm, relaxed, peaceful with an inner proudness when you find your Inner Pink Star

Comfort Zones

"It is worth remembering that the time of greatest gain in terms of wisdom and inner strength is often that of greatest difficulty"

Dalai Lama

Often in life it is easier to ignore your Inner Pink Star or shut her down because heeding her call can mean you need to take action. You may have to make the hard decisions and possibly change the direction of your life, and this can sometimes create consequences you are not willing or ready to face. We humans get used to our comfort zones; it's easy, we like them, it's cruisy. We tend not to listen to our Inner Pink Star for guidance when we want to avoid the risks in doing what is right for us. Through this we negate the potential we are capable of.

Time and time again we get used to the uncomfortable pangs and uneasiness and believe that is part of life. We believe we have to live with what is presented to us and the feelings that come with it. Yes it is part of life to feel uneasy sometimes, but not if it is because we are ignoring our Inner Pink Star. If she is trying to quietly guide us to what we should be doing with our lives or who we should be spending it with, we should listen.

If we ignore our Inner Pink Star and remain uncomfortable and uneasy, this slowly becomes a comfort zone where we choose to stay to avoid making the hard decisions. It is a comfortable uncomfortableness.

This then begs the question, why would you accept it is okay to feel uneasy, knowing inside you are the master of your own destiny?

My Inner Pink Star

As you remain in your uncomfortableness, investing in a bad situation, staying longer than you should, you keep trying that little bit harder, hoping for the miracle even when you know it is a lost cause. You become accustomed to the challenging feelings, and your level of uncomfortable becomes a new level of comfortable. You feel and hear yourself saying "This is just the way it is for me, this is my lot". You reason that feeling a little bit uncomfortable is better than feeling a whole lot scared.

You can change track at any time to access happiness and contentedness

I have worked with many people who have stood in that space, then finally decided to follow their heart and move forward. They have suffered a little short term pain and fear, then quickly risen far beyond what they could have previously imagined or dreamed of. They listened to themselves, knew what was right, trusted themselves, stood in the face of fear, acted courageously and guess what, they created their version of heaven on earth.

Yes there may still be struggles and choices but when your Inner Pink Star is allowed to run the show, life changes beyond anything you can imagine. Surrender to her and you will never regret it. Imagine those little snippets of peace you feel from time to time becoming a permanent fixture.

Reaching the right decision by accessing your Inner Pink Star does not mean you can avoid all pain. Sometimes the pain cannot be avoided in order to come to the place of peace you are seeking. These positive growth pains are very different to the anxiety-ridden pain you create when you are living behind a façade, not making wise life decisions, ignoring your values and core beliefs and listening to the ego.

Even in the face of grief when I lost my fur child Maxy, my Inner Pink Star guided me and allowed me to feel all the grief and sadness. Through the whole process I trusted myself and allowed myself to feel. I didn't pretend I was fine and ignore it; I listened and took time out. She was telling me to slow down and be there for me, be gentle and compassionate as there was healing to do. So even though it was grief, it was uncomfortable and out of my control, and it was hard, a part of it felt beautiful because I was honouring myself. I didn't feel depressed or anxious, I just felt sad and I expressed and processed it. Eventually by honouring myself I moved through it, because I had faced it head on and let it all out.

Each time you trust yourself and act accordingly, you will strengthen your emotional muscles. You will become accustomed to stopping and asking your Inner Pink Star for guidance, you will wait for the feeling she creates inside to generate the answer for you. This will create time and patience around your decisions. You will know when you are trying to force a decision because the difficult feelings will surface as a warning sign.

When you are in tune with your Inner Pink Star you will feel proud and happy with yourself. When you are not in tune you will feel the uncomfortable feelings, anxiety and a sense that something is not quite right. As you become more practised at this it will become so easy you will wonder what you have been doing all these years.

Each and every time you honour yourself, the benefits increase tenfold and you become prouder and more protective of who you are. Once you are at this point, boundaries become easier to create, assertiveness becomes easier to achieve, life starts to flow. You start to honour yourself and will only do what is true for you.

You become prouder and more protective of you

The world runs on a quick fix mentality. Everything is so fast-paced and so our impulsivity rises and we want something now rather than stopping to evaluate. We have a feeling and act on it. If you fast track you are setting yourself up for potential disappointment, heartbreak or catastrophe. Have you ever noticed when you make a decision and then ponder on it for a few days, things appear different and you wonder if you might have made a different decision given the time again? This is where the practise of patience and self trust will allow time to mull over decisions and not race into them.

You should only go as fast as the slowest part of you wants to go. Not everything has to be decided in an instant. Enjoy the journey as they say.

I didn't listen to the radio for a long time. Every time a song came on that reminded me of the relationship I would feel so sad and upset, the intensity of the emotions was terrifying and I feared I would become totally overwhelmed. I didn't want to deal with it, and thought that if I didn't hear our songs I wouldn't have to feel the emotions. So the off switch on the dashboard was easier than releasing the internal on switch to let the emotions flow and the truth follow.

It was not until the relationship ended that I allowed my feelings to surface and release. Once I gave permission to myself to heal I started to turn on the radio again. There were still plenty of tears to be shed but they came and went with no overwhelm; I was able to release them all and let the music world back in.

It's utterly astounding what we do to live a life of self denial and avoidance of our situation, emotions or fears and the dark frightening place it leaves us in. It's even more astonishing that the so-called fears that we are scared of are actually not scary at all, once we learn to face them. Facing your fears opens the pressure valve and everything is released, then settles down.

Once you have been strong enough to do this in your life you will grasp the fact that many fears are completely false and not really scary at all. It is just our thoughts about our fears that make them so terrifying and real. That is what your Inner Pink Star's arch enemy, Lady Chitter Chatter, uses as her position description.

WELCOME HOME

The relationship I'd dreamed of appeared one night
Touching all the parts of my soul with delight
Finally, The one, I believed, had been given to me

Long chats and hugs were introduced to my days
I savoured the newness, the hopes and dreams
United we stood against the odds in a world rife with pain

Love, laughter
Light, happiness and joy
Deepened the love I'd sought for life

Then came the fights and the tears
The angst and the pain
I drowned out my inner voice
and the wisdom that prevailed
This love, I thought, outweighed all the grief

Happiness to tears
Joy to sorrow
Love to loss
Hurt to anger
My soul screaming to be heard
My inner voice no longer happy to be ignored

Frozen in time, disbelief that my life would need to change
Comfortable in the pain, ignoring the truth
Indecision overload, did I stay or go
Either way became unthinkable
Terrified of the consequences that awaited me

My Inner Pink Star

Then the day appeared when I turned and really saw me
My internal self had become a skeleton of its normal health
I looked deep and listened and finally knew the truth

The consequences hurt
The life I knew changed in an instant
How I had lived had disappeared
Seeking faith in the unknown to follow

One footstep at a time
I made it through

Through the pain the light appeared
On the other side was a different version of me, or so I thought
In fact it was the true me that had been
Overshadowed and overlooked for so long

My soul started singing its tune
My heart started beating to its song
My Inner Pink Star started dancing its steps
Lady Chitter Chatter had been put to rest
Love is abundant and the truth is acknowledged
I finally found me

Calling on your Inner Pink Star

"Human beings feel more comfortable 'playing small'. We cling to comfort, thus continuing to hold our own power hostage"

Amy Ahlers

It is difficult to quiet our minds to be able to access our Inner Pink Star. Our minds are usually so busy we can't hear through all the chit chat, positive or otherwise. Even when we wish our Inner Pink Star would appear, we still struggle to find her as she can be very elusive.

To be able to hear, you will need to slow down, be quiet and still. If you practise, over time she will appear from behind the noise and the chaos. Be gentle, give her a chance. If you have ignored her for a long time it may take a while for her shyness to fall away.

Follow the steps below to call on your Inner Pink Star, practise regularly and celebrate when you finally touch her heart and honour her presence and wisdom. Then, life changes in profound ways.

> STOP, BREATHE
> Close your eyes
> Be still
> Be patient
> Be calm
> Be silent
> Be in the present moment
> Stop pushing, rushing and worrying
> Let your thoughts rest – don't attach

My Inner Pink Star

Surrender and let go
Go deep inside
Ask the question that is on your mind
Pay attention
Listen to your body and notice your feelings
You will find her; she is your voice of calm
She holds deep the answers to all your questions and fears
Trust the peace and the calm

Pink time out – Art expression

Stop and Breathe

To tap into your creative side and get a feeling for your Inner Pink Star, grab your Little Pink book of Love and a whole lot of coloured pencils. In the middle of the page, draw your version of what your Inner Pink Star looks like. You do not have to be a great artist, just be expressive. Let yourself go and see what appears. Use as much or as little colour as you like. Draw whatever you believe she looks and feels like.

Once you have a picture of her, give her a name. It may be an actual name or your own version of Inner Pink Star. Naming her will allow her to become more personal to you, to integrate her into you even more, and you will be able to ask for her by name when you need her.

Once you have her picture and name, around your picture get creative and write all the words she means to you.

Which words come to you when you think of her? Which words are good, calm, peaceful, breeding happiness and peace?

Once you have completed her picture, feel proud of the part of you that can access all the best things for you in your life. She is a special part of you, your best friend and if you haven't already done so it is definitely time to get to know her better.

Pink time out – Question time

◦ Stop and Breathe ◦

Read the list of questions below and allow time and space for self reflection. In your Little Pink book of Love, record your thoughts, feelings, reactions and any epiphanies and wow moments you may have about your Inner Pink Star. Let the pen flow and see what appears on the page in front of you. As this may take you out of your comfort zone, remember to remain gentle and compassionate with yourself, and always come from a place of love.

1. Recall a situation when you felt calm and relaxed over a decision. Can you feel how you were accessing your Inner Pink Star?
2. Recall a decision when you felt anxious and know that you went against what you knew was right for you. Was your Inner Pink Star trying to be part of this decision?

3. Do you ever say yes when you mean no? How does it make you feel?
4. Are there any consequences you are avoiding by not listening to your Inner Pink Star?
5. What is your comfortable uncomfortableness?
6. Where are you lacking courage to chase your dreams?
7. Are fears holding you back from taking a stand or making a decision?
8. Do you live in ambivalence, frozen in time?
9. Have you shut down or ignored your Inner Pink Star?
10. What does your Inner Pink Star know?
11. How can she help you?
12. Where do you believe you need help from your Inner Pink Star?

The work you are doing is admirable. Feel proud. This has been a great reflection showing willingness to go deeper. I hope this exercise has provided you with more information about your Inner Pink Star that you can use as you move forward through the process of healing. Every small step you take today adds to help create a new tomorrow and a happier and healthier you in the future.

Descending the stairs to leave the Pink Studio, you feel lighter and more peaceful. Your body feels stretched, your mind challenged, your soul honoured and your heart open. The day you spent perched on the hill was a once in a lifetime opportunity for honest and expansive growth, a mini sabbatical with an opportunity to get to know yourself even more.

As you leave, you feel tenderness for yourself as you have exposed your vulnerabilities and started to honour and trust yourself once again. It's a poignant moment to leave a sacred space like the Pink Studio, as the love and protection it provided is what you have been seeking for some time now, if not your whole life.

Walking slowly but with purpose, you hang on to every snippet of understanding you have learnt and every warm feeling within. You know you will need these gifts tomorrow when you get to meet your negative voice Lady Chitter Chatter and seek to understand what she has to say.

For now though, you gently bring your thoughts back to the present and appreciate the moment and all the gifts you have been given today. Feeling less introverted and now wanting more connection with people, you decide to head back to the reception area to people watch and enjoy a herbal tea. Perhaps you will meet other women on a similar journey to yourself and share some of your delightful gifts over afternoon tea.

Lady Chitter Chatter

"All great changes are preceded by chaos"

Deepak Chopra

You are a little nervous about today as you know you will have a one on one meeting with Lady Chitter Chatter, your negative inner voice. She acts at times like a little playground bully and enjoys taking control and making you hard on yourself. Holding onto the warm ambience and feelings from yesterday, you continue to place faith and trust in your journey. Your courage to continue moving forward should be celebrated, as each step into your wondrous unknown takes a colossal amount of willingness and strength.

The setting for today is the grounds wrapping around the Healing Sanctuary, a divinely serene space that aids in healing and growth. You stroll around the grounds and notice little nooks and benches to sit and reflect as you complete today's exercises.

You want to find exactly the right spot to invite Lady Chitter Chatter inside, so you continue to wander. Your feet take you off the bitumen and onto narrow pebble paths, twisting and turning through quiet sacred spaces.

Tall trees separate the various clearings and gardens, the sun shining through where it can. As you amble around you can hear birds chirping and water falling into water features and ponds. Sitting on the edge of a water feature, you feel the spray from the fountain land gently on your cheeks as you watch the enormous goldfish swimming around the pond. The gentle movement and sounds around you invite a sense of waking up and becoming alive.

In the distance you see the white picket fence. You keep walking and know that the secrets behind it will be exposed just as they need to be in the right time.

You find just the right spot, with the sun shining through the trees onto your head and knees. The bench offers soft pillows and rugs to ensure your time spent here is comfortable. You lie down and gaze over to the hills, where you catch a brief glimpse of your stunning setting from yesterday. You stop for a minute to become aware of your feelings, and notice that you are just as happy to be outdoors in this glorious setting and are looking forward to more discoveries. Now it is time to close your eyes and let the lessons begin.

Stop ruining my life, Lady Chitter Chatter

> "The primary cause of unhappiness is never the situation but your thoughts about it"
>
> Eckhart Tolle

Lady Chitter Chatter, now it's your turn. You create such tremendous chaos in my life and I really don't know how to control you. You constantly sandwich yourself between me and my Inner Pink Star. Just when I feel like I am progressing, there you are, unannounced and unwanted. Yelling, putting me down and making demands of me that make me feel unworthy, unlovable, frustrated, irritable and a myriad of other emotions. You render my life a misery.

I can be meandering along enjoying the day and appreciating all the beautiful things in life and poof, my mood changes and I feel terrible. I know when you have surfaced, but don't know how to get rid of you. Why can't you just leave me in peace? Then I may be able to access my inner calm and happiness. You make my life an endless struggle and I am sick and tired of you.

Do you resonate with this cry of discontent? Many of us contemplate this as part of our 50,000 thoughts daily. It is therefore crucial and sometimes urgent to acquire relevant tools in your emotional inventory to understand Lady Chitter Chatter, work with her, love her and heal her.

The time to avoid, deny and ignore the havoc she creates is gone. If you really want a peaceful life, you have acknowledged that the time has come to deal with her, as she can have an exceptionally destructive role if you permit her to run free.

She can be the prequel to depression and anxiety, and if this progresses, a mammoth amount of energy will be essential to keep her under control, which will leave you feeling emotionally, mentally and physically depleted.

Or she may be just a nuisance and a bother that is ever-lingering, just below the surface, creating unease and discomfort, stopping you from striving just that little bit further to where calm, peace and happiness lie waiting.

Today is the day to take a stand and say enough is enough. This is a big step and one you should be proud of. You will reap the benefits at a level you can only dream of. If you are seeking more lightness, freedom and happiness in your life, then working to understand and transform your Lady Chitter Chatter will effectively be the biggest gift you can give yourself and all the ones you love.

Before you unwrap the lovely gift that is waiting with a big pink bow tied around it, you must access your willingness once again, to dive deep and seek all the wonders that lay waiting to be discovered. Be honest with yourself and promise to become your own best friend move forward and let the miracles appear.

Lady Chitter Chatter's influence

"I am doing the best I can, and it's enough"

Christine Arylo

Lady Chitter Chatter has been with you for what seems like forever. You created her yourself at some point, most likely when you were young and needed protecting. She really does care for you and wants the best for you, as she is your ego. She believes she is acting in your best interests and protecting you when you cannot protect yourself.

She doesn't trust that you have the tools to look after yourself. She has felt the hurt you have suffered and does not want you ever to feel that again, so she creates strategies, thoughts and actions in your life in a misguided attempt to help you.

She does not want you to feel rejection, ridicule or abandonment and will do whatever it takes to prevent these feelings. At one point in time she may have helped you, but now that you are older she is out of control and may in fact be causing more harm than good.

Your purpose here is to understand her and the myriad of ways she manifests in you, and appreciate her for what she has tried to do for you. Instead of hating and denying her, she is a part of you. Develop patience, gentleness and compassion for her and for yourself. Integrate her into your life in a positive fashion and take the control back.

It is important not to beat yourself up in the process of trying to gain a full understanding of her crazy and peculiar ways. Acceptance and forgiveness are called for while you explore what you have allowed her to do over the years. Remember we only do the best we can with what we know at the time.

Lady Chitter Chatter

Moving forward, you will learn more so you can do better. Don't look back, criticise and condemn. Instead, look forward with excitement at what you can learn and how you can transform your life. This is the icing on the cake and the freckles on the chocolate, it's the reward waiting for you to come home to yourself and learn, grow and develop into the wonderful and enlightened person you are. It really is so very exciting and leaves me with goose bumps at the thought of it.

Draw on your self acceptance and self forgiveness

You will know when Lady Chitter Chatter is making decisions as you will feel tied up in knots, anxious, irritable or a host of other negative emotions. In comparison, when your Inner Pink Star is in control you feel calm, connected, peaceful, relaxed, happy and loved. If you are unsure of who is doing the talking in your head, stop and breathe, then go into your physical body to feel your feelings. They will tell you every time; feelings don't lie.

Don't underestimate how you feel as your feelings hold the keys and the answers. Pursue the calm and peaceful feelings and know the stars are shining down on you. Feel the challenging negative feelings and take it as a sign to stop, take notice and reassess.

To manage without Lady Chitter Chatter takes faith, confidence, self conviction, love and trust in yourself. The more you build this up the more she will fade away, as she will believe, know and honour that you are now capable of looking after yourself and her role is becoming redundant. She will be there in the background, occasionally asserting her authority, but the faith and trust you have in yourself will facilitate her silence. She will know who is in charge and will lessen her bullying words and criticisms.

Loving her may sound utterly ridiculous - why on earth would you want to do that? She is part of you, created by you and will always be with you in some form. However she has lessons galore to teach you and just wants to be heard and understood. If you can muster the courage to stop and listen attentively, you will access and honour your vulnerabilities and emotions and be well on your way to transforming her and altering your life.

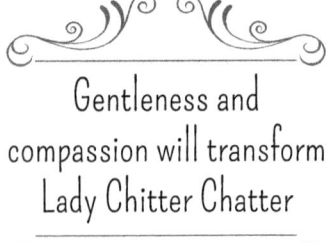

Gentleness and compassion will transform Lady Chitter Chatter

You are calling on your Inner Pink Star on a regular basis now, so Lady Chitter Chatter knows she is no longer needed. She is like a little naughty child seeking attention; she does it for good reasons but she does it in an emotionally immature way. Once she has your attention she is happy, but she needs boundaries, to know you are an adult who can run your own life and no more childish antics will be tolerated.

My Lady Chitter Chatter and a Pilates Mat

"If we are willing to do the mental work, almost anything can be healed"

Louise Hay

Attending Pilates always guaranteed me a visit from my Inner Pink Star. The environment was so serene and the nature of Pilates is to go deep into your body, focusing on your breathing, inhaling and exhaling. This miraculously switched off the constant mind talk in my head for an hour. I felt such a sense of relief every time I attended a class.

I would close my eyes and perform all the exercises with my mind turned off. I was deep into the 'Do I stay or do I go?' question in my relationship around this time, and was fraught with anxiety and indecision.

Lady Chitter Chatter

At Pilates, my Inner Pink Star would guide me to visualisations of the happiness I had experienced at my previous home, Cool and Classy. I immersed myself in feelings of wholeness, love and calm, as if I was floating on a cloud. When I accessed the quiet and really tuned into my Inner Pink Star, she knew what was right for me, and a giant screen in my head played a fabulous movie of how I wanted my life to be. It showed me all the calmness and peace I had experienced previously and I knew that this was what I was looking for again. I happily basked in the radiant glow of my feelings until I would step back into reality, where indecision overload was waiting to creep back in.

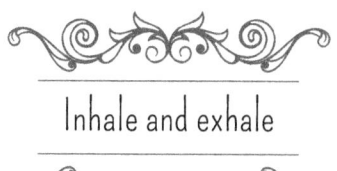
Inhale and exhale

Back in the real world, Lady Chitter Chatter was telling me I couldn't cope, I didn't know what to do, how could I leave, I loved him so much, I was hopeless not being able to repair my relationship, not being able to make a decision, I was unlovable, I was a bad person etc etc blah blah.

I didn't trust myself or my decisions so Lady Chitter Chatter kept beating me up, trying to protect me from the inevitable hurt by delivering all the ongoing negative talk.

Finally I understood that the negative talk was just getting amped up each time I listened to Lady Chitter Chatter instead of my Inner Pink Star. The yelling and chaos had to stop, and stop it did, once I made a decision, became gentle with myself and followed my Inner Pink Star to my truth. I still had the pain of grief but at least it wasn't a constant barrage of my inner self telling me I was a bad, unworthy person. The minute I truly listened to my Inner Pink Star, there was a massive difference in the way I felt.

Luckily for me, I had my Pilates escape and the truth was delivered to me slowly on a soft blue mat on the floor. It taught me to trust my inner wisdom, to access the quiet and listen for the truth. It taught me to be gentle and compassionate with myself.

But most of all it provided me with an environment that channelled my Inner Pink Star every time.

Lady Chitter Chatter often surfaces when you take on new challenges, as she becomes scared for you. If there is a lack of trust or a small waver of conviction, she will take the opportunity to jump in and deliver all kinds of criticisms. It's her job; her role is to protect. She believes if you stay in your comfort zone everything will be safe, which is why she pops up whenever you try something new.

This is when you need to ask your Inner Pink Star what she has to say. She will know if what you are about to attempt is right for you or if Lady Chitter Chatter is in fact holding some truth. Listen and you will know. If you decide the challenge is for you, put Lady Chitter Chatter to the side, access your self trust and power through. She will eventually realise you have the faith and confidence in yourself to do what is right for you, and will go back into hiding till the next challenge.

Lady Chitter Chatter's family

"Your willingness to look at your darkness is what empowers you to change"

Iyanla Vanzant

Lady Chitter Chatter doesn't work alone. She has lots of other family members who can manifest in your life. Here we will meet her family and see which of them you have got to know over the years.

All Lady Chitter Chatter's relatives take you far away from your happiness and light and make life difficult and arduous. Through their influence you can become your own worst enemy, criticising yourself in ways you would never dream of treating a good friend.

Lady Chitter Chatter

Being critical of yourself is nothing to be proud of; it is not a healthy way to access your true potential, skills and talents.

You can be proud of yourself when you turn your mindset into one of gentleness and compassion, acceptance and forgiveness. You will then soar in life, your inner world will be a place where you love hanging out and somewhere to go for solitude and stillness. This will transfer to your outer world and change how you see things, how you are treated and what you can achieve.

Let's take a look at the Chitter Chatter family tree. As you are reading about each Lady, go to your feelings for a jiffy and assess which resonate with you. You will know. Don't feel bad if you have a number of her family members residing in your head. We all do, me included.

The trick is to know them, acknowledge them, have awareness around them, work out how you think they are trying to help you and then bring in your Inner Pink Star to disperse them.

The Chitter Chatter family tree

"No matter how hard the past you can always begin again"

Buddha

Hi, I'm Lady Overworker

I am such a good little worker, I try so hard, and get everything done and more. I am so proud of myself when I can show how much I have achieved. No one can do it like me and if I don't do it, it won't get done. People always come to me to get tasks done as they know I will take care of it. My vocabulary consistently uses the word 'should'. I will work extra hours to ensure the job is finished. I have an endless tick list and continually add new tasks to it even though I know the list is impossible to complete. I have the next task or achievement lined up ready to start before I have finished what I am currently working on.

I am perpetually telling you that you will be happy when... you have the new car, the new job, the boyfriend, the new dress, the skinnier figure, the children, the degree, the piece of jewellery. The list is endless, because as soon as you fulfil one dream I create another set of criteria. I am forever taking you away from the freedom, happiness and internal peace you deserve and crave. I dangle carrots in front of you so you will run towards them, but once you have digested one there is another waiting. I don't allow you to live in the present moment and accept happiness in the here and now.

I will burn you out with fatigue and exhaustion from living with unreasonably high expectations and pressure to perform or just keep you busy working. I receive external validation through my achievements and enjoy being busy being busy to distract myself from me. This busyness gives me a feeling of self worth, so I don't prioritise self care and ignore the warning signs when I am doing too much.

Hi, I'm Lady Perfect

I am so perfect, everything I do is just right. I need to have control over everything and can never make mistakes. I will go the extra mile to ensure what I do is done to perfection. Unless every little detail is taken care of, I can't relax. I will work harder and longer to make it happen, wasting precious time to be perfect. Only one hundred percent is enough; any less than that makes me a failure. I depend on praise for doing things well for my very existence. I have exceptionally high standards for how I perform, how I behave and how productive I am. I praise myself when I do it perfectly but honestly that is rarely and I always believe I can make it just that little bit better.

Often I tell you, you are a failure. I make you frustrated and angry because you can't meet the expectations I set for you. I make it difficult for you even to get started on a project because I have already convinced you that you will not do it perfectly. Loved ones frequently feel they are not good enough because I place very high expectations on everyone. I seek external validation, because internal validation cannot be found as I am never prefect enough.

Hi, I'm Lady Pleaser

On the outside I appear so happy, willing and friendly. I want to please everyone and anyone. I am willing to put aside your values and beliefs to please others and ensure you are liked, even if this means they take advantage of you. I always say yes, but underneath I am actually saying no. I don't want to let anyone down, I don't want to be judged, rejected or alienated.

I need external approval just to exist in this world. My self esteem is not high enough to put my needs before others, as I just want to be liked. I am unable to accept the consequences if others aren't happy when I say no. I haven't yet learnt assertiveness and instead I am more passive or aggressive, constantly building resentment towards others. I get tired and irritated and send you to the cliff of exhaustion trying to fit in all the things I've said yes to, to please others.

I am the one that wants to fix and rescue everyone else. I will sacrifice your wants and needs to have the feeling of helping someone else. I get you to step up and offer unsolicited advice designed to benefit the situation. When I allow you to help others it helps you feel good about yourself and increases your self esteem.

I want everyone to love you because you do not yet love yourself enough. I haven't a solid sense of self, values or beliefs. The more others like you the more it creates a false sense of inner love but it's a vicious and exhausting circle. Your wants and needs are never met but at least people like you.

Be gentle with yourself

Hi, I'm Lady Comparison

I am the princess of comparing. I spend my time looking, evaluating and judging others. Sometimes I will tell you that you are better than others to make you feel good about yourself at their expense. I am jealous when others display traits that I would like to have, so I put them down. I am disgusted when they display weaknesses I haven't owned within myself, so I put them down for those also.

Putting others down always makes me feel better about myself. I share my opinions with anyone that will listen because it gives me an opportunity to let them know how good I am. I feel validated when they share the same opinion, so I choose to share the information with people who feel the same way. I can be quite manipulative.

At other times I will evaluate that it is you who is substandard and make you feel bad about yourself. I put you down and remind you constantly you are not living up to the expectations I have for you.

You are either better or worse than others, you cannot just be you. I do not accept you as an individual. No one wins as I will spend my time making sure you are in a constant state of comparison. I can never relax. I cannot accept you for who you are and what you offer the world.

Hi, I'm Lady Unloved

I am so good at the 'poor me' act. I persistently repeat that no one loves you. I will look for proof that this is true and then obsessively play it like a record in your head. I will look back and make you wonder if your parents loved you. I will drive away partners because I need them to constantly prove to me that they love you. They get sick of my demands and neediness. I will pick partners that won't love you so it creates a vicious circle that proves my theory to be true. I'll tell you that you are unlovable and unworthy of love.

I don't love myself so I am unable to let anyone else love you. You are miserable and under that, angry most of the time, as you never get what you want and you feel you don't deserve it. I am so scared you will be hurt again so I remain in this state because it is comfortable and safe.

Hi, I'm Lady Victim

I play the part of victim so well I could receive an award. I am sad, hopeless and helpless. I would prefer to stay put, complain, never change anything and be angry at everyone and the world because of it. I make you cry often without healing. I constantly tell you that you are hopeless. I make others uncomfortable in your presence as I sense they would like to tell you to stop whinging and move on. Your friends will listen for a while but I know they get sick of it. I confess I do enjoy the attention the victim receives. It adds drama to your life and as a bonus you don't have to think about what you need to do to pull yourself out of it. I deflect responsibility and avoid creating awareness and stepping up to own my life at all costs, it is much easier to blame and attack others.

Still the mind and remain calm

Hi, I'm Lady Strong

I am the part of you that won't allow you to feel your vulnerability. I often will beat you up for feeling vulnerable rather than acknowledging that as part of who you are and being gentle. I often arise after the downfall of a relationship, a death or loss of a job, times you feel scared, hurt and small. I can creep in when you feel like tucking yourself up in bed and wrapping yourself tightly in a blanket to protect yourself.

I don't look after you enough to allow you time out to heal and learn. I won't let you stay home and heal when you know you need it; I will make you put on a happy face and face the world. I tell you to be strong and stop being pathetic. I can send you into a spin of depression rather than just allowing you to feel the normal vulnerabilities of life. I am the falsely strong part of you that calls you weak, tells you to ignore your feelings, get up and get on with it. I don't want you to have any down time, as you may look weak to others.

I don't want to allow you to show anyone your weaker side as they may not like or respect you. I could be embarrassed, raw and exposed, and I prefer being in control at all times. Sometimes you are a little child just needing love and attention and I am a critical mother yelling 'stop being a baby'. I cause you tiredness and exhaustion to keep your vulnerable feelings packed away out of sight. I use all your energy trying to stay strong when you really need the time out to heal, repair and move on in your own time.

Find self compassion

Hi, I'm Lady Nasty

I am horrible and create an enormous amount of shame in your life, by attacking your self worth and the person you are. I attack you in any way possible and tell you in words, sentences but most likely a feeling or a sensation that you are a bad and flawed person and you do not deserve to exist. I am constantly throwing these thoughts and emotions at you, which invariably lead you to depression, despair and a sense of unworthiness. I never let you experience any good moments. I am just horrid.

I undermine your confidence and self esteem at every turn. I create a huge amount of self doubt, guilt, regret, anxiety and worry that makes it impossible for you to believe in yourself and trust yourself. I ensure that you struggle every day. I make you want to stay in your passive ways feeling helpless and hopeless. I get you to withdraw from the world as I don't believe you have anything real to contribute. I create unwelcome and scary fantasies in your mind.

Oh my dear, the Lady Chitter Chatter family has lots of lovely relatives all vying for attention doesn't it? What an incredibly dysfunctional bunch, but we love them because they are family, don't we? Which members of the family do you have taking up residence in your head? Maybe you have some that are not even on this list, so feel free to grow the family tree if you need to out them. I admit I have had most of them visit me at different points in my life, if you need to be reminded I am not straddling a high horse in my cowgirl boots, teaching you about your faults. I am here walking beside you, sharing not only my professional knowledge and education but also my own personal experiences and growth, the ins and outs of my journey.

All of your Lady Chitter Chatters will settle down when you are ready to be gentle with yourself and drape them in self love. Learning to create internal validation will release you from being inauthentic and seeking approval outside yourself. You will become more trusting and forgiving with yourself.

This will in turn create more self respect and honour internally, enabling you to trust yourself more and enjoy being in your own company. The incessant mind talk slowly becomes less invasive and you find yourself happier in the here and now, appreciating the present moment for what it is and who you are. Take responsibility and make the choice to learn more and lessen the Chitter Chatters. This will increase the love you direct deep inside.

Pink time out – Questions

Stop and Breathe

Read the list of questions below and allow time and space for self reflection. In your Little Pink book of Love record your thoughts, feelings, reactions and any epiphanies and wow moments you may have. Let the pen flow and see what appears on the page in front of you. As this may take you out of your comfort zone, remember to remain gentle and compassionate with yourself as you are answering these questions, and always come from a place of love.

1. Which Lady Chitter Chatter stands out the most?
2. Ask each Lady Chitter Chatter individually, 'What are you trying to tell me? What is your purpose in my life?'
3. What does each Lady Chitter Chatter say to you?
4. What tone of voice does she use when she talks to you?
5. Does she lie to you?
6. What are you scared of?
7. What is your biggest fear?
8. What does Lady Chitter Chatter think you could do better?
9. How does she attack you?
10. What do you stress about?
11. Where are you judging yourself?
12. Where are you pushing yourself to hard?
13. Where are you burning out?
14. What nasty words does Lady Chitter Chatter use?
15. What denial or avoidance tactics does she use?
16. What feelings does she create inside?
17. How often is she with you in any one day?
18. What negative thoughts preoccupy your mind?
19. What do you sacrifice in your life by listening to her?
20. Are these sacrifices worth it? What price do you pay?
21. Why do you do this to yourself?
22. Why do you believe her?
23. What is she protecting you from?

24. What consequences are you avoiding?
25. Are there any other Lady Chitter Chatters that are not on the list that reside in your head?
26. If you are not enough, when will you be enough?

Brilliant work. This was a hard exercise. It is difficult to come face to face with the Chitter Chatter family. I hope you are feeling a sense of knowing yourself as you unearth more discoveries about yourself.

Pink time out – Ratings

Stop and Breathe

Giving yourself a rating is another tool to use to unearth more information about yourself and how you are feeling.

Rate yourself from 0 – 10 (10 being the best) for the statements below, to help you gain further insight to how much you operate using Lady Chitter Chatter or your Inner Pink Star.

Go with your first thoughts and your first ratings. Don't feel stressed in trying to be exact and perfect. Go with your Inner Pink Star's initial thoughts. Trust yourself.

I am ready to transform my life
I have awareness for self

I trust myself
I am loveable
I am capable
I am enough
I can deal with anything
I am able to express myself
I can face my fears
I can do this
I am worthy
I have high self esteem
I can access forgiveness
I accept me for who I am today
I am significant
I am powerful
I respect who I am
I don't beat myself up
I am not self critical
I take responsibility for my self
I am unique and do not compare myself with others
I am an individual and proud of it
I am not a perfectionist
I take time out for self care and listen to what my body, mind and spirit is telling me
I have compassion for myself
I am gentle with myself
I let myself have fun and play
I don't need to please others
I say no when I want/need to
I am not afraid to admit the truth to myself
I act on the consequences the truth brings
I never should/have/must on myself
I am my best friend
I do not future happy myself. Eg I will be happy when...
I have an unwavering willingness and desire to live a happy and peaceful life

Excellent. Your Little Pink book of Love must be filling up with interesting facts and feelings about yourself. I hope you are becoming more trusting and loving towards yourself. You are now coming face to face with yourself once again after a long time of being disconnected and feeling only grief and sadness over your breakup.

Pink time out – Artwork

Stop and Breathe

To tap into your creative side once again, get your coloured pencils and choose a new page in your Little Pink book of Love. In the middle of the page, draw your version of what your Lady Chitter Chatter looks like. You do not have to be a great artist, just be expressive. Let yourself go and see what appears. Give her an ugly dress, bad hair, terrible shoes or a beard. Whatever you believe she looks and feels like.

Once you have a picture of her, now design your own personal name for her. It may be an actual name, or your own version of Lady Chitter Chatter. If you name her she can become more known to you. This will help you understand her even more. You will be able to pinpoint when, where and why she pops up and tries to wreak havoc in your life.

Around her picture, write all the words that she means to you. What words describe her? What words come to you when you think of her? What words are negative, bullying, critical and make you feel not good enough or bad? Be creative and write these words in the colours or styles that evoke their meanings for you.

Once you have your completed piece, feel proud that you have come to know her better, appreciate what she has meant to you and what she tries to tell you. Then put her aside and move on.

Reflection

"The moment in between what you once were, and who you are now becoming, is where the dance of life really takes place"

Barbara deAngelis

At the Healing Sanctuary we do not lie down and take it. We step up and use intense internal scrutiny to be the best person we can be, growths, warts and all. Sometimes it is not fun and sometimes it is dreary and sometimes it is downright frightening. But baby the rewards are mind blowing, if you dare to let them materialise.

After spending time thinking about your Lady Chitter Chatters, you may feel you have countless different personalities running amok inside you. Don't worry, so do most of us, that's why there is so much literature out there on this topic. Through having fun meeting them, greeting them and naming them you can find out what they are trying to protect you from and why they throw their miseries and hurtful remarks at you. You can grow and evolve and learn how to handle their personalities and gain some control over the Chitter Chatter bunch.

Since denying and avoiding Lady Chitter Chatter, trying to eliminate her or buying in to her destructive inner talk clearly does not work, I encourage you to attempt this strategy of listening and loving her. Accept she is a part of you and in her bizarre way is striving to help. When she emerges unexpectedly she presents the opportunity to ask yourself, 'Why now? What is different about my life at this moment? Is there a decision I need to make? Am I sleep deprived? Am I avoiding something?' Try to understand what she is trying to tell you. Don't get caught up, attached to the downward spiral of thoughts and start beating yourself up. Try to separate yourself and observe her message from a distance. Hear her messages and warnings for what they are, rather than becoming emotionally involved and attached.

More lessons I have learnt to help deal with Lady Chitter Chatter and bring myself internal happiness and fulfilment, through my evolution, study, experiences and introspection in the last twenty years is housed in the next section, the Flower Garden of Love. This is where you will learn how to apply new skills to your own life to produce a state of calm.

Now, you stand up, stretch your muscles, and thank Lady Chitter Chatter for all her insight into the special, complex person, you are. You head back to reception through the pretty gardens, thinking about how amazing humans really are. Listening to the water in the fountains, you admit you may not be ready to integrate Lady Chitter Chatter fully into your whole self, but you have taken the first step. You have moved out of denial and avoidance and are now ready to face her head on. You are ready now to learn how to heal her and make life a whole lot easier. With that thought, your pace quickens as you once again feel the transformation occurring from the inside out, and the redesigning and redecorating taking place.

You are coming to the end of the healing journey and tomorrow will relax in the Flower Garden of Love. It is peaceful and loving there, and you will wear flowers in your hair. It is light and free, a garden at the Healing Sanctuary reserved only for those who have done the work to get there.

Meditation and Me

"Love yourself first and everything else falls into line.
You really have to love yourself to get
anything done in this world"

Lucille Ball

Welcome to the Flower Garden of Love

Heading through the main grounds again, you twist and turn till you find the white picket gate. With anticipation you turn the squeaky handle and in you go, feeling as if everything is about to change.

Welcome to the Flower Garden of Love. You stop for a moment to breathe, inhaling peace and exhaling any negativity and distress you are carrying. You access the stillness and peace you hold internally, relishing being in the moment. Right now you feel it is possible to let go of yesterday and tomorrow, to just be here now and allow yourself to go deep inside.

You spy luscious green leaves swaying in the mild breeze on healthy vibrant trees. Pretty flowers in every colour of the rainbow bloom for the world to see. They blanket the ground, dotted by the stone pavers that lie in exactly the right position for you to move through the flowers without disturbing the array of beauty.

Immaculately manicured, groomed and nourished, the flowers smile at you as you pass through them, the colours leaping into your heart and making you smile.

Lacquered wooden benches surrounded by overflowing flower pots are scattered through the garden and soothing fountains trickle into the pool below. Birds are tweeting their unique tunes and sipping from the fountains while butterflies flutter past. There is something a little more magical about this garden than that on the other side of the white picket fence. You take in the atmosphere as you walk deeper into the garden, alone with your thoughts, feelings, mind, body and spirit.

You feel encompassed in love and life and know you are shifting towards healing. The absence of distractions helps make this the perfect serene and tranquil place for the last of your healing work.

The stepping stones take you to an opening, through which you can see a round grassed area wrapped in flowers. Brightly coloured meditation pillows are arranged in a circle under a white meditation tent. Coloured ribbons float in the breeze. In the centre of the circle lies a large white stone covered in candles and statues, with throw rugs lying over the sides. It is a Balinese delight delivering a spiritual and sacred space.

You allow yourself to relax. Here you will learn the tools to create an internal loving atmosphere by creating stillness with yourself and then learn to carry that wherever you go. You will soon be able to maintain calm amidst the chaos in your internal or external world.

After visiting the Flower Garden of Love, everything will look different. You will see gardens, flowers, water fountains and prettiness wherever you go. You will look inside and know that the flowers, lightness and love you see on the outside are a reflection of what you carry within you, having found love for yourself. A gift to yourself, tied up with a pretty pink bow.

This is the prize at the end of your journey of healing. You have completed an abundance of internal work that brings you to this point and you deserve to savour every moment.

This, that you have created, is your life. The only life you get. There is no rehearsal, there is no second act. This is it. Don't waste any more time settling for a lesser existence when you now know there is another option. Take the higher option every time. Every moment of introspection creates another moment of peace in your life. The work you have accomplished leads to the masterpiece you are creating.

This is the only life you get. There is no rehearsal, there is no second act

Stop and appreciate how far you have come. It was not so long ago you were a pile of rubble on the floor, with no idea what to do next. You are now here; you have achieved so much. Take in the feelings of pride, the thankfulness for who you are, what you have learnt and the lessons that have been gifted to you. Is now the right time to say that maybe your heartbreak was the best thing that ever happened to you? It became the necessary impetus for you to go inside, redesign and redecorate for the better.

What will I learn in the Flower Garden of Love?

"Life's experiences, regardless of how they show up, are the means through which we get to love one another"

Panache Desai

At the Flower Garden of Love you will build on the experience of learning how to love yourself by allowing yourself to live in the moment. There are a myriad of ways we try to fix ourselves and many are unnecessary. We are told how we need to change to be what we think we need to be, or what others tell us to be. Consider this. Essentially the only permission you need is yours, to BE YOU AND ONLY YOU, quirks, eccentricities and all. Accept yourself.

Yes there may be things you have decided to change in order to create your new dream life. However first you must allow yourself to be you. The way to do this is simply to love yourself. Melt away all the disliking, judging and loathing and make way for the love to surface. When you love yourself you will see the struggles and problems dissipate slowly, naturally. You will become not only more self loving, but more loving to others, with an enhanced ability to form true connections.

Unhealthy behaviours of the past will be superfluous and new healthy ones will take their place. You will grow your emotional maturity and be able to share this with the world, bringing enormous benefits into your life. You will always do what is right for you, making the best decisions even if they require some short term pain. Things that used to bother you will no longer be of any consequence. Life will become easier and more pleasant and you will gain a sense of inner fulfilment that brings peace, clarity, calm and happiness.

Make a promise today to unequivocally do everything in your power to create an internal loving atmosphere. Love, love, love yourself. Don't worry about the tall poppy syndrome and people that try to chop you down; they are not worth it. They are more likely jealous of your new inner-found happiness, a happiness which continues to evade them. Worry about yourself, your inner world and your soon to be shiny new fun and happy world.

The people who are meant to be in your life, the people who bring out the best in you, will appreciate everything you do to love yourself more. Positive, motivated and inspired people will be magnetically attracted and want you in their lives. You will want to be in the lives of healthy, mature, rational people. Those who do not provide calm and reason will fade away naturally, as they no longer have anything to offer you.

These people may want to stay stuck to you because of the enthused energy you bring, but you will find that you gently unleash these attachments and leave them behind. You know you deserve better. You, your friends, your partner, your life will all become more healthy and radiant. You will start to become luminous and everything around you will start to magically glow.

Be you, love you

The Flower Garden of Love helps you to ponder learning to love yourself by living in the moment through meditation. Start small and watch your love grow. Do not expect this to happen overnight; it is a slow continuing process. Drop the impulsivity and create patience and tolerance, develop a daily practice. Relish being the tortoise not the hare, they are much cuter anyway.

WHY MEDITATION?

"The quieter you become the more you can hear"

Baba Ram Dass

You may have never been exposed to meditation before, although it is becoming more widely recognised as an amazing tool in your toolbox to get back in touch with yourself and your truth. It provides a safe haven to escape the stresses of everyday living and just let your mind rest for a little.

During this time in your life your mind is working overtime. Some days you may feel like you are going crazy, the thoughts are so insistent and unrelenting. This is a normal part of the grieving process, yet even with acceptance of this fact we need tools to help us through.

In your sleep you normally rest and recover, yet during the grieving and heartbreak process it does not provide the relief you are so desperately seeking, and you often wake up just as exhausted as you were when your head hit the pillow the night before.

When our minds are off doing their chaotic rumba, it can be a dangerous time. We so desperately want to feel better we often seek unhealthy distractions. Alcohol, drugs or other destructive tendencies can look appealing, just to cope minute to minute.

Destructive traits, unfortunately, always tend to grow bigger and bigger and in time, they can become entrenched in our lives and turn into addictions that can have an even bigger injurious and detrimental effect on us and those we love.

Meditation provides the opportunity to get out of your chaotic head and just be. You have the ability to discover the quiet and the authentic self within. The part of you that is peaceful and true. The part of yourself that is trusting and gentle. Meditation gives you access to your Inner Pink Star and quietens Lady Chitter Chatter of her unhelpful chit-chat.

Meditation was one of the most profound tools to fast track my healing process, and made my struggles a bearable experience. I am not sure I can explain in words how grateful I am for being introduced to meditation and I know it has been partly responsible for creating massive breakthroughs and relief in my life.

It has enabled me to learn about myself, seek healthier ways of healing and processing many current and past hurts. In the long term this has made it possible for me to clear the past blocks I was holding onto and opened up my heart to create more love and abundance to flow in.

MEDITATION AND ME

There are a few concerns I hear from people apprehensive about trying the meditative state.

"I don't have enough time to meditate". Yes, we are very time poor in our lives. But it's about priorities. When you are going through heartbreak or a grieving process you now know how vital it is to take time to stop, breathe and introduce self love into your life in all its forms.

You do not have to meditate for long. Even five or ten minutes daily will make a difference to the calmness you experience during the rest of the day.

"It doesn't work for me" is another concern I hear regularly. Think of a new hobby you wanted to try, say the game of squash. Before you know what you are doing and how to hit the ball, how to score and move around the court, you know you need to practise. Meditation also takes practise, commitment and more practise. Don't expect perfection, just be. The more you sit on your cushion the better at it you will become.

"It's all just mumbo jumbo." Some think meditation is eccentric and a bit hippy-ish. Meditation is an ancient tradition in many countries and we all know how calm and peaceful the monks are who sit on a mountain top for months on end.

Put yourself first and allow gentleness and compassion. If you are committed and have enough desire to feel better and more relaxed, you will add into your life the tools that are required that will benefit you.

The reality is that meditation works. Your busy mind will thank you in bucket loads if you can introduce a tool that will slow it down. You can learn how to observe your thoughts rather than attaching to them. With practise, this will spill over into your

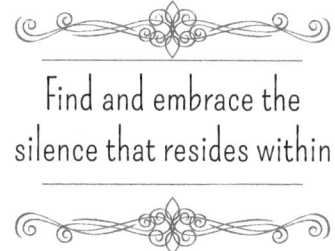

Find and embrace the silence that resides within

everyday life, creating a more balanced and calm reality, in turn decreasing negative thoughts, energy and emotions.

The benefits of meditation:

- Gain calmness and inner peace
- Gain a deeper awareness and connection to your inner authentic self
- Learn to manage your busy chaotic mind, observing your thoughts rather than attaching to them
- Increase self confidence and decision making ability
- Learn to live in the present moment
- Become inspired
- Gain energy and lightness
- Sleep better
- Create more happiness in your life
- Learn to surrender and let go
- Learn acceptance
- Learn how to just be

If you are a beginner to meditation, there are many guided meditations that make it much easier for you. The majority of meditations I use are apps on my iPhone that I have downloaded from the app store. They walk you through step by step - all you have to do is press play.

You open your eyes for a moment and take in the gorgeous scenery, the colourful pillows and what you have just learnt. You watch the meditation tent ribbons float gracefully in the wind. Coming back to the present moment, you now feel ready to put it into practice in your life and see the benefits for yourself.

Pink time out – Simple meditation

～ Stop and Breathe ～

Getting comfy on your meditation pillow of your choice, sitting in lotus pose with your legs crossed, you close your eyes once again. Allowing the breeze to skim your lips, you clear your mind as you seek to find and embrace the silence that resides within.

Follow these simple steps for an introduction to meditation if you have not delved into the practice previously. If you are new to meditation, continue to practise this until you are more comfortable with it.

- Once you are comfortable and have your eyes closed:Regulate your breathing, then take a few deep breaths.
- Now put all your focus on your breathing.
- As you inhale, say in your mind 'inhale'.
- As you exhale, say in your mind 'exhale'.
- As thoughts enter your mind, acknowledge the thought and then let it drift away.
- Allow yourself to observe and witness them and then let them go, try not to attach to the thoughts.
- Continue to inhale and exhale.
- When you are ready to come out of your mediation, wiggle your toes and fingers, bring your concentration back to the moment, then when you are ready slowly open your eyes.

- Continue to practise as above for as long as you feel comfortable. You may wish to start with five to ten minutes and build up to thirty or sixty minutes.

Pink time out – Challenging meditation

Stop and Breathe

When you feel confident with the basics of meditation, try this guided meditation to deepen the experience.

This meditation provided me with huge epiphanies. When I was at a very vulnerable and raw time and had lost a lot of my self trust, this meditation allowed my soul and my Inner Pink Star to guide me to people that I trusted. It allowed me to be truthful with myself about which people were not acting in my best interests and gave me the courage to distance myself from them.

Through a meditation you will create a circle of trust, and let your soul decide who is allowed inside that circle of trust. You will need to go deep, to really feel whether each of the people around you is helping you create your best life. Through this you will gain the power to protect yourself at a deep and authentic level.

Give it a go and see how it works for you.

- Find a comfortable space and posture for meditation.
- Close your eyes and breathe.

- ❈ Visualise yourself sitting on the meditation cushion in the meditation tent at the Flower Garden of Love.
- ❈ Relax all the parts of your body, spend some time just being in your body.
- ❈ Keep breathing and relax.
- ❈ Observe any thoughts that appear in your head without attaching. Let them go and visualise them drifting or floating away.
- ❈ Visualise drawing a big pink circle around where you are sitting.
- ❈ Make the inside of the pink circle a safe and peaceful space. Include flowers, candles or whatever you feel creates a warm safe place.
- ❈ Think about the one person that you feel most safe with in the world and visualise them approaching the circle. Ask them to step over the pink line into your space, and decide where they will sit. Go to your feelings, do you want them right next to you, touching you shoulder to shoulder, cuddling close, or just nearby, perhaps close enough to touch but not right up against you?
- ❈ Continue visualising each of the people you love approaching your circle of love and trust one by one. Take your time, and show each of them where you would like them to sit, ensuring the position feels right to you. The ones you love deeply you will want right next to you, others you may appreciate and respect so you still want them in your circle, but don't need them quite so close. As you immerse yourself in the visualisation and feel your loved ones entering the circle, their places will become more obvious. There are no hard and fast rules, just allow the process to happen.

- Let in as many people as you wish and have them all quietly and comfortably be with you in your loving circle of trust. Feel the positive and loving energy. Feel the abundance of your connections and sense of belonging you have in your life.

- Now I am going to ask you bring your ex into your vision. What are you feeling when he arrives? Do you wish to invite him into your circle of trust? Or would you like him to stand just outside the circle, close but not trusted? Or do you wish to put up a big pink wall and shoo him away?

- Do you notice your feelings change when you are considering the place your ex has in your life? Do you notice any negative energy?

- Now sit with everyone you have invited into your circle of trust and allow the loving feelings to be just as they are. If there is any negative energy, allow it just to be also.

- Now think about other people who are prominent in your life and may be loitering just outside the pink circle of trust. Go to your feelings once again and for each person, see if you wish to invite them into your circle, wish them to remain where they are or wish to ask them to leave.

- When you are ready, visualise each person inside the circle slowly standing and leaving you, knowing at a profoundly deep level where they sit in your life. Continue to breathe and relax and take in all you have learned.

- When you are ready to come out of your mediation, wiggle your toes and your fingers. Bring your concentration back to the moment, and slowly open your eyes.

Meditation and me

Sit for a moment and take in what you have just experienced before we move onto reflection. This exercise can really highlight in a deeply soulful way who you trust and would like deeply ingrained in your heart and your life. It will also highlight others who, when you are really truthful with yourself, you may not want very close, and others who you may want to go away all together.

It may be scary or eye-opening or a little of both. If you allow your authenticity to shine through in this exercise, you may have some truths to face or some hard conversations to have. Your outer ego and persona may think it needs certain people to exist, however your beautiful soul knows who is healthy for you and who is not. This may create difficult decisions and consequences.

Pink Time Out – Question Time

⸎ Stop and Breathe ⸎

Read the list of questions below and allow time and space for self reflection. In your Little Pink book of Love record your thoughts, feelings, reactions and any epiphanies and wow moments you may have. Let the pen flow and see what appears on the page in front of you. As this may take you out of your comfort zone, remember to remain gentle and compassionate with yourself, and always come from a place of love.

- How did you feel about the meditation? Were you able to let your thoughts go?
- How did you feel about bringing in the ones you loved? What feelings did it create inside?
- Think about where you placed everyone, were there any surprises about where you let people sit, or how close to your heart you asked them to come?
- Did your meditative presence let you introduce your ex into your safe circle?
- If your ex was not able to enter, what did you think or feel about this?
- If you did let them enter, where did you place them and how did you feel?
- If you asked your ex to go away and put up a big wall, how did this make you feel?
- If there are people that your meditation shooed away and yet you are still expending energy on them in your day to day life, why do you choose to do this?
- Did you experience any negative energy and if so, what or who created this?
- Are there people you seek approval or reassurance from, but your meditation showed you that they are not in the circle of trust? Why?
- Are there any decisions or conversations you need to have after doing this meditation?
- What other information did this meditation provide?

This type of soul growth can be difficult yet rewarding, so use self love and self trust and take one moment at a time. If you have highlighted a potentially difficult decision or conversation, remember it does not have to be done today. Sit with your reflections and epiphanies and let them unfold. Have faith in the process; when the time is right you will know how to act and what you need to do.

When I did this meditation it provided me with remarkable clarity about how I felt, rather than thought, about different people in my life.

There were family members that I asked in before others and were placed as close to my heart as they could get. My dogs were as close to me as I could get them.

There were friends I don't see often but were very close to me, and others I see a lot that were inside the circle but not right next to me. I wanted them there but they were not so connected to my heart in a deep meaningful way.

Each time I tried to ask my ex into the circle, a big wall went up when he got to the pink line. I simply could not invite him into my circle of peace, calm and trust. Part of me so dearly wanted him to enter, he felt so familiar, like a family member. However a deeper, more wise, knowing part of me wanted him to stay away from my heart, my recovering broken heart.

Through this meditation I could see that to keep my vulnerable heart safe and peaceful, I needed him to be outside the circle. By acknowledging and honouring my feelings, my self love was increasing. I was finally putting myself first.

Invite meditation into your life, your home and your spirit. Spend time practising with patience and compassion for yourself. Watch and wait for the calm and peace to wash over you and start to feel the differences in everyday life when you take control back of your mind. The benefits are astonishing.

Find and embrace the silence that resides within

Wow, loving yourself through meditation is a big task. The key is to be in the moment while you learn to love yourself. To be in the moment, with yourself, your thoughts, your emotions, your body, spirit and soul. Allow your thoughts to be, and be calm anyway.

As you leave through the little white picket gate, you say thank you to the flowers of The Flower Garden of Love. You pick a couple of your favourite flowers as a reminder, and put them in your hair to remind you about the learning from today.

Allow your thoughts to be, and be calm anyway

As you wander back to your villa, you reflect: one day at a time, tiptoe through life, be in this moment and grow the love you have for you. You are significant, important and worthy. You hold wisdom beyond what you see as your potential. You are you and only you. Continue to find you, meet you, welcome you but most of all love you.

READ, RESEARCH, SEEK KNOWLEDGE

"Knowledge is the life of the mind"

Abu Bakr

Sitting in your villa, you realise that tonight is your last night at the Healing Sanctuary and you hold dear to your heart every last piece of healing and nurturing you have experienced during your stay here. You decide to hop into the king-size bed with your herbal tea and spend the last night exploring the reading material from the bedside table.

You are becoming more and more drawn to learning about yourself, your heart and your soul. It is becoming a little addictive because every new tool and piece of information you learn enables you to understand yourself more, to be more self loving and authentic. These tools provide a protective coating for your heart and soul, slowly allowing your self trust to surface again.

There is so much to learn. Don't feel overwhelmed; feel excited, enthusiastic and passionate. Because now you know what you have to do, you can start doing it. Knowledge is powerful - with knowledge you can achieve anything.

Create a hunger for knowledge. There is information galore everywhere you turn. We have delicious book stores that you can wander around with delight for hours, historic buildings that house libraries full to the brim, and then we have google search, housing all the information you could hope to find in the comfort of your own home, at the tips of your fingers. There is nothing that you cannot find out about if you so wish and desire.

Every time I hit a stumbling block, I hit the books or the internet. There is nothing that isn't out there for discussion. Some of the best online courses I have attended are run from the other side of the world and have left me with absolutely incredible tools and skills to propel me forward with my healing. Become the expert at whatever you are facing. Be passionate about your healing, health and emotional state. Yearn to learn absolutely everything you can about the topics that you sense will help you. The more understanding and knowledge you have over a topic, the less daunting and frightening you may find it to be.

Attend courses, online or in real life. Read every book or article you can get your hands on. Seek out a good therapist who can help move you forward. Visit Facebook pages that address similar issues to the ones you face, and contribute to the comments and discussions. Reading about others' stories where they have overcome adversity will create snippets of hope for your situation. It creates a sense of connection and you will not feel so alone.

It is startling how much information we now have access to, so use it to your benefit. Seek and you shall find. Research and read, do whatever you need to do, find whatever you can and never give up till you find what you are looking for, to put you back into the calm and peaceful state you deserve to live your life in.

Knowledge really is power. When you understand what you are facing and are given skills, tools and knowledge it creates a means to help move you through your troubles. Give yourself a big pink gift of knowledge to help you thrive in your healing.

Your eyes feel heavy as you lean over to switch off the bedside light, grateful for your stay here, your life and your ability to be proactive to love and care for yourself.

CHECKING OUT

"Maybe she had it wrong all this time and her empty heart could never be filled by his ingenious broken spirit. Maybe this yearning had nothing to do with him, and everything to do with her"

Coco J. Ginger

You made it. It is time to leave the Healing Sanctuary and all its glorious serenity behind. You sense a knowing that all you have absorbed remains with you, to be held forever. You are astounded at the peaceful feelings you possess compared to how you felt on arrival here.

You arrived on shaky ground, but not rubble on the floor, and now leave with a sense of ease and self love. You understand what being your own best friend means and realise you are the person you should admire most in the world. You accept your individuality and feel prepared to respect and honour yourself at all times under all and any circumstances.

Your experience here has been once in a lifetime. You fully immersed yourself into the Who Am I questions and created your own Pink Heart Print to keep with you always. You met your Inner Pink Star and your Lady Chitter Chatter, integrating both into yourself to promote healing within. Finally you spent time at the Flower Garden of Love and learnt how to love and respect yourself even more.

You know you still have to apply what you have learnt in the real world but trust that, as you use your new tools, they will become easier and will soon be cemented in your skills inventory. Your boundaries are shaped, your values and core beliefs are solid. You feel you can breathe again. Life's looking good.

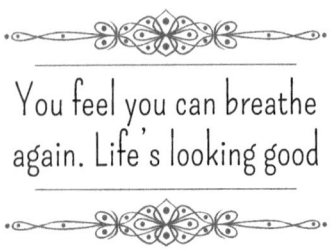

You feel you can breathe again. Life's looking good

The heartbreak really was the impetus to dive off the cliff with no harness and discover you. It was not as scary as you imagined, and the rewards have been nothing short of amazing. You have awakened the real you within, the one that holds her head high and walks with purpose and clarity. You know her well, you accept her flaws and imperfections and celebrate her strengths and wisdom. You are enthusiastic and want to share yourself with the world, yet at the same time don't want to let anything disrupt the peaceful place you currently reside.

You walk through the grounds to reception one last time, take a quick glimpse to the Pink Studio perched on the hill and remind yourself of its sacredness and the feelings it created within you.

All the promises you were given on arrival have been fulfilled and a smile lights up your face as you wait to check out. You gaze over at your favourite lounge and see the coloured rugs strewn over the arms, inviting a new soul to sit, sip on the teas and feel protected and covered in the warmth of this healing space.

You feel teary as you look at the stunning chandeliers one last time. They are shining bright as always and while you gaze outwards you feel the warmth and tenderness residing within.

The girls at the desk explain that your next destination is the Happiness Shack. Finally, after all this concentrated effort, you are going to have some fun! Beaches, coffees, fine food, water, dog parks and laughter.

Checking out

You feel your Inner Pink Star jumping for joy with what is to come. Lady Chitter Chatter is feeling a little hesitant but with your new found trust and self love, she remains at bay.

Before you leave reception you are asked to answer a few last questions:

1. What is one thing you can rave about to others about your stay here?
2. What did you like most about your stay here?
3. What is the biggest thing you learnt during your stay here?
4. Would you revisit in the future if you needed to?
5. How will you acknowledge and celebrate how far you have come in your journey?
6. Please rate your stay from 0 -10, 10 being the best.

Pink time out – Song choice
Stop and Breathe

Pick one song that relates to your stay here. Choose a song that is symbolic of how you felt when you arrived, what you achieved and how you feel now. Play it over and over and let it sink in.

In your Little Pink book of Love, record the name of your song. Let it be your reminder for ever and always of the time you spent here. Remind yourself often of the tremendous progress you achieved and the amazing journey you have been on.

Heartbreak, Healing and Happiness

At the Healing Sanctuary you created breathing space to help you to grow the love you have and to reconnect with yourself. You found your truth and truly met and discovered yourself, found self forgiveness and allowed time for respite and healing from your heartbreak.

Once you have answered the last few questions and chosen your song, you pick up all your gifts and leave the Healing Sanctuary via the black iron gates with the love heart carving. You kiss the heart for good measure, say a quick Namaste, bow to show your respect for your respite and your healing and then jump with gusto on the shuttle bus to head to your next destination, the Happiness Shack.

Thank you for staying at the Healing Sanctuary.

Love – Truth – Purpose

PART 3

THE HAPPINESS SHACK

Hello Happiness

"Leap and the cliff disappears"

Lisa Cherney

You are on route to the Happiness Shack at last. The shuttle bus from the Healing Sanctuary dropped you off at a meeting point to be collected by a jeep - something you feel a tad apprehensive about, yet you trust that you will be cared for.

The jeep is roofless, so you feel open and exposed but in a warm tingly way. You are ready to go wherever this ride is taking you. Bumpy roads manoeuvre over small hills and valleys and you hold on tight as you are carried away into the exciting unknown. As you bounce along, your fear is put to rest and your courageousness appears.

You breathe deeply and close your eyes as the wind filters through your hair and brushes over your face. You realise at this very moment in time you have no thoughts running through your head except that life is great and you feel good.

There is still so much unknown, yet you have found a space to appreciate the present moment and all the beauty it offers.

Raindrops of hope appear and you sense snippets of joy and peace bubbling under the surface. There is no forcing them, they simply arrive and ask to be acknowledged.

Appreciate the present moment and all the beauty it offers

The beachfront comes into view, a paradise of white sand and calm seas on a clear and sunny day. Bathers, tee shirts, skirts and shorts, all colours of the rainbow parade past your eyes. Hats of all different shapes and colours protect smiling faces and beautiful eyes shine with happiness and delight.

The people look light and free, oozing smiles and laughter. The serious looks you have become accustomed to are gone, replaced with calm, cool contentment. An inner peace exudes from those around you; the elusive feeling you have been seeking seems to have appeared. It is not forced; what you have desired for months appears just to be in these people; they are being, they are feeling with no internal force.

Everyone seems to be either on their way to their next adventure or loitering on the sidewalks and beach, chatting or just being. You notice surfboards, jet skis, boats, catamarans and all sorts of other beachside toys along the sand, ready to be put to use.

Cafés and restaurants line the esplanade, where lattes and green teas are sipped by patrons covered in sand and salt from their morning beach adventures, or relaxing in yoga gear after a morning of inner reflection, exercise and meditation.

Dogs of all sizes, breeds and ages nestle at their owners' feet, some resting from their morning swim and others waiting to get down to the beach, anticipating sandy paws and wet ears.

Boutiques dot the main street as window-shoppers of all shapes and sizes search for the magical outfit to match their positive mood.

Standing in the main street, you realise that this is where you now fit in. You have let happy moments come in to your waking hours and your hurts and heartbreak sit in the background. Having spent time healing, seeking internal knowledge and processing all that you have discovered, you realise the time has come to have some fun again. What's more impressive though is that you actually feel like you want to have fun; a feeling that has lain dormant for a long time.

The darkness you have been travelling through is fading and the pink light at the end of the tunnel is close. There are still times you feel low and feel you need to protect yourself, but like a flower bud starting to blossom, you are ready to take on the world. With a little nurturing and watering you are ready to go.

The skills and tools you have learnt over your healing journey have shown you how to trust that the path you are following is right for you. Now you can relax and enjoy the peaceful moments, knowing that in time this will be the norm; the low, dark times of the recent past will dissipate to hazy memories.

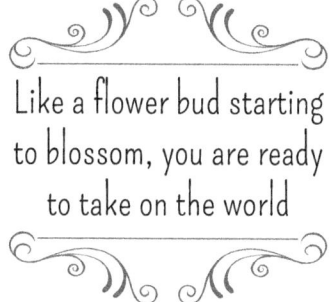

Like a flower bud starting to blossom, you are ready to take on the world

Your cottage

"Life moves pretty fast. If you don't stop and look once in a while, you could miss it"

Ferris Bueller

Your driver drops you off with a map to your accommodation and scoots off with a friendly wave.

You follow the map to the end of the beach strip and realise that the formalities and structure you had so been seeking and needing at the other destinations is not necessary where you are now in life. You sense that you are here to relax, loosen up, live life, be in the moment and appreciate what you have and who you are. The time spent internalising and processing is coming to an end. You trust that you are emotionally safe and know the diamonds will appear when the time is right.

You have done everything you needed to do to heal from your heartbreak, so now it is time to go and live it. Test it. You know there will always be new lessons and hurdles to jump in life, but for now you are happy to live, to enjoy activities the Happiness Shack provides.

The sight of your little cottage at the quiet end of the busy beach strip takes your breath away for a moment. It's beautiful. A pathway bordered by roses leads through a gorgeous colourful garden to the pink front door. As you take the walk up the garden path you see a cute little sign that reads 'The Happiness Shack'. Comfy wicker lounge chairs sit on the veranda and look straight out to the beach.

You open the door and notice is how light and bright it is, with an open, fresh living area filled with soft colourful lounges. You can see that this was once an old shack but has been lovingly renovated with all the modern amenities. The homely feel has been retained, and is accentuated by flowers and candles around the room making you feel instantly content. A state-of-the-art kitchen with snow white Caesar stone bench tops and shiny chrome tap wear sits to your left. On the counter is an envelope next to a big bowl of fresh fruits and a bottle of Moet champagne, waiting to be opened in celebration.

Glass bifold doors look out from the living area to a magnificent view that stretches out over the crystal clear blue ocean. You open the doors to the veranda and sigh. It has taken a long time, but you are finally beginning to open your eyes again, to feel happy and appreciate who you are and where you are. You are awash with gratitude for the gift of the Happiness Shack and as you allow this gratitude to wash over you, you notice hanging from the ceiling a glorious pink chandelier shining brightly, creating lightness and joy within.

Wandering around the rest of the house you discover three bedrooms decorated with funky Balinese furniture and luxurious bed clothes. The artwork is colourful and joyous, reflecting how you are starting to feel on the inside. The bathrooms are clean and crisp with big shower alcoves and fancy silver mirrors. You sneak a quick glance at yourself and notice you look healthier, with more colour in your face.

You pick up the envelope from the kitchen and return to the veranda. Peeling your eyes away from the tranquil ocean, you open the envelope to discover more about your stay here. You try to read slowly as you feel this may be the last destination you visit. You want to savour every moment, and revel in the excitement that has been missing for so long.

Your last part of the In the Pink Process is presented to you, with instructions on where each step takes place. You will need to find your own way there and you realise you are alone in this delightful place, with no reception area, just you, your knowledge, skills, attitudes and self.

In the Pink Process
Love - Truth - Purpose
Self love
Passion and purpose
A new partner
Vision and goals

The fun sparkly part is that you realise you will be discovering your dreams, passions, life purpose and the rest of your exciting future while lying on a sunny white beach soaking up the sun, boating across the waves and visiting the cafes and restaurants that line the streets.

It's your choice how you spend the time here, extracting your miracles to ensure a shiny and bright future. You decide to unpack your bags, throw on your favourite swimwear and a pretty summer dress, and go to explore the area so you will be ready for tomorrow's fun on the last leg of your journey.

You wander down the main street, taking in all the exciting new sights and smells and pass a shoe shop that tempts you to visit. Wandering in, you see all the new seasons colours and styles and immediately pick out the ones that you need to try on. Shoes have always made you feel wonderful and you know there is no way you will get to leave the shop bagless.

Your sense of guilt sneaks in as you think about the money you spend on shoes. But you decide it is time for a little celebration for your journey so far, it's time to spoil yourself after all your hard introspective work. Catching the retail assistant's attention, you ask her to bring different versions of the strappy sandals in your size. Your feet are in heaven, as you select the pair you love the most and walk out of the store joyfully, anticipating wearing your new shoes on your stay here.

You continue to wander the shops and the sights for the rest of the afternoon before you head back along the beach to the Happiness Shack, where you lie back and relish in the rest of the beautiful day.

Self Love

"You must love yourself before you love another. By accepting yourself and fully being what you are, your simple presence can make others happy. You yourself, as much as anybody in the entire universe, deserve your love and affection"

Buddha

What is self love?

You open your eyes and look out over the ocean, pondering self love whilst still snuggled in bed. As you learnt in the Flower Garden of Love, self love is the ability to accept, love, respect, honour and value the beautiful person you are, the individual that you are, that is only you.

It is the ability to be gentle and compassionate with yourself in the face of all odds. It is the ability to make decisions that are right for you, trusting your Inner Pink Star and following her signs in your journey of life. It is having the skills to competently deal with the consequences of accidentally choosing wrongly.

It is a strong, unwavering, sense of self trust and self belief, at all times and under all circumstances. It is the ability to stand proud and stand up for yourself, protecting yourself in a calm and mature way. In this place drama and chaos do not exist, as you choose not to allow them into your world.

Self love is the ability to accept, love, respect, honour and value the beautiful person you are, the individual that you are, that is only you

You are eager to learn more, internalise more. You have only touched the surface of self love and what you have learnt has already created an internal shift. So you decide to head to the beach for this next part of the In the Pink Process.

People wander happily about, but you follow the directions in your letter to a colourful Balinese beach hut surrounded by water toys. After checking in with the friendly staff you head over to find yourself a beach tent and make yourself comfortable. You lay out your hot pink beach towel, lather on the sunblock and feel the sand under your towel.

The water soon tempts you, so you venture down to the lapping waves, but find it not quite warm enough for a swim so you potter back to your tent, saying hello to all the wet fur balls on their morning walk and stopping to pat a few. You admire dogs' curiosity and their happiness with a simple life. If they could talk I am sure they would explain love for self and others succinctly and authentically. You know you wish to be around them more often, to appreciate their lessons and the love they bestow on you.

Self love

How self loving are you?

"Self love is the instrument of our preservation"

Voltaire

Despite all the work on self love, when we are honest and really look at how we have behaved, most of us at times have fallen miles short of our expectations. We constantly let ourselves down and beat ourselves up. At times we are not authentic to ourselves and have worn a mask that hides an interior of pain, instability, insecurities, bad choices, drama and chaos.

We believed we hid it well and hoped others didn't know what we were going through. We may have filled our lives with a false sense of importance, hoping it would make us feel good for at least a short period of time. Once the feeling faded, however, we found another mask to wear and hide from ourselves and others. Through your journey of healing, you have learnt that living this way means your true self is never allowed to surface, heal or shine.

You now know that those people who truly love themselves can see straight through the mask. They feel sadness, compassion and acceptance for those proudly wearing masks; they understand mainly because they have been there. They have moved through the process and found self love.

Each person can only move through their journey at their own pace, and we must honour that. Now that you have found more self love you may have noticed that you slowly separate yourself from the drama, chaos and destruction in your life. You have started to see the light and are enjoying moving to a more peaceful and contented existence.

Self love is about being able to pull yourself out of destructive situations and believing you deserve better, saying no to toxic people, places and situations and sending clear messages maintaining your self respect.

Self love is about forgiveness; having the capacity to forgive yourself for any mess ups and people you may have hurt. It also means you are able to forgive others with compassion. Forgiveness means you let go of all the bitterness, anger and resentment within and return your inner being to a peaceful calm state. People are humans and humans mess up, so use compassion and forgiveness along the way. People deserve a few chances, however not three thousand and sixty five. At some point you need to stop, value yourself and walk away.

Self love is about removing all the unnecessary childish drama from your life, whether self created or self imposed, that you use to create distraction or self importance. Instead, you can use self love to craft a life encompassed by peace and calm. You can remove the false and damaging adrenaline rush that masks itself in importance, excitement and fun.

Self love is about stopping when you feel overwhelmed, realising when you need to take time out to care for yourself and your physical and emotional wellbeing. Self love is about having a mammoth to do list and getting half way through, then saying to yourself 'enough for today. I am tired and I need to rest', then believing that you are worthy of that rest. Looking outwardly busy and important is a sign of worthiness for many of us. However it is not impressive to work so hard that you crash and burn. Self love is understanding that by continuing to push yourself beyond your limits, you risk burnout or physical injury.

Self love is the ability to say no

Self love is about having laser sharp self awareness so that you can understand what is happening internally and what you need in that moment to move forward in a healthy fashion.

SELF LOVE

Self love is about having fun, having heartfelt tears running down your face from laughter. It is being able to let go of the stresses and struggles of life, be in the moment and just enjoy. When you love yourself you know exactly what gives you pleasure and fun and will seek it daily.

Self love is about being self expressive and appreciating expression's positive impact. It may be yoga, writing, art, dancing, singing, Pilates, running or church. However you feel most comfortable, allow your being to express itself naturally in the way it has been designed to do.

Self love gives you the ability to stand solid in yourself, not needing to impress others. You are able to sit quietly with an internal love that requires only your own acceptance. The anxiety and constant energy required to impress others is released.

Self love is the ability to say 'I love me' and feel the warm tingly feelings inside that come from true gratitude, acceptance and a solid belief that it is true.

BEING SELF LOVING IS BEING...

Loveable	In control
Worthy	Peaceful
Connected	Relaxed
Belonging	Important
Good enough	Trusting
Significant	Calm
Visible	Confident
Powerful	Valued
Capable	

I love me

You stop to appreciate the white sand and the clear blue waters, bringing your focus back to the here and now. You dig your feet deeper into the sand and are still, allowing yourself to be immersed in the warmth of the day and the atmosphere on the beach.

You know the benefits of self love and know it holds the key to happiness at another level. You lie down on your beach towel in your shady tent and be with this knowledge and feeling as more lessons are delivered to you on the white sandy beach.

MINDFULNESS IN THE MAKING

"Contentment is the greatest treasure"

Lao Tzu

Mindfulness is 'the intentional, accepting and non-judgmental focus of one's attention on the emotions, thoughts and sensations occurring in the present moment'.

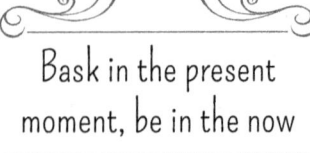

Bask in the present moment, be in the now

Wow, the definition itself creates hope of an inner peaceful and calm existence. It offers the type of happiness we seek and yet struggle to find in this life full of business and chaos.

Mindfulness is a relatively new topic in Western philosophy, however it is an ancient practice in the East, involving

Self Love

consciously bringing awareness to the present moment and its experience, with openness and interest.

Eckhart Tolle in his book 'The Power of Now' demystifies this theory. He explains how we are the creators of our own pain and, by living fully in the present moment, we can have a pain-free existence. It's that simple, really.

An easy way to see mindfulness in action is to wash your hands. Yes, that's right, such a simple way to practise a complex concept. When you are washing your hands, turn on the tap and place your hands under the water. Consciously experience the water falling onto your hands. Notice the pressure, the temperature, the feeling, the noise it creates. Enjoy and be grateful for each feeling and sensation. In this way, something as simple as washing your hands can become a pleasurable experience.

Next time you go for a walk, consciously feel the wind on your skin. Notice the temperature of the air, the sounds up close and in the distance. Look at the sights, feel your feet in your shoes touching the ground. Keep walking and keep your mind in the moment. When your thoughts wander off, gently bring them back to the now and try again. By the time you return from your walk you will notice the calm happiness that you carry.

Practising mindfulness is easier when you are doing things you love and that connect you to yourself. For me, that is walking my dogs, Pilates and swimming. I love these physical activities so I am able to achieve a mindful state more easily when I am doing them.

During the breakdown of my relationship, I would greet the pavement for about an hour every day with my pooches. No matter how inconvenient it was, I continued to invest my time and undivided love and attention to my dogs, as they bring me tremendous joy. It was on our walks that I had the space to think, feel and heal. It was here I learnt what self love was, bit by bit. I was in a walking meditation and resting my crazy thoughts for a short moment in time. A little like at my Pilates classes, my mind stopped and even if thoughts appeared, they no longer bothered me.

This enabled me to walk around our glorious park-lined suburbs, literally stopping to smell the flowers, talking to other dog owners and appreciating nature. It was like being on holidays when in reality I was just around the corner from home. My mindset was awesomely calm.

> "Whoever said that diamonds are a girl's best friend never had a dog"
>
> Anonymous

When my mind was quiet like this, any lingering anxiety and depression lifted, and a sense of clarity emerged. Things were great. If only I could keep that pattern of thought all day, but invariably it was short lived, as my thoughts returned to remind me I had a decision to make about my relationship and my insides were not allowing me to ignore it for much longer.

Each time we enter the green grass of the park, Suzy looks up at me asking me to take off her lead. I am totally captivated every single time I slip off her lead and watch the joy in her eyes and the wiggle in her butt as she races into the park and nosedives. I am fascinated by the joy a well-looked-after dog has, of being and loving life and each moment they are given.

You will notice that dogs rest a lot, love a lot, eat well and smile. They use all the self love tools so easily, yet we as humans complicate things and make self love difficult. Dogs can teach us so much about living simply.

They can teach you that you need to let go sometimes, let go of the stress and the problems. Give yourself space to breathe and figure out what you need without making it harder by beating yourself up at every turn. Switch off your mind and let the thoughts pass through. Observe them but do not attach to them. When you

SELF LOVE

are able to manage this, you will find a calm and peaceful space waiting that is a heaven in the mind.

Once you are able to achieve mindfulness doing what you love, you can incorporate it into other activities. Slowly you will be able to access this state so much more often and experience true happiness in more and more of your life. Of course there will be times you still get caught up in past/future mind games but you will be aware of what is happening. This will give you the hint to stop, move out and come back to mindfulness.

The moments of love and peace that descend on you are the moments indicating you have got it. When you are mindful is when you become the person you want to be, the person who loves everything, the weather, be it stormy or sunny, other people and their dogs, the grass at the park, the flowers in people's gardens. You can walk through your day in authentic happiness, smiling at everyone and everything because you feel so loving towards everything. It is like walking on a white fluffy cloud, so free and peaceful.

Of course it would be much easier to master this skill if you were a monk sitting on a mountain top for months on end, but you are not. So you need to practise on the background of your own life, and be grateful for the snippets that appear, that bring the realisation that this state is in fact real and attainable. The more time you dedicate to practise, the more often you will spend residing in your new loving mindful state.

 ## PINK TIME OUT – QUESTION TIME

✿ Stop and Breathe ✿

Read the list of questions below and allow time and space for self reflection. In your Little Pink book of Love, rate your responses to the following statements from a 0 - 10,

10 being the best. As this may take you out of your comfort zone, remember to remain gentle and compassionate with yourself, and always come from a place of love.

This will give you another gauge to see how you are going in these areas and how you are progressing with improving your self love.

1. I know who I am.
2. I know what I want.
3. I respect and honour myself.
4. I care for myself and put my physical wellbeing first.
5. I stop and take a rest when I need to.
6. I remove myself from toxic situations or people.
7. I say no when I mean no.
8. I laugh every day.
9. I have forgiven myself for past mess-ups.
10. I have forgiven everyone I am angry at.
11. I express myself outwardly.
12. I have an awareness about who I am and what I need.
13. I trust everything will turn out okay.
14. I am able to put aside my to do list and relax.
15. I have an unwavering self belief.
16. I have confidence and high self esteem.
17. I trust me.
18. I like hanging out with me.
19. I accept my flaws and imperfections.
20. I am able to detach and observe my mind when it gets chaotic.
21. I love me.

SELF LOVE

Well done on another reflection and your courage to go deeper every time. I hope this exercise has provided you with some clarity about how much you love, cherish and look after yourself.

If you rated highly on this exercise, take the time to celebrate how far you have come and what you have achieved on your journey so far.

On the other hand, if you rated lower than you had hoped, do not berate yourself. Remember that you are here on your journey learning new skills and tools to take into your life. You are not expected to know all these things at a certain point. Allow yourself to be in a learning phase and keep moving forward. Place trust in yourself and focus on the positive growth you have already achieved.

"All his life he tried to be a good person.
Many times, however, he failed. For after all,
he was only human. He wasn't a dog"

Charles M. Schulz

As the day warms up, you head to the water to feel its coolness on your body. Pondering what you have learnt so far, you appreciate a break from your thoughts and your lessons. You relax in the water and watch the children, parents and dogs having a fabulous day at the beach.

You stop and give thanks for today. You relish the present moment and what it is offering you and, after letting a big smile escape to your lips, you walk slowly back to your beach tent for your next lesson.

ADORABLE AFFIRMATIONS

"Whether you think you can or you can't, you are right"

Henry Ford

Our mind has about 50,000 thoughts per day and with 80 percent of these being negative it gives us motivation to improve the way our minds work and what we create in our lives.

Affirmations help you to take back control of your mind and filter the messages you choose to send to the subconscious, rather than sending your automatic thoughts. You are now on the path to happiness, and affirmations will help fill your mind with positive rather than negative thoughts.

Affirmations are short and succinct statements you can repeat through the day. Your subconscious mind cannot differentiate between good or bad, true or false, so affirmations used repetitively will form new messages that will filter to your subconscious mind.

Like a visualisation, an affirmation states something as if it is already happening. For example you would say 'I am loving' rather than 'I want be loving one day'. Speak the affirmation in the now, so you are acting as if you already have what you want.

What you think and the images you put in your mind will become your reality. Choose to put your efforts into creating positive affirmations and images to boost your thoughts, feelings, behaviours and life.

The first step is to decide which affirmations you will use. This will be guided by the specific goals you are working towards or the areas of your life you are currently improving. Use 'I can', 'I am', or 'I will' as sentence starters for your statements.

Self love

You can use an affirmation to counteract a negative thought that is recurring in your mind. For instance, if you find yourself thinking 'I am so disorganised', your affirmation could be 'I am becoming more organised every day'. When the negative thought appears, say your affirmation and repeat, repeat. Over time, this will help to minimise the negative thought, as the positive affirmation will have filtered to the subconscious and changed the pattern.

Work with only a few affirmations at once, then change them when you feel they have done their work or you are ready to move on. Each day while walking my dogs I put my affirmations on repeat in my head, along with my visualisations. The combination was very powerful and started to change my reality.

Some days this process will be easy and fill you with joy, and on other days you will feel that no matter what positive statement you say to yourself, a deeper feeling is pulling you back into the negative and you feel at a loss to stop it. That's okay; be patient, give it time, practise.

The important thing when you are having a bad day is to avoid adding more negative thoughts into the already negative mix. Allow yourself compassion and forgiveness, then try again later. Tiredness, stress and other external factors can make using these powerful skills very difficult. A 'never give up' mindset and loads of compassion will help you continue moving forward.

Pink Time Out – Affirmations

Stop and Breathe

If you would like a kickstart to find the right affirmations for you, choose some from the list below. Choose the ones that are relevant for you and say them over and over until they sink in. Trust me, sometimes you need to fake it till you make it. If you repeat affirmations enough they will eventually sink into the subconscious.

'I am enough just the way I am today'

'I am doing the best I can with what I know right now'

'I am amazing just the way I am'

'I am loved and loveable'

'I do not need to be perfect to be enough'

'I love me'

'I am a good person. Actually, I am a great person'

'It does not matter what others think of me, it matters what I think of me'

'I trust myself implicitly'

'I believe in myself completely'

'I will stay true to my authentic self'

'I am proud of what I am learning every day'

'I value me'

'I forgive me'

'I am healing'

'I respect my experiences and my losses'

'I accept myself wholly'

'I will do whatever it takes to gain internal fulfilment'

'I am calm and peaceful'

'I need to please me, not everyone else'

'I put myself first'

'I take good care of myself'

'I deserve a peaceful, beautiful life'

'I have faith in my journey, and trust in the flow of life'

'I am safe just as I am'

Self Love

'The universe will provide'

'I have everything I need inside me'

'I deserve to be loved'

'I will always be there for me'

'I am amazing'

Choose the affirmations that speak deeply to you. Make a promise to yourself that you will put them on repeat in your head.

To remind yourself of your affirmations and keep them at the forefront of your mind, post note them on your desk, lipstick them to your mirror in the bathroom, blackboard them in the kids' playroom, magnet them on the fridge, put them on your sun visor in the car or put them on a card in your handbag. Whatever works for you; just use them and wait to feel the difference.

Stop and check in every now and then, to notice any changes that appear in your internal landscape. Push the shuffle and repeat button and swap your affirmations around. Keep working on them and you will notice the surprising benefits over time.

You find yourself dosing off with your feet in the warm sand after taking in all this new information. Awakened by barking from a nearby pooch, you decide to pack up your beach bag and stroll home. Walking slowly up the beach, you feel more connected and a have a sense of belonging, even if only to yourself. You walk slowly and gracefully, practising your affirmations with each step.

You stop at the local café for a latte and a little people-watching on the way back to the shack. Arriving home, you open the bifold doors and glimpse the champagne in the corner of your eye and stop to put it in the fridge so it's chilled when the time is right. For now though, you walk to the veranda and sit on the wicker lounge, nestle in and enjoy just being and living.

Passion and purpose

*"Everyone has been made for some particular work,
and the desire for that work has been put in every heart"*

Rumi

Feeling relaxed and rejuvenated from your early night, you rise and take a long walk before the town comes alive for the day. Going over what you learnt yesterday, you are able to access the self love feelings a little more and allow them to permeate through you.

Walking along the quiet streets, you reflect on how far you have come since the Heartbreak Manor and how much you have learnt. Your emotional and physical strength is returning and you give thanks to all the learnings that have so far presented themselves to you.

Spying a few dogs heading your way, you stop to give them a quick hello and a pat and feel the love for these happy bouncy creatures. Things really are starting to appear brighter. Walking back to the Happiness Shack, you wonder about the plans for today and what will unfold.

You muster up a little skip up the garden path to the front door, then jump in the shower and gather your beach bag together once again. Heading down to the beach, you are directed to a gorgeous boat that houses a kitchen, two bedrooms, a lounge and a lovely sunbathing area on the deck.

Hopping on board, you are told your day will be spent cruising around. You look forward to snorkelling, sun and a yummy lunch along with your next lesson.

Leap of Faith

"Sometimes you just have to take the leap and build your wings on the way down"

Kobi Yamada

Faith will allow you to follow your Inner Pink Star and your passions to create the rich meaningful life you deserve. Life is too short to trudge around complaining about hating your job, not wanting to get out of bed and feeling numb about your future. You know with all your heart you don't want to live in a state of helplessness, watching the years pass by, growing grey and doing nothing about it.

Following your Inner Pink Star may be the way to proceed, but it can be hard to know what she wants you to do. Do you struggle to understand exactly how you want to live your life, and how you can translate that into earning a living? This lack of direction could see you continuing to live in your uncomfortable comfort zone and you know that you want more than that.

Imagine waking up every day, opening your eyes and feeling your body pumping with energy, jumping out of bed, excited and enthused by what the day holds, ready to live out your life purpose. You feel alive, excited, enthused and creative. You barely want to stop for breakfast because you are so keen to get started for the day. This could be your reality. For some people only a

Passion and purpose

small change is needed to energise your career and for others it is a huge shuffle around and takes resignations and business loans to see your dreams come to fruition.

This can involve you taking a risk, so you need to have your self love on board, trust yourself fully and have faith in the journey. No more excuses. The time has come to take responsibility for your life, start creating and watch your passions unfold. If you choose not to, nothing will change. Even if it is only one small step at a time, start making some changes. Small changes today can equate to big changes a year from now and a totally new life ten years from now.

Your purpose may be landscaping and pruning roses, or singlehandedly designing the best and most delicious menu for a restaurant full of hungry mouths. What lights up one person could be a daily slog for another; everyone has their own light switch.

We are all put here on this earth with a purpose, we just need to spend time uncovering the gift. When you have found it you will know, because everything feels right. Your inner self lights up so brightly you can feel the heat. You feel purposeful, connected, useful and confident. You jump out of bed every day with an inner excitement, aliveness and enthusiasm. You feel inside you are doing what you are meant to be doing, you feel you can offer the world your best self and help others, you are unstoppable.

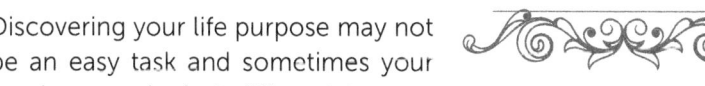

Passions and purpose create an exciting aliveness within

Discovering your life purpose may not be an easy task and sometimes your passions are in fact different to your life purpose, so be careful with your search, watch out for signs, be aware and pay attention to your feelings.

I have spent many years studying and improving my skills, completing many diplomas and certificates, always following my passions. As I would embark on a new qualification I would think 'This is it. I know what I want to do. This passion is my purpose'. My mind would get busy creating business opportunities and strategies to incorporate this new passion into my life as my new career, and then as quickly as I got started, things fell apart.

At one point I attended Pilates at least four times a week. I loved it; my body felt so good, the neck and back pain I was suffering had disappeared. It provided me with a serene space and snippets of spirituality, with meditation sessions at the end of our classes.

I decided I wanted to become an instructor, so I sought out a good school and enrolled. The diligent student I am, I completed my certificate and received excellent marks, then accepted a position teaching Pilates at the same studio.

I continued to learn, read and research and people loved my teaching style and enthusiasm. There was a minor glitch though, every time I sat at home and thought about teaching a class I felt drained. I would get to the class and enjoy teaching and afterwards I would feel rewarded, so I couldn't put my finger on the reason I felt so drained at the thought of going to teach.

I racked my brain for a while, but finally realised that as much as I loved to attend Pilates classes, it was not my life purpose to teach it. Pilates was my passion but it was not what I was put on this earth to do. I finally accepted that this was just the way it was, so continued attending classes but resigned from teaching.

After a few similar scenarios I started to lose hope. Why had I continued to follow my passions and complete these studies when nothing transpired into a life purpose? For a while I became disheartened about completing another course as I believed the same thing would happen. I would invest time, money and energy and love attending the course, get tremendously excited but it wouldn't go any further; once I finished the course my enthusiasm to make a living from it waned.

Passion and purpose

I continued seeking the thing I would jump out of bed for. I created an affirmation 'It will all fall into place at some stage'. I believed that if I continued to follow my passions in the personal development and health arena, one day they would all come together and present my life purpose to me on a silver platter. I continued to believe in myself, even though it was difficult at times.

Follow your heart

Well guess what, it worked. I found something I loved to think about doing before I did it, I loved doing it while I was doing it and I loved the feeling afterwards. I would get up early in the morning to work and at times work late into the night. I could spend a whole day working and only stop for a few cups of tea, or when Suzy wanted to be walked. It was a combination of all that I had learnt, all I had studied and all the passions in my life.

Writing my book, dreaming of many more and starting my Life In the Pink business was my life purpose. It incorporated my different studies, certificates, diplomas, knowledge, passions and experience. Once I realised this, it all felt different. It didn't drain me or cause me to lose enthusiasm when I thought about it; it felt right.

My faith in finding my life purpose was restored and I felt wonderful. Life started to appear more purposeful in general when I had a bigger picture laid out in front of me. I had a reason for being on this earth, I had a purpose. It had taken twelve years of study and life experience before I actually worked it out, but all along I knew that one day it would be presented to me, I just needed to continue to believe and take small steps in the right direction.

Please, please, please don't give up. Continue to follow your heart, appreciate the journey, try different things, live in the moment, shake it up a bit and things will change. Your purpose will appear. Staying dormant, complaining and trudging through life will never reveal your purpose, your dreams or your best self higher calling.

Diving deep into the waters for a snorkel in between lessons creates a sense of freedom and release. The water is cool and inviting and you feel liberated and alive. Exploring the waters reminds you of the self exploration journey you have been on for some time now. Never knowing what is around the corner but preparing yourself for whatever may appear, you are starting to realise you can cope with anything.

Looking down you notice a big stingray lying still on the floor of the ocean and feel yourself wanting to move away, a touch of fear lodged in your heart. You stay calm, appreciate the moment to view the ray and as you move away, thank him for his appearance. You give him the nickname Mr Ray and move on to see what else waits to be discovered. The next moment, a clown fish darts in front of you and you follow him intently with your eyes until he swims back to seek protection in his anemone.

Later, as you enjoy lunch on the deck, you think of your snorkelling experience and are grateful for a wonderful day and come to understand the value of living life like a day of snorkelling; if you search, seek, have patience and allow life to unfold, anything may occur.

The anchor is pulled up and as the engines slowly fire up, the boat gracefully moves from its spot heading to a new location, a new lesson and new experiences.

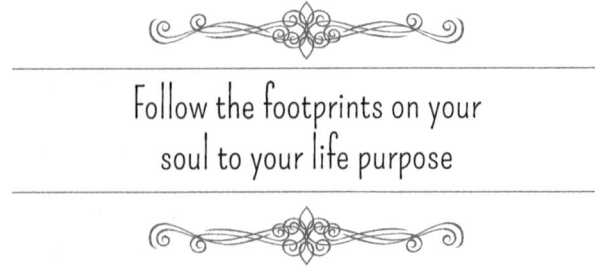

Follow the footprints on your soul to your life purpose

Pink Time Out – Question Time

Stop and Breathe

Read the list of questions below and allow time and space for self reflection. In your Little Pink book of Love, record your thoughts, feelings, reactions and any epiphanies and wow moments you may have about your life purpose. Let the pen flow and see what appears on the page in front of you. As this may take you out of your comfort zone, remember to remain gentle and compassionate with yourself, and always come from a place of love.

Create some time and space in your busy mind to fully focus on these questions and draw out the hidden gems lying dormant. Review the points in your Pink Heart Print to help you answer some of these questions.

1. Write a list of all the things you are really, really good at.
2. Write a list of all the things you love doing that make you feel excited, alive and enthused.
3. Write a list of what you loved doing when you were a child.
4. What are you doing when you lose track of time?
5. When you have free time, what do you naturally gravitate to?
6. If you were guaranteed that you would be successful at anything, what would you do?
7. If you were told today you had one year to live, what would you do?

8. If money was no object and was on continuous flow, what would you do?
9. What would you do if you won a million dollars cash, tax free, in the lottery today?
10. What is the greatest vision you have for your life?
11. What do you most enjoy doing? What gives you your greatest feeling of self-esteem and personal satisfaction?
12. If you were following your heart, what would you do?
13. What have you always wanted to do but been too afraid to attempt?
14. What one great thing would you dare to do if you knew you could not fail?
15. You are sitting at the back of the church as your eulogy is read out. What does it say?
16. Visualise lying on your deathbed. What did you miss out on, what are your regrets?
17. What will you regret if you don't do it? How can you make it happen?
18. How can you have the greatest positive impact in your life?
19. What can you do to create the life you really want?
20. What is the greatest gift you can give yourself?
21. What do you need to do to know that you have lived a full and meaningful life?
22. What do you want to be remembered for?
23. What are the ten things you still want to do in your life?

24. Are you living any parts of your dreams and life purpose already?

25. Is there any one thing you can make a change to right NOW?

26. Once more, if you had all the money in the world and you never needed to work ever, ever again what would you do to occupy your time?

Well done on your reflection and your courage to go deeper and flush out your passions. I hope this exercise has provided you with clarity that you can use as your move forward through the process of healing and discovering your passions and purpose.

DIG A LITTLE DEEPER

"Sometimes we have to dig a little deeper to reach a little higher"

AC Anderson

Listening to your feelings once again is imperative. To know, understand, trust and believe you are on the right path, you must trust yourself and how you feel. If you feel alive and renewed you may well be on the right path. If you feel drained and tied up in knots you are probably following the wrong path. Stop, be aware and check in.

The process of elimination works well during this phase, journaling about the things you love and the things you dislike, referring back to your Pink Heart Print. Try highlighting areas that you would like to be part of your ideal picture and also documenting features you want to ensure are not included.

Think about it as designing your perfect purpose. Add a little bit of this and a little bit of that. Use meditation to sit with your feelings and see if you are on the correct path as your ideal picture unfolds.

Continue adding to your picture as you try new things. It doesn't matter if you try something and feel it is not for you, there is always a gift or a learning experience that you can use to benefit the picture you are designing for your future.

When purposes entwine

"Your purpose in life is to find your purpose and give your whole heart and soul to it"

Gautama Buddha

I am blessed to have two life purposes. First is my Life In the Pink business, my book and anything surrounding personal development, and my second purpose is advocating for the physical and emotional health of our four-legged furry friends. I just have to take one look into any big or small brown eyes and I am mush. I would do anything for them.

I collect strays and return them home and spend time at the park every day entertaining Suzy and her friends. I stop and talk to every dog I pass, which drives my friends and family mad. When I travel, I take photos of all the foreign-speaking dogs. I once stopped a lady in a street in Rome to tell her the ground was way too hot for

Passion and purpose

her pooch's paws and she should pick her dog up, in my messy mishmash of Italian and English.

I am the girl that would prefer to stay home Saturday night and be with Suzy than be out dancing the night away. She is my family and I adore being in her company. She provides me love, laughter, cuddles and fun every minute we are together.

Many years ago, after leaving the corporate world that housed no soul, I was fortunate to be offered a role at a veterinary hospital as their Business Manager. For ten years our team developed, evolved and grew the veterinary business.

I loved going to work. I adored the team, the role was varied, challenging and rewarding, the location and facilities were excellent, the clients and patients were amazing and the owner an inspirational mentor, friend and boss.

The company grew, we were very successful and eventually we developed a more corporate feel and structure. That's when I started to struggle. I felt disempowered, that my voice no longer mattered after being such a big influence in the business for so long. The values of the business felt like they were changing rapidly and appeared grey to me, rather than solid as they had always been. For six months I struggled with the changes until I began to think I couldn't cope any more. This type of victim thinking of course made me feel even more flat, anxious and depressed.

After a while I realised the 'I can't cope' thought pattern was easy because I could sit in my space being uncomfortable, blaming others and not making a decision.

I started to question my thought pattern, and realised 'Actually I can cope but I don't want to'. The victim mentality left me and was replaced with empowerment and inner strength. This new thought pattern gave me responsibility for my life and allowed me to make the hard decision to resign from my much loved role.

It was a hard choice to make, and a small part of me wasn't sure that I was doing the right thing. However my Inner Pink Star held my hand as I handed in my resignation and helped me to feel free and liberated. I did not yet know what was next, but I knew no matter what it would turn out for the best and there would be diamonds around the corner, because I believed in myself. Almost straight away I was offered a role at another vet clinic, a smaller clinic with the grass-roots values that meant so much to me.

The point of my story is to follow your heart, take action, find your life purpose and get busy living the dream. I am now privileged to work in a great vet clinic doing what I love part time, which allows time for my other purpose of creating a personal development business. It took a lot of work to make it happen, but with trust and self love I created it and so can you.

The boat pulls back to the beach early in the afternoon and as your feet touch the warm sand you feel invigorated and refreshed after a day of fun, participating in the joy of life once again.

Deliberating your passions and purpose and remembering your snorkelling experience, you notice people and dogs are busy everywhere and the atmosphere is alive and buzzing. While you are a little closer to realising your life purpose, for now your only purpose is to enjoy this moment. You decide it is time to visit the shops before heading back to the Happiness Shack for a relaxing evening. Maybe there is something you can buy as a memento of your stay here and the day that you explored your life purpose.

My New Partner

"A healthy relationship doesn't drag you down, it inspires you to be better"

Mandy Hale

On awakening, you realise you've slept in, this almost never happens. A sense of peace and relaxation washes over you, as you have no place to be and no to-do list to tick off. You realise you have the whole day free to explore. You slowly get yourself ready and, closing the door behind you, breathe the warm air deep into your lungs as you take the first steps of a beautiful walk to unearth glorious local treasures, friendly people, more wet, sandy dogs and many kind thoughts.

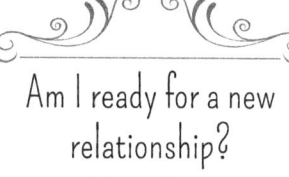

Am I ready for a new relationship?

After a satisfying day wandering the shops, swimming at the beach and spoiling yourself in the cafés, you return to the house for an indulgent nap before you get ready for your lesson tonight. It actually sounds like a dinner date - your instructions are to be at the local Italian restaurant, La Bellissima, at 8pm.

Seated at a table for one in a cute little black dress really puts you out of your comfort zone. Champagne and hors d'oeuvres are served as you sit self consciously alone. You muster your new skills and decide to stop listening to Lady Chitter Chatter, worry less about what others think, go with your Inner Pink Star and enjoy the night. You allow yourself to be on your own at this lovely restaurant as you take in your next lesson.

Throwing yourself into another relationship, or even thinking about dating can be anxiety-building and scary. For many who have been badly hurt and have spent valuable days and months rebuilding it is a daunting thought. Relearning how to treasure the new-found, healed version of you, creating self love and living a fulfilling, peaceful life is something that still needs to be nurtured. Perhaps you feel confident and alive, ready to take the plunge and test out your newly found skills and authentic self. But for some, the new version of you still feels a little fragile, as if one wrong move could tear it all down. You are still building up your trust muscles to become confident in your abilities to maintain this state.

Wherever you stand now, after the healing work you have done, knowing when the time is right to venture back into the dating world can be a really hard decision to make. You need to listen to your heart and your Inner Pink Star. Some days you may feel confident, sexy and available, excited about the prospect of a new date, yet something inside prevents you from making your next move.

Do what feels right; listen to your Inner Pink Star

Don't try to push yourself, this is all just part of the process; when the time is right you will know. If you have been attentive to your Inner Pink Star you will have started to feel when things are right for you and when you still need to sit back and wait it out a little longer. Patience is a hard lesson to learn, but one that is imperative to master to have a calm and content life. Be prepared to stop, think, be aware, listen to yourself and act in accordance with your values when you are ready.

My New Partner

Your body, your mind, your emotions and every part of you is sacred, so don't give any of these aspects of yourself to anyone until you are absolutely sure you are ready. Treat all the parts of yourself with respect, gentleness and love. After all the work you have done, it's important to avoid choosing a new partner just to fill an empty space in your life. It may feel good to have the company and attention in the short term, but disrespecting your body, mind and soul will take you backwards in the long term.

The time will be right when you feel healed, alive, enthusiastic, proud, peaceful, calm and content with your life. It will be right when you trust with every cell you are able to cope with whatever is thrown at you, do things at your own pace, and have the ability to say no when needed.

If you dive back in too early you could be too needy and not yet healed. This can drive away the person who is the perfect fit, and can also attract the same type of person you've recently spent months getting over. If you decide to have casual flings to prevent opening up and being vulnerable to anyone, you put yourself in danger of more damage to your fragile self esteem and confidence.

The only real way to put your best self out in the world is when you are truly happy and authentic with who you are. Battle all your inner demons and feel good about yourself. You then will feel better about any potential dates or relationships and this is the sure-fire way to attract a partner aligned with your solid values. You will also hold confidence to move past people that do not respect your space and values. Just be comfortable in your own skin.

Pink Time Out – Quiz

～ Stop and Breathe ～

This little quiz will provide reflection and help create awareness of how you feel about relationships and if you are ready to begin to explore this. Have fun.

- Are you able to talk about your breakup without dissolving into tears?
- Have you honesty closed the option of a reconciliation?
- Are you able to listen to sad break up songs without getting upset?
- Are you happy sitting at home on your own on a Saturday night if there is nothing fun happening?
- Do you choose to have a night in to spend time with yourself?
- Are you able to say no to invitations if you feel you want a night at home alone?
- Do you treasure and protect your space and time?
- Do you respect and honour your body, mind and spirit?
- Do you feel the time is right to look at dating again?
- Can you honestly say you want to date because you want someone in your life rather than needing someone to fill the empty space?
- Are you able to protect your boundaries?
- Have you learnt from your last relationship to prevent making the same mistakes?

- Are you open to communication and discussion in your relationships?
- Do you continue with your life without hoping a new partner will appear at every corner?
- Are you designing your life and following your dreams even while you are single?
- Are you filling your time with your own interests and friends and enjoying your chosen activities?
- Are you able to take things slowly in a new relationship to ensure you are investing time in someone who deserves your time, love and attention?
- Are you able to cope with rejection in a mature, adult way without crumbling?
- Are you able to take responsibility for your life and not blame others or play victim when things go haywire?
- Are you able to express and process all your emotions in a healthy fashion?
- Do you know beyond a show of a doubt that, regardless of what happens with your next partner, you are able to healthily deal with whatever the situation presents?
- Do you feel proud of who you are, what you say, how you treat people and your actions?
- Are you your best self?

How did you go? There are no right or wrong answers, these questions are simply a tool to provide you with more insight into yourself. Think about what the answers have revealed to you. Have they helped you to access yourself more and allowed your truth to surface in regards to starting dating again?

After completing this exercise, you may feel ready to be open to a new relationship and if so that's great, you have come a long way. If however you still are cautious and are not quite ready that is great also, you are aware of yourself and are honouring yourself and your feelings.

The main thing is that you are honouring your truth and doing what is in your emotional best interests.

Healthy vs Unhealthy

"To be fully seen by somebody, then, and be loved anyhow – this is a human offering that can border on miraculous"

Elizabeth Gilbert

Natural spring water is delivered to your table, to balance out the champagne as you take in what you have learnt so far. You can't believe you have come this far and are actually thinking about dating again. On top of that you are happily sitting at a table alone in a little black dress. You envisage one day sitting here with a new partner and although you still feel like it may be an impossibility

My new partner

to find that person after all that you have been through, you feel hope that it will happen one day.

You order your next course and choose Gnocchi Ragu as you have heard whispers from other tables that it is just like Nonna used to make. As your mouth waters waiting patiently for Nonna to deliver on her dish, you dive deeper into your lessons for tonight.

You have decided it is the time to put your beautiful self out there. It may have been a while since you dated and before you take any big steps in your life it is good to reflect and ensure you have your values solid and know what you are looking for and what to avoid at all costs.

Consider how you feel when you are around a potential partner. You will always know if he is good or toxic for you by how you feel about yourself in his presence. If you feel your solid authentic, happy self, he may be the one. If however you feel you need to constantly chase him, impress him, appease him or mother him you may be heading down a road to heartbreak once again. Trust how you feel while you are in his company. You have now done the work to know you can trust your decisions and intuition.

Watch how you feel about yourself around him

Any relationship that drains you, empties you of your precious energy, takes more than it gives, expects support but offers none, expects you to entertain them without equality is a disaster waiting to happen to your self esteem and confidence. These relationships can be labelled toxic.

A good relationship will motivate, inspire, lift you and bring out the best of your best. You will feel you can move mountains, that anything is possible. This partner will be your proudest supporter and cheerleader, making you feel you are able to achieve anything. You will be excited to speak with him and look forward to conversations. You will grow in his presence and advocate his growth. You will be by each other's sides supporting each other 100 percent of the time.

The reason a good relationship works so well is that there is peace, calm, maturity, open communication, honesty, constructive feedback and mutual respect. There are no childish tantrums, inappropriate attacks on self worth, lies, hot-headed outbursts, immature blame and shame or screaming matches. Instead, there are two individuals who are able to take responsibility for their own feelings, have rational discussions and respect, paving a way forward and preparing for when challenges occur.

In every relationship there is anger and frustration. Choose to express these with respect

It is a luxury, not a right, to have someone in your life at a close level. Never allow someone to make you feel obliged; you choose who you help, who you invest time in. Sometimes you have to pull back to look after your own heart and sanity. That is the gift at the other end of creating self love; you will know when you need this to happen and will have the strength to implement appropriate boundaries.

This is a big list of requirements and it is a big ask of a relationship. But you deserve to have a good relationship; you have worked hard and know that the best way to achieve a relationship like this is to be the person you want to find. Go inside and check that you are walking the talk of what you are looking for. Once you can do that, you will find that perfect person for you. Then you can start living your very own version of your fairy tale.

The gnocchi is served as the lesson concludes, so you decide to be in the moment and savour each piece of gnocchi as an orgasmic delight before you move on to the next exercise.

As you put your Little Pink book of Love down, you give thanks to Nonna for being a fabulous Italian cook and then notice the chandeliers glowing over your scrumptious meal and the patrons around the restaurant. The chandeliers speak to you 'Hey look at me, I'm shining brightly just for you'. Be proud of what you are achieving and remember to share the thanks with your beautiful heart and soul. Your heart which is lighting up more and more each day and glowing to the world.

Pink Time Out – Reflection

⚘ Stop and Breathe ⚘

In this exercise you will reflect on your past relationships to draw out patterns, beliefs or situations that you found yourself in. Looking at the past and waking up to your patterns can help you make a different choice for the future.

Take out your Little Pink book of Love and write the names of the partners that you have been in a serious relationship with over your lifetime. Put a line down the middle of the page and list the positive and negative qualities of each partner. On another page list the positive and negative traits of the relationship you were in with them.

1. What are the similarities in the partners and the relationships?
2. Which common traits stand out again and again?
3. Which traits do you dislike the most?
4. Were your partners the same people with a different face and name?
5. Does this help to determine your pattern in the men you attract?

This exercise can be very enlightening especially if, like me, you realise you created the same type of relationship with different partners. Spend some time thinking about this as it may surprise and wake you up enough to make a different choice for your future.

Pink time out – Magic wand

 Stop and Breathe

The fairy godmother has returned and I am waving my magic wand again. Enjoy!

You can now be in a relationship with whoever you want to. You are free of any of your old negative behaviours. When you are with him you feel like the queen of your castle, a goddess. He loves you unconditionally and admires every inch of you. He respects and honours your imperfections.

In this exercise you will create three lists to help unravel exactly what you desire in your new partner. In your Little Pink Book of Love, rule a fresh page into three columns and label them as below.

1. Important traits (Important but not imperative traits to have)
2. Deal breakers (Must have traits)
3. Red flags (Traits to avoid)

Rather than focussing on his physical qualities such as hair or height, think about the spiritual connection you wish to have, how your soul relates to his, the deep qualities you would like in this person who will be closest to you in your life.

Who is he? What attributes does he have? What do you admire about him? What do you think about yourself when you are with him? How does he hold himself? How does he treat you? How do you feel when you are around him? What type of energy does he dispel? What makes you proud of him? What do others say about him?

Make a list of all the qualities you want for him. Add all of these into the important column. Use these sentence starters for help. Dream away, think outside the box, visualise yourself with this new man. Who is he?

He is...
He feels...
He is good at...
I am proud of him for...
His best attributes are...
Others comment that he is...
Others feel jealous that he...
I so want him to be...
I hope he is...
If I could I would want him to be...

Next we are going to look at the deal breakers. It is beneficial to split the deal breakers from the important to absolutely understand what is not negotiable. This will help you know what you will walk away from immediately, versus the important traits, which are what you would like, and are important, but you may be able to compromise or negotiate around.

An example of a deal breaker may be that he must love animals and be willing to have them in his life. For me if he does not like animals and does not want to be around them I would not even enter into the idea of a relationship. For you, those deal breakers may have to do with religion, or willingness to have children, or something else that you know you must have to be happy.

Add all your deal breakers to your Little Pink book of Love.

You may have some attributes in the important column that you realise are deal breakers, so move them over to the deal breaker column in your Little Pink book of Love. Or there may be attributes that are so inherent to who you are that you haven't written them at all. This is your chance to express your deepest values.

Once you know how important each trait is to you, regardless of how charismatic someone is, or how good they look in a pair of jeans, if they don't have all your deal breaker traits it's goodbye to anything serious. Learn to prevent the heartbreak rather than blindly jog head on into it, thinking it will work itself out down the track. It won't.

Lastly take a look inside and think about red flags. The red flags are traits that indicate you should run in the other direction swiftly. A red flag may be excessive drunkenness, drug use, disrespectful behaviour, violence or any other warning sign that may pop up that warns you off taking the relationship any further.

Add all your red flags to your Little Pink book of Love.

I know it may feel too early to consider another relationship at this point, however it is beneficial to have an understanding of what you desire. By shining a light on gaps in a previous relationship, and comparing that to your ideal relationship, you will create a clearer goal to aim for in life.

Keep your lists close to your heart and keep the feelings alive for what you desire and wish to have when you are ready for a new relationship.

Pink time out - How will your new relationship look?

Stop and Breathe

By this stage you have some good information around what traits you would like in your new partner. These questions will help you envisage the look and feel of your new relationship.

- What do you want to see from both of you in the new relationship?
- How do you want it to look?
- How do you want it to feel?
- How do you want your communication to take place?
- How supportive are you of each other?
- How important is having similar interests?
- How much time do you wish to spend together?
- What shared values must you have?

- How much are you prepared to help each other with your personal growth?
- How much do you need to inspire each other?
- How much do you need each other for support?
- Do you want him to be your best friend as well as your lover?
- Do you need him to listen to all your needs?
- Do you need him to go out with you all the time or do you need time out on your own?
- How much time alone do you both need?
- Do you want children?
- Do you want to be married?
- Do you want to live together?
- Do you want to have joint finances?
- Are you happy to take on his children?
- Do you want him to act as a father to your children?
- How would you like to see him bring up his children?
- Is it important that he works? If so, how much time would you be happy to see him working?
- Is it important that he is social or would you prefer him to be a home body?
- Is it important he is fit and energetic?
- What religious beliefs does he need to have?
- What about politics, is it important that your views are aligned?
- Do you need regular presents and flowers to feel important or is a birthday present enough?

- ❈ Do you need him to be tidy and organised or are you happy to move around mess and clutter?
- ❈ Does he need strong boundaries with others in his life?
- ❈ Is it important that he can speak up and protect himself?
- ❈ Does he need to be able to feel, express and process his emotions?
- ❈ Do you need to like his friends?
- ❈ Does he need to be family-orientated?
- ❈ Do you need to like his family?
- ❈ Would you like him to enjoy travelling?
- ❈ What habits or addictions, if any, would be tolerable?
- ❈ How would you like him to handle conflict?
- ❈ How would you like him to treat others?
- ❈ How would you like him to handles stress?
- ❈ How would you like him to handle his anger and frustrations?
- ❈ Does he need to be emotionally healthy or are you happy for a fix-it project?
- ❈ Are you entering the relationship to add to each other instead of fill each other up?

You now have a solid picture in your mind and heart what you are looking for in your next relationship. These lists can be prettied up with coloured pencils and posted on your bedroom wall. Do whatever makes you feel good, allow your creative side to flourish and have some fun.

The gnocchi was divine and with no room for sweets, you sip on a beautiful coffee as you visualise being in a relationship again with a heart and soul that is perfectly matched with yours. You have finally allowed yourself to be vulnerable, authentic and honest in admitting this is what you truly desire.

Spend some time visualising your dream and start to make it a reality. Remain positive, optimistic and real, continue to spend time on and with yourself. Your ideal partner will appear when he is meant to. When he appears, your ideal partner will be one that comes with his own imperfections and flaws but sits together with you like a perfect soul jigsaw.

Finishing your coffee, you thank the waiters and almost float down the beach towards home, revelling in your heavenly dream of a blissful fun filled future.

Vision and goals

"If you fail to plan, you plan to fail"

Benjamin Franklin

Waking up today seems surreal. Today is your last lesson and then you are on your way again. Dinner was so fabulous last night and you have fallen in love with your cottage and the town, but know that the time is coming when you will have to head back to reality. A morning walk is on the agenda again before you head to Café Rosa for lattes, banana cake and your last lesson.

You find an empty table where the sun peeks in under the umbrella just enough to warm your legs. You take your cap off and adjust your sunnies and let loose a big smile full of warm and fuzzy feelings.

You remember your first day here, seeing all the people relaxing in beach attire and sunnies. You wonder, have you become one of those happy people you gazed at in envy when you arrived? You are not quite sure; it is still hard to acknowledge yourself as a person filled with happiness. Your self trust can still waver and you need to consciously remind yourself you are allowed to be happy and feel protected and loved. You are not perfect but are a perfect you. So you keep your faith, place your breakfast order and allow your concentration to be focused on your last lesson.

Now is the time to put all the hard work together, using all the tools you have learnt along the way. Now is the time to think about your dreams and aspirations as you set goals for your future and write your own personalised vision statement.

Your life is changing rapidly and you may be running behind, trying to catch up. Often when one major change takes place it creates a domino effect and the other areas of your life start to move, wanting their own declutter and rethink. Once one area is sorted and running smoothly you can shift your focus to the next, bringing the goal of a balanced fulfilled life closer every day.

This can be quite overwhelming, so having a plan can help you manage it in a positive way, in order for you to enjoy the process as it unfolds. Putting some organisation into place will ensure the changes you make today will be beneficial for the big picture goals you want to reach further down the track.

My Goals List

"When eating an elephant, take one bite at a time"

Creighton Abrams

To some, goal setting appears boring and overly structured, but a good goal will still allow you to be spontaneous and change direction. If your goal is to have fun and try different things, then that's part of your plan! What goal setting will do is break down an enormous plan into little manageable steps.

If you have a long term dream with no shorter term goals, it can be hard to get started on actually achieving what you have visualised. The gap between where you are now and where you want to be is too big to leap in one go. So instead you label it too hard and the goal is discarded.

Taking little steps is so much more achievable, and each of those little steps will ultimately bite off chunks from the larger goal.

Vision and goals

Focus on the little step you are taking today, live in the present, do what you can and in time you will look back and realise how far you have come.

Thinking about the big goal gives you somewhere to head, but the individual steps along the way will give you something to get out of bed for each morning. Ticking goals off your list is enormously satisfying, and will boost your confidence and self esteem. Each success means you'll be ready for new goals to be set and met, once again increasing your confidence and self esteem. It is a happy and healthy cycle.

You have already eaten most of that big pink elephant, through overcoming your heartbreak and healing yourself. You have achieved some serious deep inner work. Your Little Pink book of Love is full of love, goals, desires and passions. You have unearthed a wealth of needs and wants that were hidden deep below. Sprawling over many pages of white paper you could get lost in the words you have written and the journey you have taken.

Focus on the little step you are taking today

So, let's put it all into order to help you move forward and dedicate time to what matters most, and help you reach your ultimate goal.

Pink Time Out — Five Year Goals

Stop and Breathe

"Create the highest, grandest vision possible for your life because you become what you believe"

Oprah Winfrey

In this exercise you have an opportunity to list achievements you would like to come to fruition that are achievable but will take some time. Five years is a long time away, but if you start today you will make it there, one bite at a time.

Visualise how you would like your life to look and what you will be doing. Having already spent time delving into these areas, there will be some things that are bursting to be listed, goals you have held deep inside that are now excited to be acknowledged. You are now ready to commit the effort, energy and truth to assisting them to materialise in the next five years.

Think about these areas of your life. Focus on each area and brainstorm all the things you would love to achieve. Don't let your fears get in the way, have some fun, keep writing all the things you would love to achieve in:

- Relationships
- Health
- Career
- Spiritual and personal development
- Finances
- Fun
- Sport

To help you focus on the different areas of your life, sit in a meditation to clear out your mind before starting on the next life area. Doing this is like having a sorbet to cleanse the palate before trying the next taste sensation. Have your meditative sorbet and cleanse your mind to help free up space, before shifting your focus into your next life space.

Once you have filtered through all of the areas of your life and listed what you would like to achieve in the next five years, sit back and review your goals. Take it all in and see if it feels right. Does it produce a warm feeling inside? Do you feel that if you achieve all that you have listed you will be coming home to yourself?

Don't despair if there is some hesitation or fear around your goals. It can be fun to make a list but then the reality and questions bubble to the surface. 'How am I going to achieve this?' It's a big pink elephant; remember you can't eat it all at once. But you can sit back and appreciate the grandness of the pink elephant and the direction your life takes when you have a big goal in your vision.

 ## Pink time out - One year goals

⸺ Stop and Breathe ⸺

You now know how you want your life to look in five years' time, so what can you achieve in the next year that will take you closer to those goals? Are some of your goals small enough to knock them over in one year?

Using the same headings you had previously, list all the goals you would like to achieve in the upcoming year for various parts of your life. Think about the big five year goals and brainstorm the smaller steps and smaller goals you need to complete in the next year, to take you further ahead. Some of your goals may be recurring. If you aim to be a regular exerciser and maintain a certain weight, this goal will remain the same every year.

At the end of this exercise you will have a five year vision and a one year vision. You now have somewhere to head and a plan to get there. You have something to strive towards. Your passions have been awakened and your life purpose is starting to appear.

Deep in thought, you realise you have finished your latte and return to the counter to order another. You feel you could sit and ponder life in this café forever, enjoying the little slice of heaven it's providing. You are hovering on peace and contentment and want to hold on tight to this unfamiliar feeling.

What you slowly realise as the second latte is being placed in front of you is that it's not the café that is providing this safe sanctuary. It is you. Your heart and soul are healing and through the healing you are again finding the happiness and peace you have sought throughout this journey. You thank the waiter with sincere love and kindness. As he smiles in appreciation, you realise that now you have more love and kindness for yourself, you are ready to give it away to everyone you meet.

Looking back

"A goal is just a plan without a wish"

Antoine de Saint-Exupery

Looking back on the list of goals I wrote one year ago, there is a lot that I have yet to achieve. In hindsight I realise that some of my goals should have been on the five year list, so I'll adjust that next time I revisit it.

I see now that I was not ready for some things to appear in my life. I am a big believer that things need to feel right, and it was not the right time for me. As much as it is all well and good to list your goals in pen, visualise them and work towards the outcome, unless it is the right time you will not attract it into your life.

Dream big then create action

On the other hand, there are some goals that were not on the list at all that I still achieved over the past year. I wrote them in at the end, to give myself the satisfaction of ticking them off! As humans we are continually evolving and changing and sometimes we do not know what we are capable of.

Sometimes you will achieve things you did not think were possible. You don't see how they fit into your life until they are upon you, arriving at just the right time. These are the small miracles, the ones to be extra appreciative of. They come from a special creative space inside that houses all the little miracles you are capable of but have not yet rationally believed.

Some goals I looked at on my list made me realise that when I wrote them I did not truly believe I could do it. Quit smoking was one of those goals. Like most smokers, I really enjoyed having a cigarette, and although I knew I should give up to save my health and my money, my heart wasn't in it.

However as the year went on and I progressed with my personal development, I started to feel shame around smoking. I felt bad about who I was when I smoked. This was a much greater motivation to give up than money or health. I was coming into self love and shame does not live in congruence with self love. As I moved towards self love I gave up smoking without an effort.

Our goals, like ourselves, are very much a work in progress, a general plan to move forward in the direction that feels right.

A goals list is not a document that needs to be perfectly adhered to, nor is it the means to create a perfect person. It is a mud map with a healthy direction to help you feel excited about life and what you can achieve. It gives you a purpose and a place for reflection.

Vision statement

"Keep your eyes on the stars and your feet on the ground"

Franklin D Roosevelt

Most companies have a vision statement, to speak loud and clear to the outside world as to who they are, what they are about, and where their values and beliefs lie.

Your personal vision statement tells you and others where you are heading and what you want to accomplish. It is a statement of how you dream you and your life to be at their best. Your vision statement is a contemplation and a snapshot of your values and beliefs, your Pink Heart Print and your Inner Pink Star.

It helps you know who you are, even through the act of writing it. It speaks to you, whispering what you really want. Once complete, it is a constant daily reminder of who you want to be and what you stand for, to bring you back when you travel off course.

Pink time out – Vision statement

~ Stop and Breathe ~

Using all the knowledge you have mastered to this point, you are now ready to plan and write your own personal vision statement.

Be as creative as you want. Play with your words and describe you and who you are.

Think about the most important things to you. Think about who you want to become. Think about what you stand for. This is a very personal statement and you can choose what to add and how it will look.

Start fleshing out some words in your Little Pink book of Love, and putting some sentences together.

You will know you have your completed vision statement when you read it and say to yourself 'Yes, that is me'. It encompasses the most important areas of your life. It feels right inside and you are content and happy with the words.

Once you have your completed vision statement, feel proud. You are coming closer to the person you want to be. You are moving through the healing process and coming out the other end.

My vision statement is below to give you an idea of how you might like to put yours together. Maybe to the professional vision statement police it may be too long, but I could not fit all I wanted to express in a smaller paragraph, so this is it.

Don't create too many rules around your personal development – let it flow. Be true to yourself and let the essence and juice of who you really truly are bubble up, appear, and overflow into your reality, making your life easier, more sparkly and way more fun.

> **MY VISION STATEMENT**
>
> To be fully present and balanced.
>
> To love myself, and live a calm, peaceful, compassionate and authentic life seeking continual personal and deep soul growth.
>
> To be the best version of me, to follow my passions and live my life purpose, and through my own self expression inspire others.
>
> To have fun, live in the moment and be surrounded by the ones I love.
>
> To protect, watch out for, love and nurture all our furry children.
>
> To be kind to myself, others and the planet.

All coffeed out, you leave the café holding onto your vision statement and your list of goals in your Little Pink book of Love. You are excited knowing you have a purpose and a vision and it

Vision and goals

is now broken down into realistic goals. You want to get started straight away. Your head starts planning but before you get busy with another tick list, you want to enjoy the last evening at this beautiful location.

You put your Little Pink book of Love into your bag and enjoy the walk home to your cute little cottage. Tonight is your last night and as you sit on the veranda and take everything in, you get a little teary. The whole journey is coming to an end, and your tears represent happiness, joy and sadness; a myriad of emotions. You have uncovered so much and feel like you are a new and different version of the same person. You hardly even remember how it felt to be the pile of rubble that was on the floor at the Heartbreak Manor.

You let the healing tears flow until they come to an end naturally, then decide now is a good time to open the champagne, sit with yourself on the veranda and just be and appreciate the journey, this destination and you. You feel the time is now right to celebrate the new you, so you pour a glass and lift it to propose a toast to yourself 'To me, all shining and bright'. You are like the shiny and bright chandeliers you have encountered along the way, directing and gently guiding you to this precious moment in time and this new way of being.

Checking out

"Accept what is, let go of what was and have faith in what could be"

Sonia Ricotti

Wow, you have come so far. It is now time to leave the Happiness Shack and the beaches, the waves, the fun and the sun. You pick up your bags and wheel them down the front path. You turn to face the cottage one last time and thank it for its warm friendliness.

It is time to return to reality and integrate all that you have learnt and become on your journey into your amazing life. You will still have many challenges and situations in your future that will throw you back into self reflection, introspection and grief, but you now have enough tools to help you through. You know, understand and love yourself better than before. The more awareness you create and the more tools you have in your toolbox, the better you can glide through tricky times.

One of the challenges in the real world is maintaining the balance, desires, motivation and energy to create and sustain your new life, the one you have so delicately and deliberately planned and created.

Think about creating some rituals and positive daily habits that will help keep you in your sacred space and in tune with your inner being. You know that when you start a new diet you may lose weight and then a few months down the track it piles back on, with some added extra kilos as a bonus. The only true way to lose weight is to create a new lifestyle, create habits for life. It is the same with your emotional and spiritual health. To get the most benefit, you need to integrate what you have leant into your life over the long term, not just for a few weeks.

Try documenting some daily rituals that will help you stay on track. I have a weekly list to aim for. I don't always achieve it; there are certain things I don't want to do every day and need to drag myself out of bed for, but sometimes I just have to get up and do it because I know the benefits.

Create your sacred daily rituals

These rituals are quite simple and yet they bring me joy as well as emotional, physical, spiritual and mental peace and wellbeing. Over time they have become integrated into who I am. It has been a long journey to who I am today but one I am very proud of.

- Stop and Breathe
- Practise a kind gesture towards another person or animal daily
- Be still, be in the moment and practise gratitude
- Walk with Suzy twice daily
- Practise Pilates or yoga three to five times a week
- Read personal development material daily
- Meditate three to five times a week
- Write in My Little Pink Book of Love
- Eat a healthy diet including salad, fruit and vegetables
- Drink one to two litres of water daily
- Reward myself with a coffee daily

Checking Out

- Spend time relaxing, watching TV, chatting with friends or family daily
- Go to bed early most nights with a good book.

I cannot overestimate how important it is to feel good about ourselves. Often at 3pm my eyes start drooping and I get grumpy and tired. I stop and realise I have forgotten to have any water. About 15 minutes after drinking a big glass of water, my eyes are open again and I feel refreshed and recharged.

Your body is your vessel and incorporating rituals to look after it is important if you want it to see you through to older age. Be nice to your body and treat it with respect and honour, the sacred temple of who you are, that houses your soul.

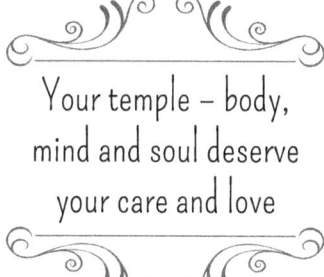
Your temple – body, mind and soul deserve your care and love

You are coming out of a massive growth phase, still practising all your new skills and tools to ensure you hang onto the self love and trust you have built up. Enjoy the moments, cherish the lessons and keep opening the gifts, as they will continue to emerge as you stroll through your life with your new found wisdom and awareness.

My Pink Manifesto

"Goodbyes are only for those who love with their eyes. Because for those who love with heart and soul there is no such thing as separation"

Rumi

Before you leave and return to your normal life, it is timely to create your own Pink Manifesto, capturing all you have learnt on your journey. This is an opportunity to ensure you are committed to the tools and attitudes you have learnt as you move forward. Reminding yourself of what you want and where you are headed will assist your Inner Pink Star to prevent you from falling into the pile of rubble again in the future.

Use the list below as a guide for you to make your own Pink Manifesto. Copy your list into your little Pink Book of Love, personalising it where you feel it is required so it speaks to your soul. Decorate your Pink Manifesto, making it colourful and memorable, and finally sign and date it to show your commitment to your personal growth, healing and happiness.

My Pink Manifesto

When I love myself I have self awareness

When I love myself I take responsibility for my life

When I love myself I feel all my feelings

When I love myself I practise forgiveness

When I love myself I create acceptance

When I love myself I know who I am

When I love myself I honour My Pink Heart Print

When I love myself I access my Inner Pink Star

When I love myself I am kind to Lady Chitter Chatter

When I love myself I practise self love

When I love myself I follow my passions and live my life purpose

When I love myself I am open to a new partner

When I love myself I have a solid vision and goals

CHECKING OUT

When I love myself I practise gratitude

When I love myself I use mindfulness

When I love myself I use visualisation and affirmations

When I love myself I create a meditation ritual

When I love myself I journal to express my feelings

When I love myself I am thirsty for knowledge

When I love myself I am able to relax, live in the moment and have fun

When I love myself I am In the Pink

When I love myself I have Love – Truth - Purpose

Now that you have this in your Little Pink Book of Love, keep it close to your heart as a reminder of everything you have learnt, how far you have come and the promises you have made to yourself. It is very special as you are very special.

LESSONS

"Forget what hurt you but never forget what it taught you"

Shannon L Alder

At Heartbreak Manor you learnt to process the initial heartbreak and move out of basic survival mode. Here you created self awareness, took ownership and responsibility for your life, met your feelings and emotions, sought forgiveness and found clarity and acceptance.

At the Healing Sanctuary you created breathing space to help you reconnect with yourself. You created your Pink Heart Print. You meet your Inner Pink Star and her nemesis Lady Chitter Chatter. You found meditation and your truth and truly met and got to know yourself. You allowed respite and healing from your heartbreak. You found your truth.

At the Happiness Shack you rediscovered your talents and gifts, your passions and purpose in life. You redesigned and redecorated internally, setting goals and creating your own personal vision statement to become an amazing new version of yourself. You also designed your next relationship. You stopped and celebrated your journey and hugged your Pink Manifesto tightly. Here you prepared to launch yourself out into the world and shower other people with sparkles from the spectacular new you.

Now you have a Pink Heart Print, a Pink Manifesto, a vision statement, one and five year goals and a Little Pink Book of Love full of insights, journal entries, lessons and miracle moments that you can take forward into your life and reflect back on when you need further inspiration.

Time to Leave

"If you're brave enough to say goodbye, life will reward you with a new hello"

Paulo Coehlo

You are distracted by the honk of the jeep waiting out the front. You snap out of your contemplation, pick up your bags, walk out the garden gate and hop into the jeep once again.

The driver stops at a café around the corner to fetch coffee for the ride, and while he collects it he hands you a questionnaire to fill in.

1. What is one thing you can rave about and tell others about your stay here?

CHECKING OUT

2. What is the one thing you liked most about your stay here?
3. What is the biggest thing you learnt during your stay here?
4. Would you revisit in the future if you needed to?
5. How will you acknowledge how far you have come in your journey?
6. Please rate your stay from 0 - 10, 10 being the best.

PINK TIME OUT – SONG CHOICE

Stop and Breathe

Pick one song that relates to your stay at the Happiness Shack. Choose a song that is symbolic of how you felt when you arrived, what you achieved and how you feel now. Play it over and over and let it sink in.

In your Little Pink book of Love, record the name of your song.

Let it be your reminder for ever and always of the time you spent here. Remind yourself often of the tremendous work you achieved and the amazing journey you have been on.

Once you have answered the last few questions and chosen your song, your coffee magically appears. The driver says "Where to now, lovely lady?" You hadn't thought about the fact that this was the last destination of your journey. Oh dear, what now? You go inside yourself, find your balance and regain your self trust and love. The words that flow from your lips are "Take me home, I'm ready to embark on my life again, I have lots to do. With love, truth and purpose, life is looking fabulous, and I need to shine brightly".

Thank you for staying at the Happiness Shack

Love - Truth - Purpose

Epilogue

*"Promise me you'll never forget me because
if I thought you would I'd never leave"*

A.A. Milne

Sitting at my desk, the sun powering in through my lovely big windows and Suzy at my feet, I feel surrounded by love, as I reflect on the journey from Heartbreak, through Healing to Happiness.

I realise it is time to say goodbye. I want to say thank you so very much for allowing me to come into your life, your heart and your soul and touch parts of you that needed help, knowledge and healing. Your soul is a sacred place and one that should be protected and loved. For you to let me in just a little is special and I truly appreciate you trusting me with your fragile, healing heart.

Remember every day how far you have come, the journey you have travelled that makes you who you are today. Live and enjoy the present moment and have faith that your future will unfold as it should. You are an amazing individual with your own special set of gifts and qualities to share with yourself and in time the world.

Find your authentic self and let your truth speak out. Be your truth, live your truth. Let any anxiety wash over you and pool at your feet as you walk away from it, knowing and trusting you can look after yourself. Be your own best friend.

I hope for you that you can walk this world in peace, surrounded by love, truth and purpose and that you live an amazing life filled with an abundance of love for every piece of your self and your shiny bright soul.

The process we have walked through together was the same one I underwent that totally changed my life and created what I have today. What I learnt about myself enabled me to create peace, contentment and joy inside. I now feel awakened and alive. I have my energy and enthusiasm back, have found my sparkle and my naughty, fun-filled, inner child that had become lost.

Even though my heart had felt so raw, and cracked wide open, it is now capable of loving like it has never loved before. I feel love for everyone and everything so much more strongly. I feel more protective of my loved ones yet I have stopped anticipating the worst and trust I can cope regardless of what life throws at me.

I don't always get it right, in fact I no doubt get it wrong a lot, but I choose today and every day to learn from my mistakes and overcome my obstacles and challenges. I believe people can change; I am living proof. To change though you must house an internal determination to be the best person you can be. To have a soul that seeks growth and aliveness instead of victimhood, denial and blame.

Through my work at In the Pink I aim to radiate healthy vibrations into the world through positive writings, powerful consultations and heartfelt services for those aiming to live a life of love, truth and purpose.

Epilogue

I would love you to stay in touch, so please share your stories with me via

Web: lifeinthepink.com.au
Email: lara@lifeinthepink.com.au
Facebook: facebook.com/InthePINKxx

Thank You

"Don't cry because it's over, smile because it happened"

Dr. Seuss

To Dad, who passed away just as I went to print on this book. You were my rock, my favourite person in the world. My whole life I felt like a princess in your presence. I felt like I was still the little girl sitting on your lap for cuddles. You had the ability to ooze love and warmth without saying a word and inspired me to be strong, to love and to follow in your family values. To me love was just being close to you. Every moment we spent together was gratifying. I am enormously proud to be your daughter and have you as my dad. Even though your physical presence is no longer here, I will move forward with you softly residing in my heart. Your soul gently guides me to my future without you. The memories I have will keep you with me forever, the tears I shed will water my soul in your honour. I was so truly blessed to have such a beautiful father to guide me through my life. Dad, it's not goodbye as you are always with me, and I send a piece of my heart with you. I love you to the moon and back forever, I thank you for everything. Rest in peace my beautiful dad.

To Mum, thank you for being an inspirational strength in my life. The things you have achieved make me understand anything is possible. I have learnt from and admire your strengths. I appreciate the mutual love of our fur children and I look forward to creating many more memories. My love for you is boundless.

To my sisters, I love you all so much. I would protect you, nurture you and shield you from anything if I was able to. At times I wish I could pick you up from your difficult times and carefully wrap you up in a nurturing pink rug, ensuring there were only love, trust, wisdom and peace available to you. You are all beautiful and amazing souls.

To Pat, you are very special, a solid loving presence in my life. You have been there for me twice when I fell into heartbreak. You listened for hours and by doing so you helped me pick up my pieces, put them back together and continue to help me grow into who I am today. I love you.

To Suzy, Maxy and Chelsea, my fur babies. When I started writing this book Suzy and Maxy, my two devoted fur children were at my feet. As my book comes to its conclusion I have Suzy and her newly adopted 12 year old friend Chelsea. Maxy my golden child, I miss you every day you gorgeous ball of fluff, and I keep the love we had for each other in my heart. Suzy my beautiful little girl, thank you for showering me with love and showing me how to love. Chelsea, welcome to our world; you make me smile and laugh every day.

To two dear friends Gemma and Anna, thank you for shining your bright angelic lights my way when mine had dulled, and for continually reminding me to love myself as much as you love me. You are angels, and life is much more illuminous with you in it.

Thank you

To my recent ex, my beautiful large silver French provincial mirror, reflecting back to me all the parts of myself that I needed to heal; you took me on an amazing journey. You brought me such love and fun, anger, sadness and fear. You were the catalyst to teach me once and for all to provide unconditional love to myself. Thank you.

To Steph, my gorgeous life coach constantly by my side to challenge me and cheer me on every step of the way. You helped me with each small step and these small steps have accumulated over time to one big pole-vault into my new amazing life. Thank you for everything.

To Alex, thank you for being a fabulous editor and for providing motivation and inspiration when mine waned. You have been amazing, you helped my dream and my purpose come to life and without you this book would not shine like it does.

To Sylvie, thank you for being a marvellous and talented designer. You have made my book look so amazing. I am forever grateful for your time and input; I love and feel very proud of the end result.

To Bruce, thank you for your photographic brilliance and your constant sense of humour. I appreciate your efforts enormously.

To all my mentors, thank you for sharing your knowledge and experiences. You all add to my growth and help me prosper in my own life. Your inspirational words and ways assist me to believe I too, can help, teach and inspire others.

BIBLIOGRAPHY

My theories and ideas are collated from my journey of many years of study, reading and personal experience. I have been privileged to find many mentors, as well as resources from others in my field. Here are some of the most influential mentors and authors I have come across to date. They will provide an additional interesting, inspirational and soul provoking read to expand your spiritual healing and journey to amazing heights.

Amy Ahlers, 2011. Big Fat Lies Women Tell Themselves: Ditch your inner critic and wake up your inner superstar. 9.11.2011 edition. New World Library.

Amy Ahlers and Christine Arylo, 2015. Reform Your Inner Mean Girl: 7 steps to stop bullying yourself and start loving yourself. Atria Books/Beyond Words.

Dr Barbara De Angelis, 2015. Soul Shifts: Transformative wisdom for creating a life of authentic awakening, emotional freedom and practical spirituality. Hay House, Inc.

Barbara De Angelis, 2009. Are You the One for Me?: Knowing who's right and avoiding who's wrong. Dell.

Brian Tracy, 1995. Maximum Achievement: Strategies and skills that will unlock your hidden powers to succeed. 1st fireside edition. Simon and Schuster.

Bronwyn Fox, 2001. Working Through Panic: Your step by step guide to overcoming panic/anxiety related disorders. Prentice Hall.

Christine Arylo, 2012. *Madly in Love with ME: The daring adventure of becoming your own best friend.* New World Library.

Christine Arylo, 2009. Choosing ME Before WE: Every woman's guide to life and love. New World Library.

Christine Hassler, 2014. Expectation Hangover: Overcoming disappointment in work, love, and life. New World Library.

Deepak Chopra, 2010. The Shadow Effect: Illuminating the hidden power of your true self. HarperCollins e-books.

Doreen Virtue, 2013. Assertiveness for Earth Angels: How to be loving instead of "Too Nice". Hay House.

Doreen Virtue, 2015. Don't Let Anything Dull Your Sparkle: How to break free of negativity and drama. Hay House.

Eckhart Tolle, 2004. The Power of Now: A guide to spiritual enlightenment. Namaste Publishing.

Elisa Romeo, 2015. Meet Your Soul: A powerful guide to connect with your most sacred self. Hay House.

Elizabeth Gilbert, 2007. Eat, Pray, Love: One woman's search for everything across Italy, India and Indonesia 25th printing edition. Penguin (Non-Classics).

Gabrielle Bernstein, 2012. Spirit Junkie: A radical road to self-love and miracles. Harmony.

Gabrielle Bernstein, 2014. Miracles Now: 108 life-changing tools for less stress, more flow, and finding your true purpose. New York Times bestseller edition. Hay House, Inc.

Bibliography

Gabrielle Bernstein, 2011. Add More Ing to Your Life: A hip guide to happiness. Harmony.

Greg Behrendt, 2006. It's Called a Break-Up Because It's Broken: The smart girl's breakup buddy. Harper Element.

Iyanla Vanzant, 2002. Living Through the Meantime: Learning to break the patterns of the past and begin the healing process. Touchstone.

Kate Spencer, 2013. Twelve Lessons. The Lightworkers Academy.

Katherine Woodward Thomas, 2007. Calling in "The One": 7 weeks to attract the love of your life. Harmony.

Lisa Nichols, 2009. No Matter What!: 9 steps to living the life you love. 1st edition. Grand Central Life and Style.

Louise Hay and Robert Holden, 2015. Life Loves You: 7 spiritual practices to heal your life. Hay House.

Louise L. Hay, 1984. You Can Heal Your Life. 2nd edition. Hay House.

Louise L. Hay, 2014. You Can Heal Your Heart: Finding peace after a breakup, divorce, or death. Hay House, Inc.

Mandy Hale, 2013. The Single Woman: Life, love, and a dash of sass. Thomas Nelson.

Marianne Williamson, 1996. A Return to Love: Reflections on the principles of "A Course in Miracles". Reissue Edition. HarperOne.

Martha Whitmore Hickman, 1994. Healing After Loss: Daily meditations for working through grief. 1st edition. William Morrow Paperbacks.

Mastin Kipp, 2014. Daily Love: Growing into grace. Hay House.

Michael J. Chase, 2013. The Radical Practice of Loving Everyone: A four-legged approach to enlightenment. Hay House, Inc.

Michael J. Chase, 2011. Am I Being Kind? Hay House.

Mike Dooley, 2014. The Top Ten Things Dead People Want to Tell YOU. 1st edition. Hay House, Inc.

Mira Kirshenbaum, 1997. Too Good to Leave, Too Bad to Stay: A step-by-step guide to help you decide whether to stay in or get out of your relationship. Reprint Edition. Plume.

Natalie Lue, 2011. Mr Unavailable and the Fallback Girl: The definitive guide to understanding emotionally unavailable men and the women that love them. 2nd edition. Natalie Lue.

Natalie Lue, 2012. The Dreamer and the Fantasy Relationship.

Natalie Lue, 2013. The No Contact Rule. Naughty Girl Media.

Paul David, 2012. *At Last A Life*. Edition. Paul David.

Panache Desai, 2014. Discovering your Soul Signature: A 33 day path to purpose passion and joy. Yellow Kite

Rachel Brathen, 2015. Yoga Girl. Touchstone.

Ram Dass, 2013. Polishing the Mirror: How to live from your spiritual heart. 1st edition. Sounds True.

Rebecca Rosen, 2011. Spirited: Unlock your psychic self and change your life. Reprint edition. Harper Perennial.

Robert Holden, 2011. Shift Happens!: How to live an inspired life... starting right now!. Revised edition. Hay House.

Sera Beak, 2013. Red Hot and Holy: A heretic's love story. 1st edition. Sounds True.

BIBLIOGRAPHY

Stephanie Dowrick, 2012. The Universal Heart: A practical guide to love. Allen and Unwin.

Steven Stosny, 2013. Living and Loving after Betrayal: How to heal from emotional abuse, deceit, infidelity, and chronic resentment. 1st edition. New Harbinger Publications.

Susan J. Elliott, 2009. Getting Past Your Breakup: How to turn a devastating loss into the best thing that ever happened to you. Da Capo Press.

Susan Jeffers, 2006. Feel the Fear . . . and Do It Anyway. 20th anniversary edition. Ballantine Books.

Tosha Silver, 2014. Outrageous Openness: Letting the divine take the lead. Atria Books.

Dr. Wayne W. Dyer, 2015. I Can See Clearly Now. Hay House, Inc.

Inner Mean Girl Reform School. 2015. innermeangirlreformschool.com.

Diploma Life Coaching: Book of readings volume 2. Life Coaching Institute of Australia, Queensland

www.ingramcontent.com/pod-product-compliance
Lightning Source LLC
Chambersburg PA
CBHW071149300426
44113CB00009B/1143